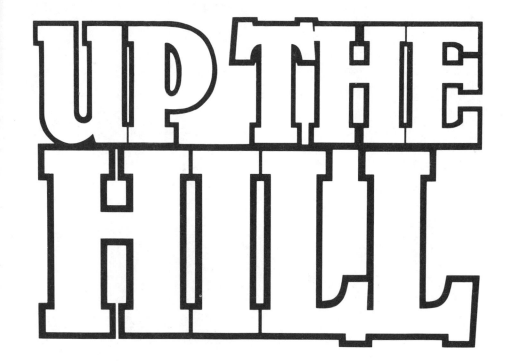

UP THE HILL

DONALD JOHNSTON

OPTIMUM PUBLISHING INTERNATIONAL
Montréal • Toronto

© Ottawa 1986, Donald J. Johnston

Published by Optimum Publishing International (1984) Inc.
Montreal

Legal Deposit 2nd quarter 1986
National Library of Quebec

Canadian Cataloguing in Publication Data

Johnston, Donald J.
Up the hill

Includes index.
Bibliography: p.
ISBN 0-88890-178-X

1. Johnston Donald J.   2. Canada—
Politics and government—1963-   .   1. Title.

FC625.J63 1986   971.064   C86-090079-7
F1034.2.J63 1986

Jacket Design: André Séguin
Cover Photograph: National Capital Commission
Frontispiece Photograph: Elizabeth Dickson

Set in Aster type by Conceptus Renaissance Inc.
Printed and bound in Canada by T. H. Best Printing Company

For information, address:

Optimum Publishing International (1984) Inc.
2335 Sherbrooke Street West
Montreal, Quebec H3H 1G6
Michael S. Baxendale, President

iv

This book is for Heather, Kristina, Allison, Rachel and Sara.

The idea of writing a book was proposed to me by my friend, Michael Baxendale, of Optimum in the aftermath of the leadership campaign. Originally conceived as following up the policy options I raised in seeking the leadership, it developed from there into a much more comprehensive work. As my editor and publisher, Michael has been closely involved throughout.

Cleo Mowers was present at the outset, listening as I dictated my initial thoughts and questioning me on the issues I raised. I appreciate his help and encouragement. His granddaughter, Susan Mowers, provided much-needed research in the early stages.

Pivotal to the whole process were members of the Dickson family, Marjorie who typed initial drafts, Rosaleen who gave many hours to constructive criticism and Elizabeth who has played a key role. Researcher, critic, editor, even typist, no part of the book has escaped Elizabeth's input. She sacrificed countless evenings and weekends not only without complaint, but with enthusiasm.

By a stroke of good fortune, my old friend, Paul Almond, arrived back in Montreal in time to review an advanced draft. His interest in the project was matched only by his amusing, insightful and sometimes scathing annotations. His comments were timely and particularly useful.

Douglas Fullerton read some early chapter drafts and his views on style and content contributed to my approach in several aspects of the book. Colleagues and friends Jim Fleming, David McNaughton, Jamie Deacey, Alice Switocz, Louis Duclos and others reviewed parts of the manuscript making several contributions.

Tisha Hutchinson, Nicole Loiselle, Vicky Harris and Tom Johnston of my staff, and Caroline Raymond all volunteered time and effort to this enterprise.

My wife, Heather, and daughters, Kristina, Allison, Rachel and Sara have shown patience and understanding because family weekends all but disappeared over the past six months. Heather has also made a number of useful editorial suggestions.

My brother, David, was helpful in recalling incidents and circumstances of our childhood and brother-in-law, Graham Watt, has given enthusiastic support from the beginning.

All of these people and others have helped make this book possible. But the motivation to undertake this book came from all those who stood by me during the leadership campaign. Believing that policy should be front and centre, they were not afraid to tilt at windmills and to attack sacred cows, even though they knew their candidate was a longshot at best. I am grateful to them all.

PART ONE

TAKING STOCK

I

Tough Choices

"Our long suffering taxpayers have paid the piper. It's time those in government began to play their tune."

How many times have you said to yourself, "What the hell is going on in Ottawa?"

Many frustrated Canadians would love to make it to the Cabinet table, whip the bureaucracy into shape and do all the good things for Canada they dream about.

Older Canadians still say to me, "Oh for C. D. Howe! He'd get this mess under control."

Does each of us not have at least one pet peeve, sometimes so strong that we yearn to throw open the window and scream, "I'm fed up and I'm not going to take it anymore."

It might be the post office, a customs officer, revelations of the auditor general or even the inanity of the day's Question Period in the House of Commons. I am no exception. For me it was our tax system.

Finance Minister Edgar Benson's 1971 tax reform bill was disastrous. That exercise in futility was the last straw. It drove me into politics and, in the end, I finally made it to that privileged Cabinet table. To my surprise, it was not as simple as I thought. The frustration remained. Nearly all solutions were beyond my reach.

From the vantage point of the Cabinet room, the vast array of society's competing interests came into focus. I saw how politicians are buffetted first by one interest, then by others, responding with appeasement here, compromise there, always keeping an eye on the weather vane of public opinion.

Although I have now left the Cabinet room I did not leave my agenda behind. My concern with the tax system has not faded. It is even greater. But there is much more than tax on my mind. Wiser, I believe, better informed and more realistic about the political process, I know we can do better. My resolve remains.

Although much was accomplished during the period from 1980 to 1984, I had the uneasy feeling that we were not meeting the broad range of social and economic challenges the country faced in a comprehensive way. Despite the financial and human resources at our disposal, it seemed to me we were attempting too much and accomplishing too little.

The absence of long-term priorities supported by adequate financing meant, for example, that short-term political priorities got the money while public property deteriorated, sometimes beyond repair. Huge sums of taxpayers' capital were spent buying service stations from Petrofina and B.P., manufacturing executive jets at Canadair, and on unsuccessful bailouts of companies such as Maislin Transport, while many vital areas were starved for money. Hundreds of millions of dollars were spent on job creation programs while unemployment climbed to its highest level since the Depression and regional economic disparities persisted in spite of massive dollar transfers.

Granted, these initiatives arose from good intentions. Some politicians sincerely believed these costly interventions in the Canadian economy would even have met with the approval of that great economic thinker, John Maynard Keynes. In fact, such attribution would more likely have caused Keynes to roll over in his grave. Keynes advocated government intervention as a means of manipulating the economy, but he was precise about the direction such action should take:[1]

> "The most important Agenda of the State relate not to those activities which private individuals are already fulfilling, but to those functions which fall outside the sphere of the individual, to those decisions which are made by no one if the State does not

make them. The important thing for governments is not to do things which individuals are doing already, and to do them a little better or a little worse; but to do those things which at present are not done at all."

Have we not learned from our own experience that a more effective role for government exists, a role more consistent with Keynes' views?

Public policy today faces an unprecedented number of critical issues. The *ad hoc* politically inspired band-aid solutions to which we have become accustomed have contributed to national decline not national recovery. We have the talent and the resources in Canada to develop an effective long-term approach. There is a better way.

Domestic trends to high unemployment, lower economic growth and mounting deficits are warning signals. The absence of a world-wide approach to protecting the environment is a glaring failure. Life itself will be threatened if ecological damage continues unchecked.

The increasing gap in standard of living between the most developed and least developed nations poses as great a threat to peace as does the inability of the super powers to reduce armaments. The $2.2 billion spent on defence every day is a monstrous drain on world resources and, if redirected, could go a long way toward bringing the standards of living of the third world and the industrialized world together.

Does not the spectre of world destruction compel us to act? What work we have ahead of us.

Many of our politicians believe themselves progressive while in fact embracing the *status quo*. Our leaders must throw off this inertia and produce coherent programs that are in the nation's best interests. If we do not, governments will stagger on trying to placate one interest then another, a little money here, a little money there, like a drunk stumbling from lamp post to lamp post. And Canada will slide inexorably into a lower standard of living and into the backwaters of the industrialized world.

We need purpose and direction. Canadians are yearning to be shown a clear path into the future. Pierre Trudeau provided strong leadership of a unique kind. Canada again needs a government that is capable of tough choices. "To govern is to choose," wrote Duc Gaston de Lévis.[2] We cannot afford a government that refuses to make hard decisions.

Canadians chose a strong majority government in September 1984, hoping it would confront today's challenges with radical new approaches. In a matter of months, those hopes were dashed as they so often are when new governments come to power.

Our latest Prime Minister speaks of changed directions. What do we see? Corporate bailouts, the expansion of Petro-Canada's retail operations, huge tax credits to finance the private acquisition of Gulf Oil, taxpayer-backed bank bailouts, increased spending by Cabinet ministers, and tax measures which increase the gap between the rich and poor.

When our government does strike out in new directions, the impact has been to align Canada with the United States, reducing our ability to act independently in the international arena, to weaken our stand on environmental issues and to undermine our social security system. Already this government has abdicated its powerful mandate and created a policy vacuum. Is there an alternative to fill this void?

From the time I sought public office in the 1970s I became deeply involved in the process of getting nominated, getting elected three times, then in cabinet trying to do some governing in three different ministries. I ran for the leadership of my party and now I find myself an elected member of a party the electorate threw out of office. It has been quite an adventure.

Now, armed with a little time to catch my breath, I have taken the opportunity to put down on paper my thoughts about the directions we should take. With time to reflect, the enormity of the job ahead comes into focus. The first half of this book is about my experiences, disappointments and achievements and the second half of the book concentrates on issues and answers.

We have a lot of work to do. Our social programs are out of date. Our economic programs lack coherence. Our tax system remains inequitable, complex and a drag on economic development. Our resource sectors, notably the fisheries, forestry, agriculture and minerals, are in jeopardy. Even the very air we breathe and water we drink are endangered. Much of our once productive manufacturing sector is obsolete. Our infrastructure, including transportation, needs updating. Above all, our education system is failing us and our children. It does not have to be this way.

To me there is one clear message. Government must withdraw from areas in which it has no business and increase its presence where it really counts—in the development of our people. This is the reason I got into politics and at least part of the reason I wrote this book.

We have seen governments past and present intervene in countless ways, ignoring our best resource, people. The record stands. The problems remain. Surely we are ready to heed the expensive lessons of history.

The world differs dramatically from that which shaped many of our policies and programs. As a result, most are now obsolete. Canadians are impatiently waiting for their governments to recognize the change, discard the tired approaches and catch up with the times. Our long suffering taxpayers have paid the piper. It's time those in government began to play their tune.

II

Into the Fray

"I could hear my flat-mate Leonard (Cohen) entertaining into the early morning hours as I wrestled with the Code of Civil Procedure. I began to wish that Frank Scott had seen poetic talent in me."

When asked by a young writer for the secret to becoming a great novelist, Ernest Hemingway replied: "That's easy, have an unhappy childhood."

By this standard, my chances of becoming a novelist are grim at best. The varied experiences of my early years, most of them happy, moved me inexorably in another direction: public policy and politics. They shaped my views on economic and social issues from the tax system to the plight of single parent families.

My life began on a small farm between Orleans and Cumberland about 15 miles east of Ottawa near the Ottawa River. Despite the proximity of Parliament Hill, politics never crossed my mind. Cows, sheep, pigs, chickens, my family and a one room school house filled my days. My mother did almost all the farm work, helped a little by my older brother David, and less by me. As far back as I can remember, Dad was away in the air force and only home from time to time on leave. I was nine when he returned after the war.

Entertainment was the radio, my mother's piano playing, her reading to us and Sunday School in the local United Church. My brother and I invented games to play around the farm. Fighting with him filled in the gaps.

Betty, our Saint Bernard, huge, lumbering and gentle, saw herself as something between our nanny and our playmate. Not once during my childhood play do I recall casting myself in the role of a politician.

Nor was politics on my mind when we sold the farm and moved for a brief period to Ottawa in 1945 where Billy Neville, later to become Secretary to Prime Minister Clark, and I became buddies and attended Hopewell School together in Ottawa South. I don't think politics was on his mind then either.

Our family moved to the province of Quebec, first St-Jean and later Montreal. I attended the High School of Montreal, an extraordinarily large downtown school whose students were a veritable cross section of urban society. HSM graduated such outstanding personalities as Oscar Peterson, Christopher Plummer, Douglas Fullerton, and our current Deputy Minister of Finance, Stanley Hartt, to name but four. At least three of my closest lifelong friendships, with Leslie Jonas, Morrie Shohet and Roberto Gualtieri, were formed at that school. All have enjoyed outstanding careers; Les and Morrie in business and Roberto in the federal public service. Indeed, the High School of Montreal provided an exceptional educational and social experience for all of us who were lucky enough to attend. In 1979, decentralization rendered our old school "obsolete." That year it closed its doors to high school students after 180 years of service to the community.

In 1948 when I was twelve, life seemed to fall apart with my parents' separation, then divorce. Single parent families, while very much a part of society today, were the exception at that time. Mother's task was not easy. We had never had much money but now it was even tougher. Happily my relationship with both parents remained strong and both contributed much to my upbringing. My brother, four years older, has always been especially close to me. Growing up together in the isolation of farm life probably created that enduring bond. It was reinforced by the disintegration of my parents' marriage.

My father was generous with his limited resources, always prepared to share what he had with my brother and me. Neither of my parents had much formal education. My father did not even make it to high school. But he was self-educated and talented. He joined the Royal Flying Corps and was commissioned as a flying officer in World War I. His interest in flying continued after the war and he received the twenty-sixth Aviator's Certificate awarded in Canada.

A jack-of-all-trades, he worked on survey teams in the far north and in the oilfields of Alaska and California. At other times he installed lighting plants for Fairbanks Morse, mostly in eastern Ontario. It was while visiting my Great Uncle's home in Pendleton, Ontario that he met my mother, Florence Tucker. They were married in 1928. The youngest of four daughters, she was born in Clarence, Ontario, on July 29, 1899. Two sisters survive her—my Aunt Irene, now 94 and living in Smith Falls, Ontario and my Aunt Corinna, 91, living in Rockland near Ottawa. Both are independent, vigorous and alert, participating fully in community life.

To me Dad seemed able to do everything mechanical. On our modest farm of forty-four acres to which my parents had moved in the 1930s, Dad was the carpenter, plumber, and electrician. He could fix any motor. His native ability with animals was also impressive. Aside from hunting, fishing and even keeping bees at one point, he was especially adept at caring for sick animals. I vividly remember him performing an autopsy on one of our sheep that died suddenly, intent upon finding the cause to save the others. David and I watched in fascination—from a distance.

When World War II was declared Dad was too old to be retrained as a pilot so he enlisted and in due course became a flight sergeant. At the end of the war he was stationed in St-Jean, Quebec. When the base was converted to Dawson College, a branch of McGill University formed to accommodate returning veterans, Dad was invited to stay on as Superintendent of Buildings and Grounds. Then, when Dawson closed in 1950, he moved to Montreal and finished his working days as Supervisor of Athletic Facilities on the McGill campus.

In 1960 he married Shirley Hope and they spent eight happy years together at their home on Meech Lake in the Gatineau Hills. Shirley was stricken with cancer and soon Dad was alone once again. He moved west, first to Comox, British Columbia, then to Victoria. He married once more in 1974 to Wynn van Alstyne and lived with her in Victoria until his death at Victoria's Gorge Road Hospital in August of 1982. Knowing Dad was happy and well cared for during his declining years was a great comfort to my brother and me.

In high school and university my friends and I found summer jobs to help make ends meet. I did every kind of work: delivery boy for a grocery store in Montreal; fruit picker in the Okanagan Valley, B.C.; door-to-door salesman of Fuller brushes; maintenance man for tennis courts; manual labourer; and my favourite, tennis coach at a girls' camp in Maine. In September 1953 I entered the Faculty of Arts at McGill University.

After two years in Arts I decided to switch to Law. This was easier said than done. Because a B.A. was a prerequisite for admission to the Quebec Bar, students were expected to complete it before beginning law studies. Professor Gerry Le Dain, now Mr. Justice Le Dain of the Supreme Court of Canada, interviewed me for the Faculty of Law. He was understandably skeptical. Not only was I two years short of completing my B.A., my marks were less than outstanding. Most of my time had been absorbed by the Red & White Revue, the annual college musical which I had directed that year. But 1955 was a small class, and after an anxious wait I was accepted. Le Dain probably thought I would not make it past Christmas when the first year class was routinely trimmed by over one-third, but I managed to hang in.

My attention was soon diverted toward public policy, especially in the areas of language and education, largely because of the incomparable Frank Scott, lawyer, teacher, poet, politician and social engineer. It is said that Scott greatly influenced Michael Pitfield, my classmate, who later gained recognition as the precocious Clerk of the Privy Council. I suspect that Scott's respect for process and the rule of law played their part in Pitfield's subsequent responsibilities in government.

Scott also played a decisive role in the life of Leonard Cohen, who entered Law with me. At the end of Leonard's first year Frank persuaded him that his poetic genius far exceeded his legal potential.

When I was in my last year of Law school Leonard and I were reunited as co-tenants of a cold-water flat on Stanley Street. His nights were spent singing at Dunn's Birdland on St. Catherine Street while I laboured over my books. Then he would return, usually with a female friend. Through the thin walls that separated us in the flat, I could hear him entertaining into the early morning hours as I wrestled with the Code of

Civil Procedure. I began to wish that Scott had seen poetic talent in me.

But Frank Scott did have a profound influence on my own career, and continued as a close friend and mentor for many years. I often visited his home on Clarke Avenue in my riding, enjoying the hours spent with him and his wonderful wife, Marian. I never knew where the conversation might lead, his interests and accomplishments were so varied. As a founder of the CCF and chief drafter of the Regina Manifesto, his perspective on political affairs was a little different from my own. A relentless reformer, however, he never lost sight of the human condition and the need for protection of the disadvantaged.

I saw Scott more as a liberal than a socialist. His thinking was always progressive and reform oriented. He had a knack for seeing things as they were, going to the "Pith and Substance" of issues, be they legal or social.

For example, he was pragmatic on state intervention. One evening in his living room as we commiserated over the state of public finance (I was President of the Treasury Board at the time), Scott declared: "It is appalling. Imagine a government-owned company (Canadair) manufacturing *executive* jets!"

On another occasion he confessed to me that much as he deplored the concentration of power and capital in large corporations, they had done much to put glue into our Canadian federation by establishing national networks, holding national conventions and creating an environment in which employees frequently relocate, moving across the country within the corporate family. Scott maintained that these large corporations actually do more for Canadian unity than most of our public institutions. It was a perceptive and fair observation, typical of Scott.

In 1982, when I was involved in the fight against inflation as Treasury Board President, I sent him a congratulatory letter on a literary prize he had received. For most, a simple acknowledgement would have sufficed. Not for Frank Scott. Back came the following note, handwritten, putting his finger on the key issues:

F. R. SCOTT
451 Clarke Avenue   11 July 1982
Montreal, CANADA
H3Y 3C5

"Dear Don,

Thank you for your congratulations. My delayed acknowledgement is due to this clinging arthritis. It ties me down and burns me up. Haven't even been to Hatley once yet.

I am glad you are coming through on the political side of the economic arguments. Why is everyone so scared of the word depression? We are clearly in one. It's like pretending you haven't got cancer when you know you have. Delays the right cures. Controls of prices as well as wages. It must haunt you!

'Nil carborundum' as we used to say in the early 30s. Don't let the bastards wear you down.

Frank"

Frank Scott's death in 1985 marked the passing of a truly great Canadian. In many ways it was Scott's influence which persuaded me to practice law instead of pursuing business administration as I had intended. The practice of law now appeared to me as the most noble of professions. Business held no ideals of comparable value. I put my heart and soul into the study of law for those tough years and, to everyone's amazement, particularly my own, graduated at the top of my class as gold medalist.

John Turner and Jim Robb, young associates of the Stikeman and Elliott law firm, invited me to lunch at *Chez Son Père* to discuss future employment. Although we did not discuss politics, I remember being aware that everyone assumed Turner would one day be Prime Minister. I sensed he knew it too. After a short articling period at Stikeman and Elliott, I left for France to study at Grenoble on a travelling scholarship. I returned in 1959, wrote my bar exams, and was accepted to the Quebec Bar. Stikeman and Elliott took me on and John Turner and I became close working associates until he plunged into politics in the 1962 election.

One memorable case together involved John's client, Stewart's and Lloyds, a U.K. oil pipe producer. The company wanted the benefit of low transportation rates available to its Canadian competition. Under contract arrangements, railways could give special transportation rates to manufacturing companies but they could not be discriminatory. Our client believed it was also entitled to the lower rate. John invited me to be his junior on the case. We made a good team; John's performance was superb. He faced a formidable phalanx of renowned Canadian counsel including the late Arthur Pattillo, Roy Kellock, then recently retired from Canada's Supreme Court, Charles Brazier from Vancouver, Roger Doe and Don Wright, both with Toronto firms.

The case was argued in the courtroom of the Board of Transport Commissioners above the old Union Station, now the Convention Centre in Ottawa. From this vantage point we were treated to a perfect view of President John Kennedy and Prime Minister John Diefenbaker laying a wreath at Ottawa's War Memorial. Afterwards, John went to watch Kennedy's famous tree planting at the Governor General's residence which resulted in the widely publicized recurrence of the President's chronic back problem.

An incident in the Stewart's and Lloyds case impressed me with one important aspect of John's character. Having lost our case before the Commissioners, it still appeared that we might win before the Supreme Court of Canada. Somehow the appeal date had slipped my attention, and his. It looked as though we might be time barred (denied the right to proceed with the hearing). We were faced with the lawyer's nightmare.

As it turned out, through imaginative interpretation, we were able to proceed. What impressed me was John's determination to take full responsibility for the oversight, never even hinting that I should assume responsibility as the junior lawyer on the file. A lesser person would have responded otherwise.

In December of 1965 I married Heather Bell Maclaren of Halifax, Nova Scotia. Her strong family ties there have made Nova Scotia a second home for our entire family, all of us spending as much time on the beautiful south shore as duty permits.

23

In May, 1966, my mother passed away after four pain filled years fighting cancer. My dear Aunt Corinna, one of mother's older sisters, now ninety-one, nursed her until the end. Mother had always been particularly close to me. Her illness and death were the most difficult personal experiences of my life.

It is twenty years since her passing but the emotional emptiness remains. I always wanted to do more for her, to repay in some way what she had done for David and me through her lonely years. Mother always had projects and dreams she could not afford. Most of them went unfulfilled. For several years before her death I recorded her conversations, her laughter, her piano playing, knowing she would not live long enough to see our first child. Those tapes sit on a shelf untouched. I still cannot bring myself to play them.

The birth of our first daughter, Kristina, later that same year, went a long way toward filling the void that death brings and only time can diminish. Over the next few years we had three more daughters, Allison, Rachel and Sara, all now teenagers.

After several challenging and rewarding years at Stikeman and Elliott a few of us left to start our own law firm in late 1966. Although relationships with our former firm were understandably strained for a short period they were soon mended and many of its members, including Fraser Elliott and Heward Stikeman (who prides himself on his conservatism), have been most generous in supporting my own political career. A senior partner of that firm, Jim Grant, has been the principal organizer and moving force behind my political adventure from the first day.

I missed my friends and associates at Stikeman and Elliott but the record shows that our departure hardly caused them to break stride. New structures were adopted, the partnership was broadened and Stikeman and Elliott embarked on a road of prosperous expansion.

One branch of our new law firm which was opened in 1967 at Place Ville Marie became Johnston, Heenan & Blaikie. It continues under the name of Heenan & Blaikie with almost fifty lawyers. After the Liberal defeat in 1979 I returned to the firm as Counsel and brought Jean Chrétien with me. In 1984,

Pierre Trudeau came aboard as Counsel and I rejoined in the same capacity.

Building a law firm with Roy Heenan and Peter Blaikie was an exciting experience. We were utterly committed to establishing a successful practice. Place Ville Marie was one of the most convenient locations imaginable for clients in Montreal at that time. Overhead costs seemed crushing but we worked hard, clients came and the firm soon began to prosper. The daily burden of keeping up with ongoing work and cultivating new clients was sometimes overwhelming. In addition I was teaching taxation at the McGill Law Faculty and writing professional papers and topical articles to attract clients. These activities enabled me to broaden the practice into areas such as construction law where there was little expertise at that time. Although little time was left for leisure, it was worth all the effort. The firm remains a source of considerable pride to me.

Both Roy Heenan and Peter Blaikie had public policy interests far beyond the practice of law. Blaikie gave concrete expression to his by twice running, unsuccessfully, as a Tory candidate against Rod Blaker on the West Island and then winning the National Presidency of the Progressive Conservative Party. Heenan has been more neutral politically while actively pursuing public policy issues, especially in labour-management relations, through lectures, teaching, and writing.

No doubt much of my thinking on public policy matters was developed in those years of active practice. My clientele was so diversified that I gained perspectives seldom seen from a highly specialized discipline in a large firm—the financing requirements of small and medium sized business; the paper burden imposed by government; the complexities of taxation for the little guy who cannot afford expensive tax counsel; the unfortunate but profitable lure of international tax havens and the inequities of our legal system where justice is eroded through delay.

My frustration with government grew day by day. Clients were shown little respect by government, often being bounced from agency to agency in search of endlessly elusive answers. Foreigners wishing to establish themselves in Canada after the Foreign Investment Review Agency came into effect had an especially difficult time. I recall a European client with

25

decades of experience in a highly specialized manufacturing process being enraged by the arrogant interrogation on the merits of his complex multi-million dollar proposal by an uninformed and inexperienced review officer.

Yet for all the frustration and anger with the bureaucracy, I did develop some sympathy when I began to appreciate the magnitude of the challenge facing government in a rapidly changing and increasingly complex society.

Some of those challenges became apparent when I negotiated on behalf of the California-based Lockheed Aircraft Corporation (now Lockheed Corporation) to obtain the largest procurement contract in Canadian history up to that time for the acquisition of Long Range Patrol Aircraft. Boeing Aircraft had the alternate proposal and the competition was fierce. Days were spent in seemingly endless negotiations with senior bureaucrats.

For Lockheed it was a challenging period. The company had been rocked by scandal surrounding alleged bribes on foreign procurement contracts while fighting for its life to survive the financial crisis brought on by the failure of Rolls Royce, the supplier of engines to the Lockheed 1011 Tristar. It seemed enough to scuttle Lockheed's opportunity to sell approximately one billion dollars worth of aircraft to Canada. It was a trying period for those on both sides of the negotiating table. Ultimately, objectivity prevailed, Lockheed won the contract and I emerged from the experience with renewed respect for a number of senior bureaucrats who had refused to be spooked by the atmosphere of scandal and crisis and acted in the country's best interests.

One standard I felt we established in the early days of the firm was to be creative. We used the law aggressively to help clients further their own interests rather than simply to defend them. For example, tax knowledge enabled me to put together the first Canadian film tax shelters in the late 1960s, starting with Claude Jutra's film entitled *"Wow,"* followed by others including the celebrated *"Mon Oncle Antoine,"* which we financed with the National Film Board and a U.S. tax shelter group. In a sense, working with the U.S. Counsel, the American film tax shelters also began in Montreal because we had identified feature films as a new tax shelter for U.S. investors as well.

26

Geneviève Bujold joined with me in a film distribution company, Gendon Films Ltd., a combination of our first names. We subsequently sold the company to Astral Bellevue Pathé, Canada's largest independent film producer, headed by the incomparable Harold Greenberg with whom I established an enduring personal and professional relationship. Our work together took us on memorable adventures to Hollywood, New York, Paris and London. Always exploring new ways to finance films, Harold and I were even joint executive producers of a forgettable horror movie starring Troy Donahue entitled *"Seizure."*

My interest in construction law brought new challenges and new friends. Much of 1969, for example, was spent fighting the New Brunswick Electric Power Commission on behalf of contractors who had built the magnificent Mactaquac Power Dam near Fredericton. The contractors felt they had legitimate claims into the millions of dollars for additional work done to complete the project. Neil McKelvey of St. John was our local counsel. We became close friends over the many months it took to prepare and then argue the complex case before an arbitration board chaired by my old professor, Maxwell Cohen.

The day to day practice of law, working with interesting clients and making money, tends to isolate most of us from public policy issues. Occasionally, however, an opportunity presents itself to address fundamental questions that lay bare the very fabric of our society. So it was when a group of lawyers decided to challenge the provisions of the Parti Québécois' notorious Bill 101 which were intended to suppress the use of English in Quebec Courts and in the National Assembly. My partner Peter Blaikie and two colleagues, Yoine Goldstein and Roland Durand, had resolved to challenge the constitutional validity of the Bill. Blaikie invited me to be one of the counsel, for no fee of course. I accepted.

Robert Litvack, Batonnier André Brossard and I argued the case in the Quebec Superior Court, then in the Court of Appeal and finally before the Supreme Court of Canada. Armed with solid, well-reasoned judgements from both provincial courts, we anticipated a favourable outcome in the nation's highest tribunal. The case was argued in the early summer of 1979, just after the Liberals were defeated at the polls and I was a member of the Official Opposition in Parliament.

I brought my fellow lawyers back to the Parliament Buildings where we visited briefly with John Diefenbaker who had just moved into new offices in the Centre Block. He had been following the Bill 101 case with considerable interest and was anxious to hear about it. After our more serious exchanges, he regaled us with the story telling for which he was so famous and a few one-liners. As we left, one of us noticed a colour photograph of Dief decked out in fishing gear, proudly holding up an enormous fish.

"Was that in Saskatchewan?" we inquired.

"Gracious no," he chuckled, "in Saskatchewan we'd throw that one back!"

That was the last time I saw him before his death on August 16, 1979, a few weeks later.

On the day of the Supreme Court judgement, December 13, 1979, I was chairing the Committee of Public Accounts. Erik Nielsen, now Deputy Prime Minister, was appearing before the committee in his role as Minister of Public Works. I excused myself to go to the Court. I was tingling with anticipation. We were not disappointed. The Supreme Court, in a unanimous decision, confirmed our position. We had won the first counter attack against the narrow-minded linguistic nationalism of Camille Laurin and the Parti Québécois. A depressed and discouraged English-speaking minority in the province received a shot in the arm.

Not all English-speaking Quebecers were satisfied, however. Pleased with the decision, they still argued that our Liberal government should have either disallowed Bill 101 (through a constitutional provision not used since 1941) or at least referred the entire Bill immediately to the Supreme Court, bypassing the long road through the lower courts in Quebec.

Those questions will long be debated. For me, the strategy chosen was the right one. Pierre Trudeau in his wisdom knew that the price of federal "disallowance" could be social unrest or even the outbreak of violence. He also agreed with our view that lower court decisions in Quebec would give moral authority to the ultimate decision which a straight reference to the Supreme Court could never provide.

28

While many aspects of my law practice pointed me in the direction of public life, it was our tax system which finally pushed me into the fray. It seemed to me that the Canadian system of taxation was both oppressive and regressive, a blunt club in the hands of government rather than a useful instrument to serve the best interests of Canadians, to further prosperity and to encourage enterprise.

In 1973 I wrote a critique of our fiscal system. It was published in book form entitled *Fiscalamity: How to Survive Canada's Tax Chaos*[1]. After I had become a Cabinet minister selected passages from that book were gleefully thrown at me across the floor of the House of Commons by Conservatives Sinclair Stevens and Perrin Beatty. They seemed to agree with what I had written and were challenging the government of which I was a part to take action.

In July, 1974, shortly after my book was published and a few days after Pierre Trudeau had been returned with a majority government, my wife Heather and I were invited to have dinner with the Trudeaus at Harrington Lake. I gave a copy of my book to the Prime Minister when we arrived. As we enjoyed a beautiful summer evening over dinner on the screened-in porch of the Prime Minister's summer home in the Gatineau hills, conversation focussed on taxation, a subject of little interest, it seemed, to anyone but me.

Testing me with his characteristic probing style of questioning, Trudeau noted that the "gross-up and credit" system for dividends as I explained it seemed unnecessarily complex.

"That's not what we were led to believe," he said implying that those who had briefed him on the subject had fallen somewhat short of revealing the true complexity of the situation.

Heather later registered her astonishment that the Prime Minister had not read the Tax Bill itself, nor did he seem to appreciate the intricacies of the tax system his own government had introduced. No one should be surprised.

Many federal budgets have come and gone since that evening, including Allan MacEachen's celebrated November 1981 exercise. I can now attest to the fact that no minister, including the Minister of Finance himself, has the time to master the complexities of the Income Tax Act. That is one of the points I made in my book. I now know first hand the problem of providing politicians with even a modicum of understanding of such complex matters.

My book on tax reform was well received eventually going into three editions but I knew that, on its own, it could not bring about the kind of fundamental change that preoccupied me. Writing the book had given me some degree of satisfaction but the underlying frustration remained. Gradually, the notion that an active role in politics might be the only way to influence the process began to take hold.

III

Winning Sure Beats Losing

"One can imagine the torment of the media when their intimidating adversary, Pierre Trudeau, not only returned to the political scene, but won the next general election."

The decision to embark upon a political career was not an easy one to make. If I should succeed it would mean leaving a lucrative law practice I had helped to build and accepting a lower standard of living. It would mean less time to spend at home with my growing family. Heather and I would also have to face the difficult question of whether to move the family to Ottawa or keep our residence in Montreal.

On the other hand, I reasoned, there would be compensating factors. As a member of the government I would participate in decision-making that would affect twenty-five million Canadians. That would be a reward in itself. I was forty, healthy, energetic and curious. Being solution-oriented I believed that, given half a chance, I could contribute to effective change for my country.

Finally, with Heather's blessings, I decided to give politics a try. Only on rare occasions have I regretted that decision.

I told Pierre Trudeau of my political interest in the summer of 1976 just after my 40th birthday. It seemed like a good time to jump into a different career.

Trudeau was most encouraging. There was little he could do to help, however, since it would have violated Party convention for him to give the nod to any particular person in a Liberal nomination race. I had my heart set on the Westmount

31

riding which included that part of the city of Montreal where we lived. My friends and supporters in Westmount represented a small "c" Liberal constituency which shared my criticisms of government financial mismanagement and the outrageous tax system. It was the logical place for me to run.

It looked as though Bud Drury, the sitting Member, would be retiring after an outstanding career which included senior Cabinet posts under both Lester Pearson and Pierre Trudeau. Bud had recently left the Cabinet and seemed unlikely to spend a long period on the back benches.

Prior to Drury's retirement, Trudeau had suggested Verdun as a possible riding for me. It had been left vacant by Bryce Mackasey's departure. I did not feel as comfortable with that constituency at the time, however, and so did not pursue the nomination there. This turned out to be a wise decision because it came to be represented by the hard working Raymond Savard, an active member of the Verdun community and a City Councillor. He would have been a difficult if not impossible candidate to beat in the nomination race and went on to become an excellent riding man. Unfortunately, Savard was a victim of the Tory tidal wave in September, 1984 but with his political touch he has quickly rebounded and is now Verdun's mayor.

For those who aspire to a career as a Member of Parliament, let me tell you it's tough getting nominated to a safe seat. It may be easy for a Liberal in the Canadian West just as it was a cakewalk for many Conservatives to get nominations in Quebec in 1984. But when a seat is perceived as an easy mark, and thus a ticket to the House of Commons, the fight is on. Winning that nomination was one of the toughest challenges of my political career.

In late 1977 when the fight for the nomination began, it was not at all clear whether the Prime Minister would opt for a general election or a by-election. This complicated our situation since St. Henri was to be added to Westmount and parts of the old riding, including downtown Montreal, would be dropped for the next general election. These boundary modifications would not apply, however, in a by-election.

Liberal popularity across the country had been going up and down like a roller coaster; mostly down. The business and professional communities had turned against the Party in

top: *My Mother, Florence, 1965.*

above: *My Father Wilbur, his aviator's Certificate, dated January 1919. His was the twenty-sixth to be issued in Canada.*

right: *My maternal grandparents Martha Moffat and Stephen Tucker, January 1886.*

left: *Father, friend, and brother David with me on the farm 1940.*

below: *David and me with friend, 1940.*

bottom: *Uncle Livingston Johnston with my father, California, 1924.*

below: *Author, mother and the faithful Betty, 1943.*

right: *On the farm with brother David and pets, 1942.*

bottom: *Cumberland School, 1943. I am in the back row, second from right.*

Off to Africa,1957. Believe it or not, in the photograph can be found the author, former Prime Minister Trudeau, former Solicitor General Bob Kaplan, former Canada Council Head Timothy Porteous and acclaimed author Lionel Tiger.

Author with fellow counsellors. Camp Walden, Maine, 1955.

McGill University./Faculty of Law 1958

G.E. Le Dain

F.R. Scott

M. Cohen

P.M. Pitfield

D.J. Johnston

Y. Fortier

My talented McGill law professors included Supreme Court Justice Gerald Le Dain, the renowned Max Cohen, and the incomparable Frank Scott — lawyer, educator, poet, and a founder of the CCF party.

Among my illustrious classmates were future Privy Council Clerk Michael Pitfield and future Quebec Bar President, Yves Fortier.

top: *Planning the legal attack on Bill 101, 1978.* left to right are: *lawyer Robert Litvack, partner Peter Blaikie, lawyer André Brossard and author. (Montreal Star)*

right: *With brother David and Aunt Corinna at nephew's wedding, November 1985.*

Beginning the 1978 campaign. With me left to right are *daughters Sara, Kristina, Allison, Rachel and my wife Heather.*

Author with family, Nova Scotia, 1983. (Barbara Collins)

Trudeau visits the Johnstons at Murder Point, Mahone Bay, Nova Scotia, 1980. (Barbara Collins)

droves by the mid 1970s. Despite this, the results of by-elections held in 1977 were reasonably good for the Liberals. Among those returned was the dynamic and talented Dennis Dawson from Louis Hébert, later to preside over the Quebec caucus.

As the Westmount nomination convention approached there was still no word on whether we would face a general election or a by-election. The resultant uncertainty about our electoral boundaries meant that candidates for the Liberal nomination had to draw support from all areas of the old riding as well as the new. Beginning with just over 300 members of the combined associations of St. Henri and Westmount, the membership swelled to 4,006 by the night of the convention on April 5, 1978. The nomination meeting had been slated for the auditorium of my Alma Mater, the High School of Montreal, but the numbers forced a move to the Ballroom of the Queen Elizabeth Hotel.

There were three other candidates: Dale C. Thomson, the renowned historian, author, and former secretary to Prime Minister Louis St. Laurent; Mark Feifer, an accomplished Montreal attorney; and Richard Rhone, an insurance executive. Thomson and Feifer led well-organized, well-financed campaigns. Much of the local Party establishment, particularly those directing the Quebec wing of the Federal Liberal Party, were solidly behind Dale Thomson, although their public declarations were non-committal. As expected, the Prime Minister's Office stood discreetly aside, although I believe Jim Coutts' sympathy lay with me.

My supporters wanted to see a change in direction, a return to liberal principles and the abandonment of interventionist social democratic views. A former associate and close friend, Jim Grant of Stikeman and Elliott, headed our campaign. Before long, we had a strong team of volunteers, including the capable and effervescent Brenda Norris, John Turner's sister, and Margaret Bruneau, organizer *par excellence* as demonstrated in her previous work with the Canadian Open Golf Tournament. Friends held countless receptions and coffee parties, contributed funds and, most importantly, showed up to vote.

Public Affairs adviser, John de B. Payne, Turner's political guru, made a solid contribution to my convention speech, and

41

film producer and director, Paul Almond, put me through several rehearsals in his house on Redpath Crescent the day before the convention.

Paul and I had worked together on many film projects and while I had watched him direct Geneviève Bujold, Donald Sutherland and others, I had never been his creative subject before. He was patient, helpful and, above all, encouraging.

More than 2,600 people crowded into the ballroom the night of the convention. It was an awesome experience to find myself suddenly, after so many weeks of work, on the platform in front of thousands of Liberal militants, 60 per cent of whom proceeded to vote for me on the first ballot. Our stunning victory was almost entirely attributable to the efforts of my talented workers, many of whom had played critical roles in John Turner's Montreal organization in the early 1960s.

It was my first experience of that kind. It seemed such an abrupt ending to the long, grueling campaign. I floated out of the ballroom surrounded by family and friends. At a victory celebration which followed, my campaign chairman, Jim Grant, a person of many talents but few words, finally had to speak. More than a friend, Jim has always been one of my most valued critics, to be counted upon for his nuggets of wisdom. He did not disappoint us that evening. He said: "Winning sure beats losing!" That is all I can recall him saying. He made his point.

For a few hours our nomination meeting may have been the largest in Liberal Party history. If it was, the record was broken the next day when Dr. John Evans won the nomination in Toronto's Rosedale riding. As the president of the University of Toronto, John had enjoyed a high profile and an outstanding record of achievement. It was a shame that he had to face Toronto's "tiny perfect Mayor," David Crombie, in the by-election. He took defeat with grace and his own delightful brand of self-deprecating wit. He once told me that during this election fight his family did a voting preference poll around the breakfast table, and Crombie won.

The fortunes of the Liberal Party were in obvious decline in 1978. Having crested at 51 per cent in June and July of 1977, Liberal popularity as measured by Gallup fell to 42 per cent by December of 1977 and 41 per cent by September of 1978. Rejecting a general election and certain defeat, Trudeau called fifteen by-elections for October 16, 1978. One of them would be in Westmount.

During the campaign I was visited by several prominent members of Cabinet (one of the benefits of running in a by-election) and the Prime Minister himself who came to my headquarters on Victoria Avenue and gave a good stump speech. Standing with me on a table top, microphone in hand, he announced to the overflowing crowd: "I have known John for 20 years." Thus I joined the ranks of Bill (Denis) McDermott and Allan Framingham (Fotheringham), earlier victims of Trudeau's penchant for confusing names. Trudeau likes to say he does it on purpose but it sure didn't look like it that day on Victoria Avenue as my assembled supporters shifted uncomfortably.

Iona Campagnolo and Otto Lang each contributed a day of door-to-door campaigning, Iona declaring that after having campaigned in Tory Ontario, Montreal was like awakening in heaven. It was the same for Otto. He had been subject to wide press criticism which unfairly camouflaged the fact that he was one of the most competent ministers in the Cabinet. But in sharp contrast to the reception Otto might have experienced elsewhere, at the first home we approached together in the Notre Dame de Grace section of my riding an enthusiastic French-speaking Liberal rushed from his door to greet Otto, proclaiming him to be a great minister, one of Canada's finest Canadians, a family man and a good Catholic to boot. Otto was overwhelmed and, from that point forward, quite prepared to knock on every door in the riding.

The two other cabinet ministers who helped me out were Norm Cafik (Minister of Multiculturalism) who worked the streets with me in the Snowdon section of the riding and the late Dan Macdonald of Prince Edward Island and Minister of Veteran's Affairs at that time. Dan, a great Canadian by any measure, travelled to Montreal to meet with a handful of veterans in Ma Heller's restaurant in Notre Dame de Grace. The measure of the affection and respect with which Dan was held by veterans was legendary, generated not only by his direct down-to-earth personality, but also because of his outstanding war service. He was much heralded for the courage and compassion he showed in battle. For example, after convincing his commander to spare a church in the midst of a battle during the Italian campaign, he was fired upon from within the church at the cost of an arm and a leg. The deep respect in which he is held by Canadian veterans was matched by his colleagues on both sides of the House of Commons.

My major competitor in the 1978 by-election was the Conservative candidate, Bernard Finestone, an insurance executive and outstanding member of the local community. As recently as my nomination convention just four months earlier, he had been a member of our Liberal Association. His defection to the Tories was one of many examples of the revolt of the business community against the Liberal Government. He ran an energetic campaign under the direction of Joan Price Winser, a talented and tireless Tory supporter and now Canada's Consul General in Los Angeles.

When the votes were all counted on October 16th, only two of the fifteen seats in the by-election were won by Liberals. By good fortune the Liberal tradition in Westmount remained strong permitting me to be among the winners. Bob Rae, now Ontario NDP leader, and current Tory Cabinet Ministers David Crombie, Robert de Cotret, and Tom Siddon were also elected for the first time in those by-elections.

A state of depression pervaded all levels of the Liberal Party following that loss in thirteen ridings. Understandably, my workers and I were unaffected at the outset, basking in the afterglow of victory. The swearing-in ceremony and the march down the centre of the House of Commons led by the Prime Minister and House Leader is an exciting experience for any political neophyte. I was no exception.

Members of the Opposition went out of their ways to be helpful and cordial. NDP House Leader Stanley Knowles, Oppposition House Leader, the late Walter Baker, Ray Hnatyshyn and John Diefenbaker were especially kind. Diefenbaker even stopped by my office on the fourth floor of the Centre Block to offer his congratulations on my freshman speech.

In my own caucus the welcome was spontaneous and warm. Marcel Prud'homme was most helpful. Lloyd Francis and Tom Lefebvre directed me toward the Public Accounts Committee, one of my prime areas of interest. John Reid, one of the Liberal caucus experts on parliamentary procedures, was always ready to share his insight and help a newcomer.

But it was the late Bob Andras who became my closest friend and supporter and remained so until his death as a victim of cancer on November 17, 1982. Few politicians deserved and enjoyed such affection and respect from colleagues and constituents as Bob did.

My mood of excitement and adventure was quickly dampened by the smell of inevitable defeat that permeated Liberal ranks in the late 1970s. A bunker mentality had grasped the Prime Minister's Office, the Cabinet and the caucus. The writing was on the wall for all to see and the Prime Minister seemed reconciled to it.

Trudeau's interest was temporarily aroused by the Pépin-Robarts Report which, in a number of respects, disagreed fundamentally with his own view of the country. The Report argued that, because of its distinctive character, Quebec should have "special status," a concept long rejected by Trudeau. The Commission stated:

> "In the case of Quebec, it should be assured of the full powers needed for the preservation and expansion of its distinctive heritage. This would require either exclusive or concurrent jurisdiction, assigned to all provinces generally or to Quebec specifically, over such matters as language, culture, civil law, research and communications, as well as related power to tax and to establish some relations in these fields with foreign countries."

Coming in the wake of Quebec's Bill 101 which constituted a frontal assault on English language rights, this proposal shocked many of us, including Pierre Trudeau.

Trudeau seemed to be angry, especially with Jean-Luc Pépin, a faithful lieutenant who had rendered him great service for so many years. One suspected the Report tainted forever his view of Jean-Luc.

We soldiered on until Trudeau called a general election on March 26 for May 22, 1979. Our popularity was tied with the Tories at 26 per cent, 10 per cent supported the NDP and a giant 35 per cent were undecided. We were in the fifth year of our mandate. Our time had run out in more ways than one.

This time I ran in the new riding of St. Henri-Westmount. The St. Henri portion had been represented for more than twenty years by Gérard Loiselle, one of the most respected members of the House of Commons and much beloved by his constituents. It is unilingual French, economically deprived but has many proud traditions. Here there are strong family bonds that transcend generations. It is a veritable village within the City of Montreal. Thanks to Loiselle I quickly became acquainted with St. Henri, and with his endorsement I won with a comfortable majority.

Joe Clark became the first man to defeat Pierre Trudeau. The vote reflected anti-government rather than pro-Clark sentiment. While support for the Liberal Party held firm in Quebec, the West was a disaster. We retained only three of the fifteen seats we had held west of Ontario prior to the election. Our ten seats in British Columbia were reduced to one, Art Phillips in Vancouver; Alberta remained unchanged at zero; we lost all three previously held by us in Saskatchewan; and Lloyd Axworthy of Winnipeg-Fort Gary and Bob Bockstael of St. Boniface managed to hang on to our two Manitoba seats.

Trudeau, I believe, had long been resigned to Liberal defeat. If disappointed, he did not reflect it either in his humour or his actions. Speculation was rampant on the subject of his future. After eleven years as Canada's Prime Minister would he be willing and/or able to adapt to opposition?

Stornoway, which would become Trudeau's home as leader of the Official Opposition, was in a state of disrepair, evidently its chronic condition, so Trudeau and his sons spent a week with my family in Nova Scotia, went canoeing in northern Canada and then visited China. As usual, nobody, including those he visited, knew what Trudeau had on his political agenda. If he had made any decisions he shared them with no one.

There followed the bizarre tenure of Joe Clark's minority. Our stint in Opposition was uneventful. At first no one expected us to return to power for several years. After all, Liberals had managed minority governments in the past. Presumably the Tories could make it work by balancing the interests of the 26-strong NDP caucus under Broadbent and the six Social Credit MPs under the leadership of Fabien Roy. Trudeau himself believed the Conservatives deserved the chance to govern.

But only nine months were to separate Clark's oath of office from the swearing in of his successor. During this period Parliament only sat for seven weeks.

For Liberals, especially former Cabinet ministers, this interlude presented an opportunity to devote more time to long neglected personal projects. I recall Marc Lalonde, for example, extolling the virtues of his magnificent onions, the product of many hours in his garden on Ile-Perrot.

For me, the change was a profound disappointment. Ahead of me lay the prospect of four years in opposition. I was uncertain as to what contribution I could make. But the initial period was agreeable enough. The election had been in May but the House would not sit until late fall. While Lalonde tended his garden, I built a shed at our cottage in Glen Sutton and finished some legal work for my old firm.

As I now know, the shift from government to Opposition is much more traumatic for ministers than for back-benchers. Suddenly the limelight, demanding schedules and scurrying staff are gone. Your input is no longer needed on burning issues that were under your daily control only the day before. The new minister and his government announce programs you yourself worked hard to introduce. Worst of all, you just are not "on the scene."

On the other hand, being a back-bencher in Opposition is much more stimulating and provides more scope for personal initiative than does the back bench in government. In 1979 I took on the Chairmanship of the Public Accounts Committee, a post reserved for the Opposition. It was there that I came to know the Auditor General, Jim Macdonell and his staff, particularly the talented Michael Rayner, now Canada's Comptroller General. It was during this time that my interest in the role of the Auditor General took root. Before long I became a staunch advocate of Macdonell's favourite hobby horse, comprehensive auditing.

On Wednesday, November 19, 1979, in the fourth week of Clark's first (and only) session, Trudeau did not arrive at our weekly caucus on time, a most unusual occurrence. As we waited for him, Monique Bégin turned to me and said: "Donald, il y a du malheur à la porte." ("There is misfortune at the door.") As usual, Monique's sensitive antennae were working well and, of course, she was right. When Trudeau entered, his message was simple. He had decided to resign.

The eulogies poured in, beginning in the House of Commons, and then across the land. Representatives of the media who had despised Trudeau now seemed to love him. They had beaten him and were eager to bury him. The time had finally come to pay last respects. How generous they were. Even Allan Fotheringham, long viewed as a Trudeau baiter, wrote a column that almost brought tears to my eyes. I had suspected Fotheringham and other astute media personnel of harbouring mixed feelings about Trudeau, secretly admiring his talents and strengths while publicly trying to hobble him with unrestrained criticism. They had seen no place for sympathy because they assumed, correctly, that he could defend himself. His departure enabled many to confess their true feelings, like Cyrano de Bergerac to Roxane in the classic play.

Everyone found something good to say about this old warrior they so long sought to dethrone. One can imagine the torment of the media when their intimidating adversary, Pierre Trudeau, not only returned to the political scene, but won the next general election.

After Trudeau's resignation, activity in Liberal circles picked up because of speculation on the Party's leadership. John Turner was a favourite of many but after closeting with John de B. Payne and other advisers he announced that he would not be a candidate. That left the field clear for Don Macdonald, considered Trudeau's choice. Few Liberals recognized how little time we had.

The unexpected fall of the Clark government on December 13, 1979, threw everything into a cocked hat. There were mixed feelings on both sides of the House and considerable surprise when the amendment condemning Crosbie's budget passed by a vote of 139 to 133. Three Conservatives and one Liberal were absent. All six Social Credit MPs abstained from the vote.

During the dinner break, I came upon the solitary figure of Jim Coutts sitting on a bench outside the Common's Chamber. He seemed deep in contemplation.

"Jim," I interrupted his thoughts, "is it true that the government will lose the vote tonight?"

"Yes, they don't have the numbers."

Coutts' deserved reputation as a brilliant political strategist is the product, in part, of his reliable information network.

His facts are seldom wrong. This was no exception.

Many Tories saw the unexpected defeat as an opportunity to win a clear majority in the 1958 Diefenbaker tradition. The Liberals were in total disarray, had no leader, and were about to launch a leadership fight that was bound to be divisive. Many Liberals feared they had not regained enough strength since the previous election to fight another election effectively. And how, they wondered, could they choose a new leader and emerge united in such a short time?

The Tories bungled magnificently. Joe Clark was ill-advised. Those who believed Tory popularity to be on the rise had not appreciated the deep erosion in public support. They did not reckon that gaffes such as Clark's promise to move the Israel Embassy to Jerusalem, reinforced by the unpopular Crosbie budget could possibly result in such rapid decline of support. Nor did they count on the return of Pierre Trudeau. They no doubt assumed they would be contesting the next election against Don Macdonald, the obvious front runner in any hastily called leadership race.

I doubt that Trudeau really wished to return. He is not given to hasty decisions of any kind, especially career decisions. The process he went through in determining to resign would not be reversed simply by the prospect of imminent defeat of the Clark government. His own reservations about returning were unquestionably reinforced by the heated caucus debate which, only after many hours, brought forth a consensus in favour of his return. He was not present but I imagine he received detailed accounts of what transpired. It was hardly the kind of endorsement that would make him enthusiastic.

I telephoned Trudeau several times after that caucus meeting, hoping to persuade him to reconsider the leadership. He was non-committal. Ed Lumley called me in Montreal and suggested that the two of us see Trudeau together. I rushed to Ottawa. Ed and I spent the better part of an hour reviewing with Trudeau the pros and cons of his return. Neither of us could fathom what was going on in his mind although he referred several times to the caucus fight.

Why was it so important to us that Trudeau return? Each of us probably had different reasons and, of course, a large number of Liberals did not want it to happen.

49

Most, I suspect, wanted him because they thought he could win. In my case, I shared that view but I also saw Trudeau as the key player in the forthcoming battle against the Parti Québécois. I knew of no one else who could play that role more effectively.

Furthermore, despite serious misgivings about several of his policies, I believed then, as I do now, that Trudeau is one of the great Canadian leaders of all time. The strengths of great men have invariably been matched by great flaws. Trudeau is no exception. But by any objective assessment, Trudeau was the logical leader of the Liberal Party in 1979.

On the day of decision a number of us, meeting in Parliament's Centre Block, slipped into the Opposition lobby to watch Trudeau's announcement on television. Art Phillips and Lloyd Axworthy were there. Nobody had any idea what Trudeau was going to say. Bets were going both ways. Rumour has it that he had statements prepared for both alternatives.

We waited in nervous anticipation for his announcement. When it came, it was no surprise: Trudeau would lead our Party into the next election. With a man of Trudeau's complexity, the opposite result would also have been no surprise. I was delighted with his decision. It even occurred to me that perhaps Lumley and I had contributed in some small way to writing this chapter of Canadian history.

Others were much less enthusiastic. They feared his return would reinforce the east-west split that was confirmed by the 1979 election. Quebec influence would continue to dominate the national agenda and western alienation would continue unabated.

The election was on. It was to be one of the most cynical campaigns in Canadian history, with the Prime Minister keeping as low a profile as possible. Some said he read his speeches with the enthusiasm of someone reciting a laundry list. At least a laundry list has colour; his performances did not.

I was exposed to the strategy at the very outset. We opened the Quebec campaign with a luncheon rally in the east end of Montreal. I was one of two warm-up speakers to be followed by Pierre Trudeau. The atmosphere was electric, the room jam-packed, everyone buoyed up by polls that would bring us to power if they were to hold throughout the campaign.

Just as Trudeau rose from his table to go to the podium, one of his aides handed him the text of his speech. Judging by the delivery, he had probably never seen it before. But it did not matter. The response was overwhelming. According to our strategists, because Clark and his Conservatives had fallen into disfavour, the Liberals would win the election by default if they could just keep their heads down and steer clear of controversy. At all costs Trudeau had to be prevented from asking farmers why he should sell their wheat for them or engaging in that wonderful tongue-in-cheek repartee for which he was noted. It was obviously the right strategy.

In 1979 I had widened the gap between myself and my Tory opponent, Bernard Finestone, to 24,882 votes when I won 71 per cent of the total votes cast. While the margin slipped to 18,243 votes between myself and Tory candidate, Claude Dupras, in the 1980 election, I still had 67 per cent of the vote, a safe margin no matter how you look at it.

The same story repeated itself across Quebec many times as Liberals won 74 of 75 seats. In sharp contrast, rejection of the Liberals in the west was even more extreme than in the 1979 election. While Lloyd Axworthy and Bob Bockstael managed to hold on to their seats in Manitoba, Party fortunes were dealt a serious blow when Art Phillips lost his seat in Vancouver Centre. He was our last member west of Manitoba and as such carried a heavy burden. Furthermore, his vigorous defence of a pragmatic common sense approach to management of the economy would be sadly missed in caucus. Despite the devastating situation in the west, we were able to win the election because of our safe edge on the Tories in Ontario (52/31) and the Atlantic provinces (19/13).

We had successfully ridden the wave of anti-Clark sentiment back into power, a decisive loss for Clark rather than a resounding victory for the Liberals. Many Liberals to this day will argue that a longer retreat to the political wilderness in 1979 would have been much better for the Party and would have allowed it to return with renewed strength and vigour in 1984.

The Party may have been better served by such a period out of office but let us not forget that, faced with the greatest constitutional crisis since Confederation, Pierre Elliott Trudeau finally realized his destiny as the articulate spokesman of national unity. He could only play that role from the office of the Prime Minister and even his greatest detractors will admit he played the role magnificently.

IV

Countdown to Defeat

*"We did not even pretend to chart a new
course. No one seemed to care what the electorate felt. It was as if they had served our
purpose and now we had no time for them."*

On January 29, 1981, while in a meeting in Edmonton
with my deputy, Jack Manion, and members of the Alberta
government including Lou Hyndman, the Province's treasur-
er, I received a telephone call from the Privy Council Office
(PCO). It was Bob Rabinovitch on the line:

"Don, I called to tell you that there was a special meeting
of Priorities and Planning this afternoon."

"Oh," I answered. I was astonished. As Treasury Board
President and a committee member this was the first I had
heard of any special meeting. "On what subject?"

"On Petrofina. We have acquired it."

There was a pause.

"We will be paying $1.7 billion."

I was dumbfounded. A commitment of that magnitude
made without any advance notice to ministers, especially the
President of the Treasury Board? Whatever the merits of the
acquisition might have been, and I held definite views on the
subject, all cabinet ministers should have been consulted, not
just those who, by accident of timetable, found themselves in
Ottawa that January afternoon. Good lord, I thought, are my
views irrelevant? Does the Cabinet no longer count?

The last mandate of Pierre Elliott Trudeau was a remarkable chapter in Canadian political history. From its bizarre and unexpected beginnings with Joe Clark's defeat to Trudeau's resignation on February 29, 1984, the period is at once a story of great national achievement and political failure.

It was a time when the whole western world faced difficult challenges: mounting inflation, high unemployment, soaring interest rates and ballooning deficits. In Canada these were combined with constitutional problems and a referendum on sovereignty association in Quebec.

It seemed that wherever Trudeau focussed his attention and brought his own political, legal and intellectual skills to bear, success followed. Striking examples were the Quebec Referendum and Constitutional Reform. In each instance, Trudeau was fully involved. Unfortunately, most other issues were left to others.

A senior official observed to me that after 1980 Trudeau no longer took home three binders of briefings for thorough study the night before cabinet meetings as he had previously. In the 1970s he had played his role as cabinet chairman with zest, arriving in the cabinet room informed and spoiling for debate. Now many agenda items tended to founder, suffering, I believe, from the absence of his day-to-day attention.

The National Energy Program (NEP) was one such example. Developed by Marc Lalonde and a small coterie of officials, it was accepted by Trudeau and MacEachen and imposed upon the country as the centrepiece of Allan's first budget rather than as a Bill introduced by the Energy Minister. Through this technique much of its content was hidden from Cabinet until it was a *fait accompli*. Certainly the tax implications belonged in the budget but hardly the entire program. Most of the measures should have gone to caucus for discussion given their significance. However worthy the ideas that underpinned the NEP, its glaring flaws caused enormous political damage.

The point is, this could have been avoided. But no one was willing to come down from the ivory tower to find out what was going on in the world below. They had not even bothered to consult with the oil and gas industry, nor with the provinces affected, before designing and launching the program.

The political agenda was controlled more by Trudeau's advisers led by Jim Coutts and later by Tom Axworthy than by elected members. It coloured both the tone and the packaging of our substantive program. History has shown that the colouring was wrong. Instead of creating a positive public image of change, we reinforced the same perceptions of arrogance and insensitivity which had led to our defeat in 1979.

I was there. As early as 1981 I felt we were on the wrong political course. I was not alone. But only a handful of fellow cabinet ministers seemed to agree. Together we watched the spectre of defeat loom larger and larger. What could we have done? What should we have done?

In 1984 I watched in amazement as some cabinet ministers and advisers suddenly shifted gears and embraced the neo-conservatism of John Turner. John was known to be against many, if not most, of our major policies. Yet, Keith Davey, Herb Gray, Lloyd Axworthy, Monique Bégin and others seen as defenders of the Party's social democratic coalition rallied to support his leadership. Perhaps they judged, correctly as it turned out, that his positions could be softened. When the 1984 election campaign stumbled and virtually collapsed, Turner returned to Trudeau policies on many fronts, notably the NEP. If the public was confused, so was I, along with many other Liberals. The Party and its policies were bobbing up and down like a cork on a sea of public opinion polls.

Polls have a major role to play in the political process in *selling* a policy that the government believes to be in the national interest. Public opinion is capricious and cannot serve as a basis for *creating* coherent long-term policy. On the other hand, obtaining informed views through consultation is imperative to responsive government.

I hoped that a new leader just might get us back on track. Yet instead of acting as a launch pad for a revitalized Liberal Party, our abysmal performance in the election campaign of 1984 proved to be the last nail in the Liberal coffin.

But it was only one nail. The others had been hammered into place over the course of many years. Any leader would have had to wage brilliant war to win. John Turner was not up to the superhuman task. In retrospect, I am convinced that the style of our government, not the substance of our programs, destroyed any chance of a Liberal victory in 1984.

When Pierre Trudeau was confirmed as Prime Minister in June of 1968, he had won an overwhelming mandate from the Canadian people. A six-layered pyramid of Liberal support was firmly in place. It had a broad base of Canadians who had voted the Party into power. Next came the members of riding associations, many of whom had been active in the election. Party members at the regional and national executive levels made up the third level. Fourth were the elected members. Then came the Cabinet; and finally the Prime Minister's Office (PMO). The pyramid was strong and secure. Everyone felt a sense of value to the Party. They were sharing in the excitement of a new age for Canada.

The day after the 1968 election Canadians woke up feeling great. They knew that a contemporary man was in charge; a man who could forge a strong alliance between French and English Canada and endow public policy with the realities of the day. Above all else, they believed that Canada was at last led by a world class statesman. What a feeling. It was mass euphoria.

We were unconcerned that our parliamentary democracy supported by strong party discipline places enormous power in the hands of the Prime Minister and his non-elected advisers. As we were to learn, Lord Acton's dictum that "power tends to corrupt and absolute power corrupts absolutely" would find few better applications in modern democracies than our own in the years that followed.

As the years passed, the corruption of power began to destroy the pyramid of support upon which Trudeau's initial success had depended. Power and influence were sequestered and jealously guarded by those at all levels with ambitions of moving up the pyramid. The base of the pyramid became smaller and smaller. Party militants were forgotten with the exception of those squeaking wheels who continued to get more grease than they deserved. The party structure, including the office of the national executive, became less and less relevant to the operations of the parliamentary wing, the Liberal caucus. The caucus in turn had much less power than party supporters supposed.

In the riding of Westmount the grass roots of the Party were moribund. That the Party survived at all in that riding was largely due to the tireless work of Diana Weatherall and a handful of loyal co-workers who held things together through sheer personal effort. Most of the Liberal stalwarts of the 1960s had drifted away, dismayed by what they saw as the "socialism" of the Trudeau government. Some returned to support me in the 1978 by-election and more became involved as supporters of John Turner in the 1984 Liberal leadership race. Many others did not. They remain outside the Party.

Over the past six years I have seen that same general pattern play itself out in most parts of Canada, especially amongst middle and upper income Canadians.

By the time I arrived in Ottawa in 1978 the Liberal caucus was little more than a voting mechanism in the House of Commons to support government initiatives. Its co-operative members were rewarded with travel, parliamentary secretaryships and invitations to choice state affairs. Those Liberal MPs brave enough to criticize the government were marked for reprisal and could forget about aspiring to Cabinet posts or any other advancement for that matter.

Among the rare exceptions to this rule was Serge Joyal. Labelled a maverick in the late 1970s for having the guts to speak his mind on language issues, he received a Cabinet appointment after redeeming himself through solid work as co-chairman of the joint House-Senate Committee on the Constitution.

Louis Duclos was not so lucky. An articulate, intelligent and fluently bilingual MP from the Quebec City area, Louis had enjoyed a previous career in the Canadian Foreign Service. The government had promised changes to Canada's immigration laws and Duclos was dissatisfied with the status of refugees as provided for in the Bill. Duclos had brought his objections to the attention of Cabinet and caucus but to no avail. As a last resort, to underline his disapproval, he voted against the Bill on third reading. As he left the Commons chamber, Marc Lalonde, Trudeau's Quebec Lieutenant, said:

"You never vote against the government on third reading." It was a short but clear message. Duclos never made it to Cabinet.

The reprisals extended beyond the caucus. For example, Gordon Gibson, a thoughtful and intelligent contributor to Liberal politics and a former executive assistant to Trudeau, was ostracized by reason of his independent stand on constitutional reform. This highly respected Party insider whose advice was often sought, suddenly found himself frozen out and very much on the outside looking in.

The list of the favoured few who received generous personal rewards in return for servile support became shorter and shorter. Those who still had the ear and favour of the PMO were well rewarded, sometimes repeatedly, while other party stalwarts went without even a word of thanks.

The control of power went further. Many senior cabinet ministers were denied control or input over key policy formulation and implementation in their own portfolios. On occasion, major initiatives were developed by Trudeau's entourage of non-elected advisers, sometimes with the participation of Lalonde and MacEachen, then sprung on unsuspecting ministers in a most insensitive fashion.

The process seems to have begun prior to 1980. A case in point was the humiliation of Jean Chrétien in 1978 when he was Minister of Finance. The Prime Minister is said to have been impressed with Chancellor Schmidt's message of restraint at the Bonn Economic Summit. As as result, it was decided to cut two billion dollars from federal spending, reduce regulation and, in Trudeau's words, "do more with less." Chrétien was not even consulted.[1] The media of the day quickly ascertained that Trudeau and the PMO were calling the shots, and decried the shocking and unfair treatment being accorded the loyal Finance Minister and the office he held.

When the Liberals were returned to office in 1980 after Joe Clark's brief administration, no serious attempt was made to rebuild the pyramid even though it was clear from the defeat of 1979 that our Party structure and our policies needed desperately to be renewed. A platform committee of which I was a member, under the joint chairmanship of Allan MacEachen and Lorna Marsden, worked out some policy options at the beginning of the 1980 campaign. The backroom boys largely ignored them. The real strategy was to coast to victory on the proven reliability of public opinion polls, keeping Trudeau out of the limelight. In other words, Liberals would do best by doing and saying as little as possible.

As soon as Trudeau was re-elected, he lost no time in recalling Michael Pitfield as Clerk of the Privy Council and Jim Coutts as his Principal Secretary. He proceeded to name a

Cabinet that was substantially a continuation of the one that had been defeated a year earlier. A few new faces were added in lesser portfolios, but the only major surprise was Mark MacGuigan's appointment to External Affairs.

I was delighted to be named to Treasury Board. There I could get at government management and spending practices, an area of activity I believed must play a central role in developing responsible approaches to restraint. It is also true, however, that this appointment placed me within a central agency whose accent was on administration, effectively isolating me from economic policy initiatives. It was an open secret that my views on government spending were seen by key insiders as being more compatible with fiscal conservatism than social democratic liberalism. On Treasury Board I could not rock the boat.

A few talented Cabinet ministers who had been outspoken in their criticism of members of Trudeau's entourage were disposed of at this time. Judd Buchanan, a devoted Liberal who continues to do more than his share for the Party, was an early victim of the revived Trudeau government. He was not invited to rejoin the 1980 Cabinet.

Jim Fleming, an articulate and enlightened Liberal, fared better than Judd but not for long. He was shuffled out of the Cabinet in early 1983. Many of us were surprised and upset because Jim always made a solid contribution. The rumour says that when Jim Coutts was defeated in the Spadina by-election in 1981, Fleming celebrated with champagne. Many fellow ministers assumed that was why he was chopped.

In essence, the Clark government had been like a rain shower interrupting a tennis match, with the same players returning to the court to resume play after the downpour, as though nothing else but a little rain had fallen.

But much more than a brief downpour had occurred. Canadians had rejected the Trudeau government in 1979. They returned it in 1980 by default. The media, pleased by the 1979 change of characters, had no reservoir of good will to offer Trudeau in 1980, resenting the old warrior's return, and anxious to destroy his government and its individual members as quickly as possible.

The perceptions that drove Canadians to reject Liberals in 1979 were still there: the arrogance of the leader, the government and the Party; the waste of taxpayers' dollars; the bloated and growing bureaucracy; and the kind of interventionism that arises from a social democratic approach to management of the economy. The style of government that Canadians rejected had not changed. If anything, it had been reinforced.

The public, our ultimate judge, could not be blamed for holding fast to these perceptions. They were not about to change their views of Liberals just because they had rejected Clark. To earn and hold their support we had to chart a course that was clearly different from the one that had brought about our defeat in 1979. For some reason we did not. We did not even pretend to chart a new course. No one seemed to care what the electorate felt. It was as if they had served our purpose and now we had no time for them.

The mood invited confrontation. Something in our style was seriously flawed. There was a sense of "us" and "them": those who were friends, those who were foes. We seemed always to be spoiling for a fight with our adversaries rather than using every effort to bring them on side. I gradually began to see that our economic nationalism was much less pro-Canadian than it was anti-American. Similarly the National Energy Program was more anti-multinational U.S. oil companies than pro-Canadian oil interests. And there was a pronounced sense of being against business rather than being for a growing and prosperous economy led by business. Even federal-provincial relations were cast in an anti-provincial light rather than being for the national interest. The whole attitude was not born of dedication to our principles but prejudice toward others. It disturbed me deeply.

These sentiments were founded in an intricate evolution of relationships and personalities which predated the last Trudeau mandate. The extent to which they had become doctrine amongst many influential Liberals came as a surprise to a number of us who joined the Cabinet for the first time in 1980. Liberals, myself among them, who, during the last government had argued for a return to a less interventionist posture with a greater reliance on the market forces, had won a brief hiatus. But the Clark victory in 1979 was used to shout down any return to the "less government" approach.

In my opinion, Trudeau's 1978 statement on reduced spending, doing more with less and so on, was realistic and responsible. Its detractors, however, were quick to label it neo-conservatism. Thus, when the brief flirtations from 1976 to 1979 with fiscal responsibility, privatization, regulatory reform, improved management and accountability were not rewarded by the electorate in 1979, any chance of continuing along that road upon our return in 1980 was destroyed. The views of social democrats close to Trudeau were reinforced and Trudeau seemed to be listening to them.

I was alarmed to find that advisers to the Prime Minister armed with nothing but opinion polls, were willing to narrow the traditional Liberal base, focussing exclusively on the so-called social democratic coalition. Tom Axworthy made the point in a *Canadian Forum* article in November of 1984[2]. He described the Liberal party of 1968 as attracting support from all parts of the country and from every group in society. He then argues that a generation of Trudeau activism changed this base so that:

> "by the mid 1980s, the affluent, and especially members of the business community, had deserted the Liberal Party in droves. They had been replaced, however, by an almost classic social-democratic core of the young, women, ethnic supporters and the disadvantaged."

Axworthy's statement is essentially correct but the shift in support began much earlier. It started in the early 1970s. In my judgement it did not need to happen. Most important, it should not have. The wedge between Liberals and liberals was driven by design, not by default.

The message Canadians received was that the Trudeau government did not stand for liberal principles but only for the interests of the nation's underprivileged. No longer offering to represent all Canadians, Liberals had become captives of narrow social democratic interests.

Yes, I was concerned. On rare occasions we held political Cabinets. They were unbelievably frustrating. With thirty odd ministers in attendance as well as our political oracles, there was no room for real debate. Goldfarb's poll results presented by Coutts or Axworthy were embraced without question. I felt manipulated, never believing that the Liberal Party should draw its strength from only a narrow coalition of economic self-interests. Surely our policies should appeal to more than single working mothers, youth and ethnics. As far as I was concerned, all Canadians who believed in liberal principles were our potential supporters. It had nothing to do with economic deprivation or economic success.

I got nowhere in those meetings. I had to do something else. Here I was, an elected Member of Parliament, a Cabinet minister, and the very liberal principles I believed in were being set aside in what I saw as a sell-out to narrow self-interest groups. What was I going to do? Certainly I was not going to sit back and watch it happen without trying to stop it. I reasoned to myself: Trudeau will listen; he will see through the narrow interest coalition; he will see the danger in abandoning the traditional liberal base. Perhaps all he needs is a little prompting. I will call him, or better still, write him. He always responds to well-reasoned argument.

And so there followed a series of letters between me and Trudeau. One such letter and his response is reproduced here with his consent.

HOUSE OF COMMONS
CHAMBRE DES COMMUNES
CANADA

Honourable Donald J. Johnston P.C., M.P.
St. Henri-Westmount

April 3, 1981

PRIVATE AND CONFIDENTIAL

My dear Prime Minister,

This letter is further to our political discussion on March 26th. The meeting was stimulating and informative, and I hope that such discussions will be held on a regular basis.

As I have mentioned in the past, I remain concerned about maintaining the very wide spectrum of "non-doctrinaire" centre support which has served us so well. I refer particularly to the business and professional community. From conversations with various colleagues and the discussion of last week, I believe that many of us tend to confuse our "electors" with our "supporters." There is no doubt that ethnic communities, single working mothers, youth, lower and middle income groups, etc. are for the most part Liberals, and that to retain and increase that support, we must "outflank" the NDP as Senator Davey suggested. In making that point, he in fact reinforces the traditional policy of the Liberal Party from the introduction of unemployment insurance, through family allowance, pension legislation, medicare, etc. While we have always outflanked the NDP with focussed social programs, we have at the same time successfully retained our supporters in the business and professional communities. Many of those supporters are also electors, but they are understandably far outweighed numerically by the rest of the Liberal "coalition" which spans the entire non-doctrinaire centre. (I would also point out that some Liberals tend to confuse the "barons of Bay Street" who report in the Financial Post that they will not be voting Liberal, with the wide diversity of business interests in this country ranging from the independent "dépanneur" in the St. Henri district of my riding through the small and medium sized business interests to the executives of our largest Canadian corporations. It also includes our professionals, e.g. doctors, dentists, lawyers, engineers, etc.)

My point is that the success of the Liberal Party, electorally and financially, has been through outflanking the NDP at the one end of the non-doctrinaire spectrum through the introduction of well-focussed social programs of benefit to the vast majority of Canadians, while not losing the support of the more affluent Liberals. Consciously or unconsciously, we seem to be abandoning this very successful formula.

Apart from the fact that I represent one of Canada's largest communities of business and professional interests in St. Henri-Westmount, I have attempted to maintain and expand contact with those communities across the country. It is not an exaggeration to state that relationships between the Federal Government and the business community have never been as hostile as they are today. The feelings of mistrust on both sides run deep. The Liberal Party has always stood for a strong and vigorous private sector. There is a growing belief in the private sector that we are abandoning that philosophy. Put another way, the business community has for the most part accepted our philosophy of outflanking the NDP with specific social programs. Many now believe that we not only want to outflank the NDP, but that we are becoming the NDP. This hostility and loss of support points to a number of dangerous consequences for the Liberal Party.

The first consequence is an erosion of our financial base. The NDP has union financial support; the Tories will gradually take away more of our business community financial support. We cannot look at the coalition described above, e.g. youth, low to middle income groups, etc. for any substantial financial support. In time, our fortunes could be in serious jeopardy because, as one of our colleagues has stated, money is the "mother's milk" of political action. (You will have noted that in 1980, the Tories obtained financial support numerically superior to us by more than two to one and I do not believe that the reason lies only in the direct mail program.)

The second problem is our capacity to govern effectively. It may be possible to be elected without the co-operation, if not the support of the business community, but it would be difficult to govern effectively. Nearly all our economic programs are directed to stimulating programs and activities initiated and pursued by the private sector. Co-operation is essential.

The third consequence is that most of the managerial talent required for fund raising and for effective political organizing must be drawn from the very sector we seem to be losing. This is particularly evident to me in the west where Liberals from professional backgrounds, active in the past, appear to have withdrawn from political participation. (For example, at a recent Financial Post conference in the west, a prominent businessman from Saskatchewan who I understand has raised hundreds of thousands of dollars for our Party in the past, is discouraged to the point of abandoning us.)

This situation is totally unnecessary and clearly counter-productive. With the right approach, nearly all our current programs would be acceptable to our traditional business-professional constituency. The policies and programs of this Government by themselves are not the root cause of the problem. Rather, the current alienation of these interests is based on the perception that they are not being listened to; that they have little policy input; that there is no genuine consultation; in brief, that we have no interest in them and their concerns. These are the views I receive.

In conclusion, I would urge my colleagues to consider means within their areas of interest and jurisdiction whereby the bridges to our business and professional friends can be rebuilt.

Yours sincerely,
Donald Johnston

PRIME MINISTER • PREMIER MINISTRE
OTTAWA, K1A OA2

May 11, 1981

Dear Don:

Thank you for your insightful letter of April 3rd. Your letter attests to the fact that the political Cabinet certainly served its purpose in stimulating thought on what the political priorities of the Liberal Party should be.

As the latest polls demonstrate, the government has done very well in retaining the support of our political coalition. Despite the reservations of the business community, we now stand higher than we did on election day, February 18, 1980. This is a significant achievement given the magnitude of the constitutional and energy positions that we have taken, and the controversy which has ensued. While rightfully being concerned about our lack of support from business, we cannot forget the people who put us here in the first place.

I am sure that you and I do not disagree about this point. The history of our party demonstrates that we do best when we are perceived to be progressive. Since King, the Liberal Party has always positioned itself as a moderate voice of reform between the conservative and socialistic camps. I believe that this political tradition must be continued.

Yet, as your letter ably argues, our tradition of reform does not preclude us from establishing a useful relationship with business. Like you, I am concerned about the distrust and distance which exists between the business community and our government. We cannot, perhaps, ever hope to win majority support from business, but as a centrist party we must have some links and supporters within it. In particular, we must have a strong relationship with small business. The Liberal Party cannot afford to ignore any part of our society, particularly one as powerful and important as business.

So, I commend your efforts to establish links with the business community, and I hope that all our colleagues follow suit. For my part, I plan to actively consult business leaders as part of our consultations for the economic summit in July.

Thank you again for taking the time to write me on this subject. You have a perspective that must be considered in any long range political strategy.

Yours sincerely,
Pierre E. T.

As I pointed out in my letter, it was really our style that was alienating all but narrow interest groups, not the substance of programs themselves. Many of our more laudable initiatives were camouflaged by poor packaging and passed unrecognized. Other achievements were undermined by the manner of their implementation. Sadly, our rhetoric and behaviour overshadowed the value of many initiatives in the public's mind.

The occasions were rare indeed when anyone, especially our political adversaries, commended us for our accomplishments. Perhaps that is why I so well remember the day the Constitutional Resolution was adopted in the House of Commons[3]. I passed the PMO on the way to the Cabinet room. There stood George Hees outside Trudeau's door. When I inquired as to what he was about, George said:

"Don, I am waiting to shake Pierre's hand and tell him what a great thing he has done."

There always seemed to be a certain mutual admiration between Trudeau and Hees which found expression in occasional witty repartee between them in Question Period.

Returning to the subject of our undoing, our style was destroying us. Worthwhile features of the National Energy Program disappeared in a swamp of acrimonious controversy which escalated to a state of federal-provincial hatred. When compromises were made, it was too late to retrieve any good will. Imagine a federal Cabinet minister requiring RCMP protection while in Alberta. It happened to me.

Similarly, the achievement of constitutional reform and the patriation of the Constitution were undermined by fighting with provinces and native groups. After many painful months our government compromised and acted wisely and effectively. It was too late. There was no good will left to herald the significance of the achievement. Hostility to Trudeau so permeated many of our communities and our media that reaction to almost any policy was knee-jerk and negative. We were paying a high price for the style of our government.

We had also shot ourselves in the foot with the infamous MacEachen budget of November, 1981. The fallout lasted well into 1982 and was nearly all negative. The good intentions of many proposals designed to eliminate inequities and anachronisms from the tax law were almost entirely overlooked. The budget not only reinforced the hostility of business where our support had already sunk to an all-time low, it also opened up new fronts of antagonism by attacking employee benefits, the deductibility of interest for investments, even the incomes of life insurance salesmen.

It was typical of the style of our government. Who had been consulted? Certainly not Cabinet ministers, I can vouch for that. The budget documents had been preserved from the eyes of all except key officials in the Department of Finance and, I presume, the Prime Minister himself. I was both offended and amazed that, as the Treasury Board President with more than a passing knowledge of tax matters, I had not been consulted about a budget that involved major changes to the Income Tax Act.

So many problems were inherent in that budget that the only practical response was to retreat. With each retreat a national chorus sang "incompetence," led by Tory cheerleaders in the House of Commons. I am sure Trudeau hated the whole exercise but, once again, his fundamental wisdom prevailed and he knew that to retreat was the right thing to do.

By spring of 1982 we had moved on so many fronts in an uncompromising way that we had managed to offend or alienate just about every group in the country. Organized labour was an exception but the 6 & 5 restraint program in the budget of June 1982 soon took care of them.

It was about this time, perhaps because the pressure on all fronts had become so intense, that a concentrated effort was launched to change the style of the government, at least vis-a-vis the electorate. Allan MacEachen began extensive consultations. Inflation which had crested at 12.9 per cent in June and July, 1981 had become public enemy number one. It threatened our very society, distorting economic relationships, savaging those on fixed incomes and driving capital into non-productive investments seen as inflation-proof.

For the first time, the government listened carefully. In the words of a respected private sector economist: "In Ottawa, consultation is in." Cabinet Ministers had input. The Prime Minister involved himself directly. The result was instant success with the 6 & 5 restraint program introduced in the June 28 budget of 1982. Allan MacEachen recovered much credibility as Finance Minister; the government was seen as leading public opinion, not following it.

Indeed, the life of a Cabinet minister during the period from the summer of 1982 until Trudeau's resignation was paradise compared to what had gone before. During this period we negotiated and signed the first ever Economic and Regional Development Agreements with a number of provinces.[4] Even the National Energy Program was updated and some concessions made.

From the day of his appointment in September 1982, Marc Lalonde turned in a stellar performance as Finance Minister. He had no doubt learned from his experience with the NEP and by observing MacEachen's torment following the 1981 budget that consultation was critical. He kept his colleagues informed and consulted interest groups at a pace never seen in the past. He listened and acted, incorporating useful ideas into his two budgets. We at last had responsible, informed government which was listening, watching and responding effectively to a plethora of economic and social challenges.

But the cancer could not be cured. Nothing seemed sufficient to change earlier perceptions, restore our popularity and arrest the countdown to defeat. The style of earlier years had pre-ordained our downfall.

Furthermore, while our government was becoming more open to input from groups and individuals during this period,

I do not believe that the PMO itself changed its style during the entire mandate. The Prime Minister's staff continued to treat Cabinet as irrelevant, increasingly isolating Cabinet and caucus from much critical decision making. They seemed only to bring Cabinet into the decision-making process at their own pleasure. The combined power of the PMO and Privy Council Office (PCO) had grown far beyond anything reasonable in a parliamentary democracy.

As a minister I often found myself discouraged. Not much was said but I could tell by the looks on the faces of my colleagues that the same malaise was creeping among them. Several believed that management by destabilization was being deliberately practiced upon them. They sensed they were being kept off balance, sometimes by the arbitrary addition or subtraction of authority, sometimes through doses of flattery or intimidation, all in the interests of keeping them within the bounds of an agenda they had little part in setting.

Known as the "envelope system," The Policy and Expenditure Management System (PEMS) contributed to the paralysis of ministers who felt that the system dulled their authority. Far from streamlining the funding process, valuable time was consumed in haggling over a piece of the pie in Cabinet committee "like so many fish wives," as MacEachen once remarked. If the PMO and PCO were unhappy with that result, they lifted not a finger to change it.

Only a handful of ministers had sufficient reserves in their own Departmental budgets to fund new initiatives. Those lucky enough to have large discretionary funding, such as Employment and Immigration, were able to operate largely outside the new PEMS process, much to the disgust of others like Agriculture Minister Eugene Whelan and Environment Minister Charles Caccia. In desperate need of funding for agriculture and forestry programs, these ministers had to look on in enraged impotence as the Minister of Energy, for example, created one expensive program after another, many of dubious value, beyond the discipline of Cabinet committees.

The PCO headed by Michael Pitfield, speaking in the name of, and presumably with the authority of the Prime Minister, did not hesitate to interfere with ministerial authority, even to the point of killing ministerial initiatives. Many of us became victims of this machinery at one time or another.

Minister of Fisheries Romeo LeBlanc, for example, was seriously wounded by actions emanating from either the PCO or the PMO. The restructuring of the Atlantic fishery was assigned to the Kirby Committee which reported to the Chairman of the Economic Development Committee, not to the Minister of Fisheries.[5]

When, I wondered, would it be my turn? It didn't take long. I proposed legislation to improve the accountability and management of Crown corporations. On its way to Cabinet it was intercepted and unceremoniously disembowled by the PCO. I was very upset because, God knows, the legislation was badly needed. Finally we did introduce some amendments to the Financial Administration Act which provided improved accountability and control of Crown corporations. These measures were not as comprehensive, nor did they go nearly as far, as my proposals. Even these changes were not made until Gordon Osbaldeston had followed Pitfield as Clerk of the Privy Council.

Crown corporations were the most rapidly expanding area of the public service. It had been obvious to me, as it had to others at that time, that Cabinet had virtually lost control over many of them. As President of the Treasury Board I could not fathom why we would nitpick the performance of public servants in Departments, regulating them to a fault, while handing the managers of Crown corporations a blank cheque. Both were spending taxpayers' dollars.

As things stood, examination and approval of capital budgets of Crown corporations was inadequate. Other Crown owned companies, like Canadair and De Havilland, were not subject to even that minimal discipline.

One of the outcomes of inadequate control of Crown corporations was that Ministers to whom they reported could be duped. In fact, we know from the public record that in the case of executive remuneration in Petro-Canada and the Canadian Development Investment Corporation, Cabinet itself was duped. The remuneration paid to some executives by both companies far exceeded that approved by Cabinet. That this could happen reinforced my conviction that the Auditor General must have unimpeded access to every area where taxpayers' dollars are spent.

Then there was the Petrofina acquisition. Since the Mulroney government assumed power, there has been a publicized dispute with the Auditor General as to what information could be made available regarding the acquisition of Petrofina by Petro-Canada in 1981. The Auditor General has sought clarification as to what material was examined by Cabinet ministers before the decision to purchase Petrofina was made, and to what extent they were apprised of the real cost of the acquisition.

The truth is that full Cabinet never deliberated on the acquisition of Petrofina. It was a matter left solely to the executive committee of Cabinet, the Priorities and Planning Committee of which I, as President of the Treasury Board, was a member. However, as my opening remarks to this chapter reveal, I, like so many fellow ministers, was absent when the decision was taken.

One further example of Cabinet emasculation was the appointment of the Macdonald Royal Commission on the economy. On November 5, 1982, Liberal MP David Collenette rose during Question Period to ask the Prime Minister the following question:[6]

> "According to press reports, an announcement will be made of a special Royal Commission to deal with the economy. I should like to ask the Prime Minister if this is true and, if so, if he is at liberty to reveal its membership?"

The Prime Minister answered in his usual relaxed manner:

> "Madam Speaker, I am happy that the Honourable Member has shown interest in this matter. I can assure the Opposition that, as far as I know, the interest is purely spontaneous. I am glad to have an occasion to answer this in the House because it is a matter of some embarrassment to me that this leak has occurred, and I am sure it is of great embarrassment to Mr. Donald Macdonald who has been approached to be the Chairman of such a Royal Commission.
>
> "With your indulgence, Madam Speaker, I am happy to give what details I can of the Royal Commission ... the purpose of which would be to inquire into the economic prospects in Can-

ada in the middle and longer term, and to look at the institutional arrangements which might be necessary for the strengthening of that economic union."

When Mr. Collenette continued with a question on the terms of reference for the membership of the Royal Commission, Trudeau said:

". . . to add to my embarrassment, I have not even consulted my colleagues in Cabinet or caucus on this project, although the Deputy Prime Minister knows about it . . . I think this Royal Commission will be extremely important, in terms of the change in thinking regarding the future of the country. I hope it will play a role as important as that played by the Rowell-Sirois Royal Commission in the years after that was produced . . ."

The Prime Minister's announcement struck me with the force of a lightning bolt. As Minister of State for Economic and Regional Development, it was inconceivable to me that such a Royal Commission would be named without prior consultation with the Minister of Finance, Marc Lalonde, and myself.

Hearing that exchange on the floor of the House, my feelings were better imagined than described. The Prime Minister had just told Canadians that a Royal Commission on the economy, which he judged would be of equal importance to the Rowell-Sirois Commission, had been named without consulting Cabinet, and that the terms of reference had been completed and would be submitted to the Governor General that same day.

Not to have consulted me was incredible enough, but not to have consulted or informed the Minister of Finance was unbelievable, comparable to the humiliation inflicted on Jean Chrétien in 1978. I have often seen Lalonde annoyed, even angry, but seldom had I seen that jaw as set and those dark eyes flashing as they did that day. Even Deputy Prime Minister Allan MacEachen confessed that he had just learned of the creation of this Commission during Question Period when he inquired about the leaked newspaper item which was in front of his seatmate, the Prime Minister. At least we had all received equal treatment.

The handling of the whole Macdonald Royal Commission was such a high-handed affair that, at the outset, its credibility was undermined. Only through the labour of Macdonald himself was it able to acquire a sense of importance. Initially it was widely seen as an effort by the Prime Minister's entourage to give Donald Macdonald a profile from which he could move forward into a leadership context as a strong alternative to John Turner. In other words, the creation of the Commission was seen more as a political move in the interests of the anti-Turner forces than in the interests of the economy. Macdonald's even-handed approach to his task, his disinclination to jump into the leadership race and the quality of the Report itself have served to reinforce the credibility and significance of the Commission's work.[7]

I am driven to the conclusion that, in this case as in others, Trudeau and his advisers decided to pursue certain objectives on their agenda and damn the consequences even if it meant alienating the caucus and Cabinet. His advisers scorned the views of elected representatives who might question their judgement. We all gradually became resigned to such treatment.

This attitude of indifference by the Prime Minister, the PMO and the PCO to Cabinet, to the caucus, and to the Party, contributed significantly to the disintegration of the pyramid of Party support. It was virtually in shambles by the time Trudeau stepped down in 1984. Only a handful of ministers continued to contribute their own time and energy to work with Liberal Party members and Associations across the country. Announcements of federal projects and federal programs that affected particular regions were all too often made by ministers without the participation, involvement or even advance knowledge of local Liberals.

And so it was that the style of government, having alienated the public, had also done much to discourage grass root supporters and depress caucus members. With the exception of the Quebec wing, caucus had lost any clout it might at one time have had in decision-making. Liberal MPs were indeed "nobodies," even on Parliament Hill. They watched bitterly as the electorate slipped further and further away from them. It was not a happy time to be a Liberal.

73

V

On the Record

"When all is lost, the cry goes up: 'Where is Superman?' And like Superman, Trudeau's arrival with his opening broadside in the House of Commons lifted that cloud of despair and brought new optimism to those Quebecers who would see their province forever Canadian."

It was April 9, 1984. The House was in session and about to vote on Monique Bégin's controversial Canada Health Act which denied extra billing. It was an historic moment. Conservative free market doctrine dictated that they support doctors in charging over and above the fee set by Medicare. They had argued long and battled hard in committee against the Bill.

The Speaker called the House to order and the poll of members began. A strange scene unfolded. Not only were Liberals and, predictably, the NDP, voting *yes* but one by one every Tory in the House including Brian Mulroney, the Leader of the Opposition, was voting *yes* too.

Many of our members were incredulous. Then it dawned on them: the public opinion polls. The Tories realized that public opinion was so solidly behind what Monique was suggesting that they dared not vote the courage of their political convictions. When the final vote was counted not a single Tory had voted *no*. Even more interesting, with her acute political intuition, Monique had predicted the Tories would come onside despite her colleagues' skepticism. The end result, another triumph for Monique Bégin in her Health and Welfare portfolio.

For all the frustration, even anger at how we were functioning, being a member of the 1980-1984 Trudeau Cabinet was a stimulating experience. There were great achievements largely because of the hard work and daily attention of individual ministers. While these success stories usually failed to attract much attention in the media, they demanded enormous efforts from the individuals involved and became the source of considerable satisfaction when completed.

Monique Bégin, for example, had many other triumphs in Health and Welfare. While she may have been frustrated with the amount of progress made on pension reform, she was able to bring the matter to centre stage and generate dialogue among all the interested parties. She debunked myths surrounding the issue and moved the entire subject substantially further than it had been in the past. If the current government succeeds in bringing legislative reform to this difficult area, it will be in large part as a direct result of ground work laid by Monique.

Gene Whelan may have been frustrated with his agricultural initiatives but he also had many accomplishments, including a national agri-food strategy. The same is true of the forest strategy for Canada produced by John Roberts when he was Minister of the Environment with responsibility for the Forestry sector.

Jean-Luc Pépin set about to butcher that sacred cow, the Crow's Nest Pass Statutory Rates for grain transportation. A new regime was necessary to provide diversification and economic development in Western Canada. For many the issue was never fully understood and likely to draw a big yawn whenever mentioned. But for the agricultural community, East and West, it was as controversial as the NEP and every bit as important. The final result was an enormous step in the right legislative direction.

Lloyd Axworthy wrestled with employment strategies and pioneered new approaches to cushion unemployment during the worst recession since the 1930s. Then in Transport he completed the Crow initiative started by Pépin and moved on deregulation in the air transport sector, an initiative which is being further developed by the current minister, Don Mazankowski.

Hazen Argue negotiated record sales of western wheat that assured Saskatchewan a strong economy throughout the recession. Bud Olson put together the federal participation in British Columbia's Northeast Coal development.

Bob Kaplan spearheaded the creation of the Security Intelligence Service. Jack Austin and Ray Perrault combined to make Expo '86 a reality through substantial federal participation. They were adroit and effective in garnering support for the project as was Gerry Regan in bringing federal money to the Calgary Olympics.

I have already commented on the fine job turned in by Marc Lalonde in Finance. His much maligned National Energy Program merits re-examination:

Faced with the escalation of world oil prices under the pressure of the OPEC cartel, some government intervention appeared to be necessary. On the other hand, many argued a better solution would be to give full play to market forces. Armed with the benefit of hindsight, that position today looks good. At the time, however, all credible predictions including those of the oil industry itself pointed to steady increases in oil prices leading to a 1986 price of more than seventy dollars per barrel. The actual price turned out to be less than half that predicted. The NEP was simply not designed to cope with this eventuality. The fault lay not in the prediction but in the program's rigidity.

Then there was the 25 per cent back-in.[1] Great confusion surrounded the proposal. On the eve of the budget some senior officials still thought the 25 per cent retroactive interest was to be paid for. Some other politicians supported the proposal thinking it was a substitute for the reversion to the Crown of checkerboard acreage. Neither scenario was true but even when explained in detail few could grasp the full measure of the 25 per cent back-in.

I drew an analogy for one government economist which I hoped would explain why investors from the United States were so enraged. I described a farmer who is told that he will be subject to a 15 per cent tax on the value of all his farm produce. He accepts the measure, albeit reluctantly, because taxation has historic, legal and social justification. Then he is told that, instead of being taxed, the government will simply take 10 per cent of his land. Wise economists advise him that this is "economically" the same, or perhaps even better for him than the tax. The farmer is enraged. So were the Americans.

77

I return to my point. The NEP was not all bad. Even the 25 per cent back-in had good intentions. An energy policy was necessary and few argued with its objectives of fair pricing, security of supply and Canadianization. On the other hand, its massive intervention with confiscatory provisions were excessive and unnecessary.

Quite apart from the issues that grabbed public attention, the accomplishments of the last Trudeau government were remarkable.

In my own case, I felt a strong sense of accomplishment in a number of areas, especially during my days at Treasury Board. The President of the Treasury Board is the manager of the government and, as such, the employer of all public servants. One of the most difficult situations I faced was negotiations with public sector unions.

As unions watched inflation escalate, the demand for higher incomes and cost-of-living adjustments in union contracts also increased. The negotiation posture of the unions was founded on the principle that every settlement had to be higher than the rate of inflation. That principle enjoyed broad popular support.

Just after assuming office, I faced the strike of our own federal clerks during the summer of 1980. They were not a militant group and had never struck before. The wage demands seemed exorbitant and could have set a dangerous trend, not only for other public service unions, but also for the private sector. We managed a reasonable settlement for taxpayers but only after a strike and much inconvenience to ourselves and to the public.

More difficult were the 1981 negotiations with the inside postal workers who were led by Jean-Claude Parrot. Negotiation of those contracts had been delegated by Treasury Board to the Post Office for some years. The record of costly settlements convinced me that the negotiations should be re-assumed by the Treasury Board. Post Office workers had previously won levels of benefits far in excess of other departments by holding the public hostage until negotiators caved in.

Once again, the demands of Mr. Parrot for higher wages, reduced hours, vacation benefits and so on, were out of the question. I determined to take a hard but fair position.

Mediation by Mr. Justice Allan Gold[2] finally brought a resolution to the dispute. We had successfully resisted the costly demands of CUPW. We came under criticism at the time for giving improved paid maternity leave but that concession had been offered before the strike began, a fact unnoticed by much of the media. Mr. Parrot tried to portray it as a major concession gained by the strike. I strongly believe that realistic maternity leave is the way of the future and feel the workers should have that benefit.

A major showdown seemed to be looming with the Canadian Air Traffic Controllers (CATCA). Their President at the time was Bill Robertson, an intelligent, personable union leader with whom I enjoyed a good relationship. They were asking for parity with airline captains. It seemed quite excessive.

Our country cannot tolerate a strike of air traffic controllers. In the past they had almost immediately been legislated back to work, a procedure I find incompatible with the right to strike itself.[3] In addition, the travelling public does not understand why there should be so much uncertainty, pain, suffering and cost inflicted on them while the government dilly-dallies about back-to-work legislation.

At Treasury Board we had been agonizing over the best approach to take. Obtaining a reasonable wage settlement while guaranteeing the national air service and being fair to union members looked like an impossible circle to square.

My deputy, Jack Manion, came into my office:

"Don, our legal branch has come up with an interpretation of the law that could be helpful. We could try to 'designate' the controllers."

(The Public Service Staff Relations Act, the governing legislation, does provide for "designation" of certain employees whose services are required in the interest of the safety and security of the public. This permits the government to go before the Public Service Staff Relations Board with a list of union members who fit that category. In the event the union to which they belong strikes, these designated employees must remain on duty, like doctors, nurses, fire fighters and so on. It had never been contemplated that the provision could be applied to air traffic controllers.)

We invited in our lawyers, labour negotiators and personnel officers. Together we hammered away at the pros and cons of trying to designate the air traffic controllers. Knowing we

79

were perceived as "hard-liners" at Treasury Board, there was some concern that this move might appear as insensitive, ham-fisted and anti-union. Clearly we would have to establish that our interpretation of the law was not simply an attempt to remove the strike option but was in keeping with the spirit of the legislation. It was a tough call but I elected to give it a try. We would have to convince the Staff Relations Board, and perhaps the courts, that the government had the right to deter-mine the level of air service required in the nation's interest. To do that, *and* ensure the safety and security of the public, a large number of air traffic controllers would be required.

It was not a matter that needed Cabinet approval but the potential impact of this move on all unions in the public sector was something that had to be taken into account. A number of ministers were nervous, believing that the move would resem-ble Reagan's tough stance with the U.S. air traffic controllers of which many disapproved. It did require the approval of Jean-Luc Pépin, Minister of Transport at the time. After some deliberation he supported the move.

Before launching the designation application I invited Bill Robertson to my office. Over coffee I explained what I intend-ed to do and why. It was a cordial meeting. We parted on good terms but it was clear he was not pleased and would fight.

To the astonishment of some, the relief of many, and to my delight, our interpretation of the law was upheld not only by the Public Service Staff Relations Board, but also by the Federal Court of Appeal and ultimately, by the Supreme Court of Canada. In the end we succeeded in designating about 1,700 operational controllers, enough to keep our air systems fully functional and safe. In subsequent negotiations, the union asked for arbitration realizing that the strike weapon had lost its cutting edge. I often wondered whether the union leaders themselves did not welcome the Court's decision. They had been relieved of the awesome responsibility of shutting down Canada's air travel, disrupting business, vacation plans and in-curring the wrath of millions of Canadians.

In all, I found our labour negotiating team at Treasury Board extremely effective. It was led by George Orser and sup-ported by legal counsel Robert Cousineau. I was pleased with our record of keeping settlements under control despite the enormous pressures brought by inflation.

In many ways, my greatest sense of accomplishment came with the 6 & 5 restraint program. Inflation in 1982 was out of control. Wage settlements across the country were dangerously high. Something had to be done. The 6 & 5 program was the government's response. It limited federal public service wages, regulated fees and prices to 6 per cent and 5 per cent increases in years 1982 through 1984. Because Treasury Board is the employer of the public service, we took the lead in its conception and implementation.

At the time the program was unveiled in Allan MacEachen's budget of June 1982, inflation was running at 11.2 per cent. Our proposal to cut this to 6 per cent in the first year was seen by many as totally unrealistic. Some laughed at our optimism. NDP member David Orlikow even bet me ten dollars that we could not do it. Columnist Richard Gwyn bet me a dinner. As it turned out, we got inflation down to 5.6 pcr cent by June 1983 and to 4.1 per cent by June 1984. David promptly paid up. Richard also came through and insisted on paying for my wife Heather as well.

We could not claim all the credit for bringing inflation under control. The recession had been partly responsible. But even government detractors acknowledged that public sector restraint had a major psychological impact on all sectors and greatly accelerated the process. The notion that the rate of inflation should be the starting point for wage negotiations had finally been broken. That was the most important legacy of the 6 & 5 program.

When the Cabinet shuffle came in the autumn of 1982 and Lalonde assumed the Finance portfolio, I thought it was time for me to leave the Treasury Board. Having missed the opportunity at Finance, I wanted to get into a line department. In the end, Trudeau elected to keep me in central agencies. His preference was probably that I stay at the Board. The other option he offered me was Economic and Regional Development combined with Science and Technology which, it was thought, should be brought into the mainstream of economic development. I opted for change.

When I left the Treasury Board, I looked around at my friends and co-workers of two years and realized how much I would miss them. We had been through a lot together.

I went on to my new posts with enthusiasm. Again I was blessed with first class colleagues. In short order we developed an ambitious science policy. Through a number of initiatives such as the Canada Tomorrow Conference, we helped raise the consciousness of the public with respect to the importance of managing the new technologies which were sweeping through our industries. I got increased funding for science and for the Natural Sciences and Engineering Research Council (NSERC), the granting council under my control.

At the same time, I began negotiations with the provinces on Economic and Regional Development Agreements (ERDAs). For all the frustration, we were making progress on that front. I also gave as much personal support as I could to the efforts of our Federal Economic Development Co-ordinators in each province. This was a Trudeau initiative which I believe will put more glue and harmony into federal-provincial relations in years ahead.

Marc Lalonde introduced Special Recovery Programs in his 1983 budget which had a total value of $4.8 billion. I was especially pleased to assume the management of the Special Recovery Capital Program, one half of the total amount allocated.

Working with Ray Hession who was seconded to me from the Department of Supply and Services, we set up a special organization to "fast track" $2.4 billion of capital projects right across the country. Ports, harbours, airports, research centres and other public works were commissioned in each province. I secured several key projects for the National Research Council for which I held responsibility. The most significant was the Bio-technology Centre in Montreal which I hope will play a synergistic role in bringing together Canadian expertise in bio-technology and support new wave industries in that sector. The beneficial effects of these projects are visible the full breadth of Canada.

I also had responsibility for Canada's Astronaut Program and the selection of the astronauts themselves. It was an unprecedented selection process drawing upon over 4,000 applications. I did not actually meet with the potential astronauts until the numbers had been reduced to 17. What an impressive gathering of talent! It seemed a shame that only six could go forward into the space program.

When James Beggs, the head of NASA, offered us a place on the space shuttle earlier than originally planned, I promptly accepted. Some senior officials had reservations, arguing that our experiments would not be ready in time. For me the benefits of putting a Canadian astronaut into space at the earliest feasible opportunity far outweighed the difficulty of accelerating the pace of preparing our experiments. We succeeded in doing both. With a superb effort by the National Research Council under the capable leadership of Larkin Kerwin, our experiments were ready in record time and our first astronaut to travel in space, Marc Garneau, soon became a national hero. The exercise added momentum, interest and credibility to our space program. I much regretted being out of government when Garneau was sent up in October 1984, the election having intervened.

It is only fitting that I leave the most distinctive accomplishments of our mandate to the end. While each of us was trying to carry out our ministerial duties, where was our leader? What was he up to? No small task fell at Trudeau's feet. His challenges were the preservation of the constitutional fabric of the country itself; first in the referendum fight against the Quebec separatists, and then the patriation of the Constitution and the entrenchment of a Canadian Charter of Rights.

Like so many issues where national unity is concerned, the great referendum debate united Canadians from coast to coast. In our quest to beat the separatists, issues that otherwise polarized us were forgotten.

The period leading to the referendum itself brought Trudeau's finest hours in public life. His very presence as Prime Minister gave confidence to those directly involved. The timing of his participation was critical to the outcome. At first, for what seemed like an eternity, he was nowhere to be seen. The separatists were on the march, dominating the debate. Popular singers and other entertainers rallied to their cause.

"Where is Trudeau?" people asked in despair. It reminded me of scenes from Superman movies: When all is lost, the cry goes up, "Where is Superman?" And like Superman, Trudeau's arrival with his opening broadside in the House of Commons lifted that cloud of despair and brought new optimism to those Quebecers who would see their province forever Canadian.

Trudeau's speeches, well spaced and brilliantly crafted, were like rapier thrusts into the very heart of the separatist option. Jean Chrétien was his lieutenant, throwing himself into the contest with exhausting enthusiasm. Claude Ryan, the leader of the Quebec Liberal Party, led the "NO" forces against René Lévesque and the Parti Québécois. Chrétien has documented[4] the difficult personal relationship between himself and Ryan. To their credit, differences were set aside and each made a tremendous contribution to the outcome. Ryan campaigned tirelessly from early morning to late at night, seven days a week. Chrétien worked so hard he endangered his health.

Within our caucus the burden fell largely on our French-speaking colleagues. But we all pitched in as if it were an election campaign. Speaking at public rallies and going door-to-door, I found myself working closely with Conservatives who had been busy trying to defeat me just weeks before.

While our rhetoric was optimistic, we were worried. It was a living nightmare for those of us who had strong emotional beliefs in a united Canada with Quebec an integral part. To many, the Parti Québécois was an evil force intent on destroying our country. Fortunately, the protagonists on both sides succeeded in keeping the debate within the bounds of civility, most arguments appealing to reason rather than emotion.

As the referendum recedes into history, it is easy to forget how frightened and insecure we were, especially within the Quebec anglophone and ethnic communities. Yet through it all Trudeau was serene, confident, a strong stabilizing force. No one had shaken his belief in the future of the country he led.

Shortly before the vote, Trudeau invited one of my former law partners, Jean Potvin and me to lunch at 24 Sussex. The referendum dominated our discussion. Trudeau allayed our concerns, observing that "le bon sens des Québécois va prévaloir" ("the good sense of Quebecers will prevail"). His game plan for the referendum was predicated on that principle. He appealed to the reason of the people over the separatists' arguments which he systematically destroyed with logic, often spiced with ridicule.

By the day of the vote, a victory by the "NO" forces seemed assured. Less clear was what the winning margin would be.

That was critical. When the results were finally counted they left no doubt that a majority of both English *and* French-speaking Quebecers were against giving René Lévesque any right to negotiate sovereignty association and victory was complete.

The triumph for federalism was a great milestone in our history, one with which all of us in government were proud to be associated, even in a modest way.

VI

Who Was
Pierre Elliott Trudeau?

*"Whether he is in Cabinet, at a First Ministers'
Conference, at an international summit or on
a lonely stretch of river bank miles from nowhere, Trudeau will not back down or run
away from a fight."*

I marched into his office barely suppressing my anger.
Fellow ministers, even some key ones in Montreal, were supporting a transfer of domestic flights from Dorval to Mirabel.
To me the proposal seemed so outrageous that even to dignify
it with debate was demeaning. At a time when Montreal was
on its economic knees, desperately seeking some small advantage to make it more attractive and with head offices being lost
daily to Toronto, why would anyone add to its problems by
making travel more difficult?

Mirabel had been a mistake. Everyone outside government knew it at the time. Why compound that multi-million
dollar gaffe by transferring flights from Dorval at great cost
and inconvenience to the travelling public?

When I faced Trudeau squarely with the issue, I received
an indifferent reception. He had been briefed and was not
about to cave in to the complaints of my Westmount business
constituents. I had an ace up my sleeve though:

"You realize," I said, "that a taxi fare with a modest tip
from downtown Montreal to Mirabel is $50 or $100 return?"

He raised his eyes to meet mine. As he did so he removed
his glasses and placed them before him on the desk.

"Are you serious?" he asked in disbelief.

I nodded. Those of us with Celtic blood understand such

things. For Pierre Trudeau, isolated so long from the real world, $100 still meant a stylish weekend in New York, a ticket to Europe, perhaps even a second-hand car. I knew that those recommending the transfer were now into an uphill battle. To this day domestic flights leave from Dorval.

Trudeau is at once a great Canadian and an unfathomable being. The fortunes of the Liberal Party have been so intertwined with the life, personality and policies of Pierre Elliott Trudeau that no understanding of the state of the Party in the 1980s could be complete without reference to that intimate, complex and often unhappy relationship.

Trudeau set about to accomplish specific objectives and achieved them. While his interests were broad, his focus was narrow. Within that focus he was singularly successful. Trudeau always wanted, in his words, "to be on the right side of history." On the major challenges of this period, he will be.

There will be critics, and I am one, who will argue that Trudeau's lack of the human touch with his Cabinet colleagues, with the provincial premiers, and with business and union leaders, contributed to a perception of arrogance and intellectual disdain.

Personal relationships and camaraderie had no place in the Trudeau management style. He treated others rationally, not emotionally. Gut feelings or personal chemistry never appeared to get in the way of his Cartesian reasoning.

No public person of this period was the match of Trudeau's finely honed intellectual equipment which depended on reason, not on facts. He scrupulously kept his mind uncluttered by unnecessary detail, whether of events or individuals, quite often to the point of forgetting names, a cardinal sin for most politicians.

Trudeau's organizational style was efficient, disciplined and precise. He went about his tasks meticulously, relying on the skills and judgement of trusted advisers in areas where he lacked the necessary expertise in politics or policies. By the time he reached his last mandate this meant that control of the Government of Canada was concentrated in the hands of Trudeau, his principal secretaries Jim Coutts and later Tom Axworthy, Clerk of the Privy Council Michael Pitfield, and ultimately, only one member of Cabinet, Marc Lalonde. With few exceptions Lalonde's advice carried on all matters in Quebec and most elsewhere. From policy to appointments Trudeau seldom appeared to take seriously advice from other Cabinet ministers if Marc recommended something different.

On the whole, Trudeau seemed to have little more than passing academic interest in the machinery of government and the operation of the bureaucracy. He no doubt believed financial management and accountability to be good objectives, but as long as statistics told him we were doing well by comparison with the past and with what was happening elsewhere, these subjects did not engage him. While he supported policies of privatization, regulatory reform and fiscal responsibility in the 1970s, they were not high on his agenda in the 1980s. When some senior ministers began to label these approaches as neo-conservative, the writing was on the wall. Such ideas were not likely to go far.

Attempts by ministers to add to the agenda set by Trudeau's insiders frequently came to grief. Undermined at every turn, their carefully planned projects were derailed by the PCO under Michael Pitfield who did not hesitate to speak unctuously in the name of the Prime Minister. Were these actions carried out with Trudeau's blessing, or was he simply indifferent? I never knew the answer to that question.

The patriation of the Constitution and the introduction of the National Energy Program, both controversial but substantial accomplishments, dominated the agenda in the first two years of the mandate. In the meantime, the recession and runaway inflation were screaming for government action. The response to the 6 & 5 restraint program was a singular success. Happily it too received Trudeau's full attention. As President of the Treasury Board, and therefore responsible for implementing the program, I was delighted by his interest. For my own part, I was so enthusiastic about the potential of 6 & 5 that I wrote a song extolling its virtues. Keith Davey, in charge of selling the program across the country, incorporated my song into his strategy with a world premier rendition and release of a recording at our annual caucus Christmas party. Trudeau loved it. Since everyone knows about the 6 & 5 program and only I still whistle the song, it is easy to see which was the greater success.

From time to time Trudeau's interest seemed to fix on

challenges other than those which brought him into public life. But his principal focus was always on bringing Quebec into the mainstream and forging a lasting Canadian unity. He found himself, as did Laurier before him, torn between the anti-French sentiment outside Quebec and the pro-nationalist forces inside Quebec. He knew that a unilingual Quebec outside the social and economic mainstream of Canada would become ghettoized, with *de facto* separation to be followed inevitably by *de jure* separation.

Within that perspective, Trudeau set about to enhance the role of French-speaking Canadians. Federal services, federal publications and the federal bureaucracy became distinctly bilingual. While some gaps remained, his achievement was remarkable. Through his efforts the prospect of a unilingual French Quebec in a unilingual English Canada became unthinkable.

Notwithstanding the enormous contributions made by Claude Ryan and Jean Chrétien, Pierre Trudeau was the field marshal opposite René Lévesque in the war against the Parti Québécois. In the referendum debate culminating in the victory of the "NO" forces, it was Trudeau who stood head and shoulders above all others. He delivered the most impassioned and important speeches of his public life. Even his most ardent critics acknowledge that he made an indelible mark upon the history of this country.

But did Trudeau's preoccupation with language and the Constitution cause the government to neglect major economic challenges, allowing Canadian business and industry to slip badly in international competitiveness?

Trudeau never had much time for, nor understanding of, business and the micro-economy. With the exception of a select few businessmen whom he regarded as friends of the government, he seemed to tolerate rather than appreciate the business community. Yet, in my opinion, he was instinctively and fundamentally a believer in the free-enterprise market system. He did not see the state as an efficient manager of industrial enterprises. Many seemed to have forgotten his outspoken criticism of the nationalization of Shawinigan Power by the Quebec Government in 1963. He was really arguing the case "if it ain't broke, don't fix it." By 1979, however, offended by declarations of business support for the Conservatives shown in a survey published in the *Financial Post*,[1] Trudeau and some of his Cabinet began to see business interests only as necessary evils. I was sad to see members of the business community, once viewed as important constituents with valid concerns, relegated by the Liberal Party to the status of unfriendly adversaries.

Many of us in Cabinet thought this hostility to business smacked more of doctrine than common sense. Not so for the Prime Minister. He seemed curiously bored and almost puzzled by the complaints of bankers and others whom he perceived as receiving good treatment. Although the record bore him out, he had no interest in trying to tell his story to businessmen. They, in turn, were inept in dealing with him.

For example, I recall a round table discussion with senior businessmen at the Mount Royal Club during the 1979 election campaign. Instead of using this golden opportunity to level with the Prime Minister on the issues that concerned them, they commended his performance. They were in awe of him. He did nothing to improve the situation. After all, what was there to say in the face of such untempered flattery. Besides, small talk of any kind is not Pierre Trudeau's long suit, and for him business small talk is an anathema.

Trudeau's puzzlement about the business community reflected his need for rational explanations. When he looked at the statistics generated by the Department of Finance on the performance of Canada, business profits, and the strength of the banking sector, he could not for the life of him understand what they were complaining about. In fairness, Pierre Trudeau did have a valid point.

For example, in the period 1968 to 1984, growth in the Canadian economy averaged 3.3 per cent per year, which is higher than that of the United States, Germany, Italy, and the United Kingdom, equal to that of France and second only to Japan's. The size of the Canadian economy increased by 64 per cent, almost 10 per cent more than the average for the other six most powerful industrial nations.

In 1984 there were three million more Canadians employed than in 1968 for a 40 per cent increase. Employment of women alone almost doubled in those years and the Canadian standard of living, measured on the basis of real personal disposable income per capita, increased by about 60 per cent in

Canada, twice that of the United States over the same period. An increase of 74 per cent in consumer spending was recorded from 1968 to 1984, as well as construction in Canada of three million homes.[2]

True, those Canadians who like to wallow in doom and gloom predicting Canadian failure at every turn spent much unproductive time criticizing Pierre Trudeau for the terrible state of the economy. The comparative record does not support their position.

Pierre Elliott Trudeau inherited the mantle, the issues and the conflicts of Sir Wilfrid Laurier. The two men were alike in several ways. Laurier's management style as a Prime Minister, his tolerance of failings in those he trusted, his unchallenged intellectual superiority amongst his peers and, above all, his refusal to speak ill of those who differed with him or crossed him, such as Israel Tarte and Clifford Sifton, all bear striking similarities to Trudeau's management style and personal philosophy. For example, despite the media's repeated attempts to find evidence suggesting a bitter relationship between Trudeau and John Turner, Trudeau gave them nothing to support it. Never did I hear him utter a disparaging word about Turner.

Laurier and Trudeau both achieved international respect and renown unequalled by any of their Canadian contemporaries in public life. Both men became bigger than life in the eyes of Canadians and, unfortunately, bigger than the political party they each led. Both became stars who commanded attention in every part of Canada but who, at the end, had solid voting support only in Quebec. After a triumphant trip across western Canada as leader of the Opposition in 1917, Laurier spoke prophetically for Trudeau saying: "Yes, they cheered for me, but they didn't vote for me."[3]

After our 1979 defeat, Pierre Trudeau and I were in the town of Mahone Bay, Nova Scotia in the overwhelmingly Conservative South Shore riding. Despite his rejection by the local voters, it was as though a local hero had returned. People sought him out in stores and on the streets for autographs and handshakes. It was the same everywhere we went. Trudeau, the man, like Laurier before him, triumphed far above and beyond the political process.

In each case the man had become the party. If a football

team could win through the efforts of a star quarterback alone, the other players would soon become fat, lazy and ineffective, their incompetence camouflaged in the shadow of the great leader, and fundamentals of team play forgotten. So it is in politics. Unused, organizers slip quietly away. Aggressive fundraising becomes less significant as parasites and profiteers take over, currying favour and worming their ways into positions of influence. The energy of the party, so evident and crucial during the ascension to power, rapidly dissipates.

While Trudeau's strengths camouflaged the party's weaknesses, they also hid from view the abilities of many ministers. It was common for the media to heap scorn and derision upon the ministers who sat at the table with Trudeau. That constant barrage no doubt contributed to our deteriorating fortunes. In fact, the press knew little of the capacities of those men and women, or of the time and energy they expended in carrying out their duties.

The public, encouraged by the media, tended to view the Cabinet as a bunch of also-rans. That was far from being an accurate reflection of reality. Many of my colleagues were exceptionally able. Unfortunately, most have now left public life and the loss has been great. The list of competent people on the Liberal benches, in and out of the Cabinet, was a long one. Their qualities and talents will never be known except by those of us who worked closely with them.

The star quality of the leader played a large role in the undoing of the Liberal Party in the 1980s, as it did under Laurier many years before.

A major difference is that the party in 1911 went down fighting for a policy: trade reciprocity with the United States. O.D. Skelton wrote:

> "Half a generation of power had slackened energy and attracted parasites. It was immensely better that the Liberals should fall in the endeavour to carry through a fundamental Liberal policy than that they should die ingloriously of dry rot like the federal Conservatives in the nineties and the Ontario Liberals ten years afterward."[4]

In the 1980s it was the abandonment of liberalism that undid the federal Liberals. Then in 1984 we offered no policy to a hungry electorate and we had no Trudeau charisma to fall back on.

Trudeau and Laurier dedicated themselves to the integration of French and English Canadians into a full partnership to build a strong, united Canada and, as a result, became targets of vicious attacks from extremists in both camps. Laurier's detractors were Henri Bourassa, the Quebec nationalists and the Conservative imperialists of Ontario (the London "Round Table" group); Trudeau's were René Lévesque and his Péquiste separatists of Quebec and the largely Conservative elements in the rest of Canada who believe in a French Quebec but an English Canada.

As I read Laurier's words of 1911, it is the voice of Pierre Trudeau that rings in my ears:

> "I am branded in Quebec as a traitor to the French, and in Ontario as a traitor to the English. In Quebec I am branded as a Jingo, and in Ontario as a Separatist. In Quebec I am attacked as an Imperialist, and in Ontario as an anti-Imperialist. I am neither. I am a Canadian. Canada has been the inspiration of my life. I have had before me as a pillar of fire by night and a pillar of cloud by day a policy of true Canadianism, of moderation, of conciliation. I have followed it consistently since 1896, and I now appeal with confidence to the whole Canadian people to uphold me in this policy of sound Canadianism which makes for the greatness of our country and of the Empire."[5]

Trudeau will always remain an enigma to me and to future historians. At most we will capture small glimpses from many sources and attempt to assemble them into a complete picture, as Richard Gwyn did with some success in his entertaining book, *The Northern Magus*.[6]

Anecdotal material on Trudeau's parsimony, his difficulty with small talk, his shyness, his intellectual powers, and his taste for young women are all widely circulated, exaggerated in some instances, understated in others. As with others of his complexity and accomplishment, the full measure of the man will never be known.

I first met Trudeau in May, 1957 on a two-month World University Service (WUS) trip to West Africa. I had won a scholarship to attend as a McGill student along with Tim Porteous and Lionel Tiger. Trudeau had been invited to participate by the leader of the excursion, renowned botanist Dr.

Pierre Dansereau, a friend of many years, and a neighbour of Pierre's in Outremont.

The entire group of forty-odd students, organizers and teachers from all over North America congregated in New York at the outset for a series of orientation lectures on the government and flora and fauna of regions we would visit. When I arrived in a conference room of the old Hudson Hotel in New York City where our first session would take place, Trudeau was sitting by himself at the back of the room absorbed in his thoughts. As we introduced ourselves awkwardly, I became aware that Trudeau was neither a student, nor an organizer, nor a teacher. Why, I wondered, is he here?

I never did find out what Trudeau's specific duties were but he added interest to our adventure and, as history has shown, an important dimension for many who first struck up a friendship with him in West Africa. His basic shyness was gradually broken down by those who became close to him. We debated the Quebec issue and other serious concerns at length but also saw the fun side of Trudeau, partying well into the night with him at local clubs in Accra. He seemed bent on adventure and, having already travelled the world extensively, he knew what to do or say in any situation. It gave us a feeling of security just to have him as a travelling companion. I enjoyed his company and developed a great respect for his intellectual ability over the course of that summer but it never crossed my mind that he would one day be Prime Minister. Nor, as far as I could tell, had it occurred to him.

It is difficult to reconcile the shy, withdrawn Trudeau of that trip with the spectacular performances millions have witnessed over the years at press conferences, television interviews and from public platforms. I liken him to the actors of the Stanislavski school who project themselves completely into the role to be played. Playing roles may also account for his love of costumes and hats which most public figures would shrink from for fear of being photographed in unorthodox attire. He has worn a cape at one Grey Cup, a Dutch Boy Hat at the next and western garb at the Calgary Stampede. Among his most celebrated was the "Great Gatsby" panama hat he wore at the Williamsburg Economic Summit.

At times Trudeau's demeanour can be hard to handle, especially for those who believe that social gatherings are for small talk, however banal. Trying to produce small talk when isolated with Trudeau at a stand-up cocktail reception has proved discomfitting for the most accomplished social lioness. "Isn't it a nice party?" doesn't seem quite appropriate, nor does "I enjoyed Kant's *Categorical Imperative*, didn't you?" Perhaps somewhere in between. But if you are lucky, someone will come to the rescue.

Even on the international scene Trudeau had his problems with social gatherings. Alexander Haig told me about his first White House meeting with Trudeau. Trudeau's reputation as a wealthy debonair bachelor had preceded him to Washington. In consequence, the evening's event had been well stocked with women anxious to meet this exciting new international personality who drove fast cars, quoted Aristotle and wandered the globe in his quest for knowledge.

Unfortunately, the evening did not go according to plan. The guest of honour failed to perform. As Haig tells it, Trudeau spent most of the evening leaning against a wall, uncommunicative, an enigmatic smile on his face, while the female guests hovered on the periphery, waiting to meet the great man but afraid to approach. Whether Trudeau was gripped with an attack of shyness, was preoccupied with concerns of a more serious nature, or was obstinately enjoying his own refusal to play the game his hosts had prepared for him, Haig could not tell me. As Haig recounted his version of the event, I wondered whether Trudeau's behaviour that evening had inspired the unflattering expletive that found its way onto President Nixon's White House Tapes.[7]

Although Trudeau is a great performer at times, there are situations in which, because of the setting, the chemistry or his own will, he is singularly awkward and out of place.

But place Trudeau in a debate and then watch. He is a skilled debator, vicious with those whom he seeks to destroy in the parry and thrust of verbal exchanges. Time and again I have seen him seize one trivial exaggeration or inconsistency in an opponent's argument, skilfully dissect it, and watch as the whole merit of his opponent's argument collapses.

When dealing with those he considers peers, or with those he believes should know better, he is ruthless on the attack. With others, especially children, he is warm, kindly and gracious, and could aptly be described as a gentleman of the old school. It is a characteristic seldom seen by the general public who have more commonly seen a combative and arrogant person. How one deals with subordinates, not how one deals with peers, is a true test of one's character.

I have learned from personal experience to exercise caution in arguing with Pierre Trudeau. Perhaps hoping to calm my ruffled feathers the day he appointed Marc Lalonde as Minister of Finance (which turned out to be a brilliant choice), Trudeau invited me to lunch alone with him at 24 Sussex.

In the course of the meal, I voiced my concerns about the flight of businessmen, professionals and the entrepreneur from the Liberal Party. Trudeau nodded and waited. With the wind in my sails I continued. To hammer the point home I stated that the business community is more than Bay Street, but includes everyone from the bank president to the *dépanneur* (corner grocer) in the St. Henri section of my riding, who believes that our government is interventionist and anti-business:

"Yes," I said, "the entrepreneurial spirit beats in the heart of the *dépanneur* as much as in that of the captain of industry, often even more when the latter is more of a corporate bureaucrat than an entrepreneur."

That was the opening he had been waiting for.

Trudeau replied somewhat as follows: "I believe I understand why some of the large business interests may be uncomfortable with a number of our programs, perhaps the NEP and elements of the MacEachen budget, but I am puzzled by this hostility towards us of your *dépanneur* friend in St. Henri. Could you elaborate?"

I knew I was in trouble. I set about to explain that the spirit of the entrepreneur has little to do with the size of the business.

"It is spawned and nourished," I said, "by the spirit of the individual who wishes to make his own independent way and resents heavy taxation and regulatory intervention by government."

I hoped that would put the matter of the *dépanneur* to rest. It did not.

Trudeau continued: "Are you saying, Don, that the provisions of the MacEachen budget with respect to interest deductions and so on had an adverse impact on that *dépanneur* friend of yours? Besides, I always thought that our tax rates for small business were quite generous and, in fact, better than those in the United States. Am I wrong?"

I felt like screaming, "Forget about the damned *dépanneur*. It was a bad example."

I had lost. I knew it and he knew it. I returned to my soup. However interested in the entrepreneur, the grocery store owner or the banker he might have been, he was much more interested in winning the debate. That was not the only time I came out on the short end of such an exchange.

Despite my admiration for the man, sometimes his office, his actions, his attitudes and his general behaviour brought my anger to the surface. In September, 1983, I dictated some notes to myself about Pierre Trudeau. I had just returned from Quebec City and a tour of Louis Duclos' riding. I was in the midst of planning the Canada Tomorrow Conference on Technology, a national event designed to bring together business, government, academics and experts from the science community to address the challenges of the new technologies. The Prime Minister had been invited to deliver the opening address. With six short weeks to go to a national conference, his office had still not confirmed his participation. The following unedited excerpt from my note illustrates the frustration this situation evoked.

> "In all, the reflection upon my own position, the attitude in the Party, the attitude of the Prime Minister, etc. I am angry and frustrated, most recently over the failure of the Office of the Prime Minister to confirm whether or not he will speak at the opening of the conference on Science and Technology to be held in November. He's had the invitation since August. I had speaking notes prepared for him by Douglas Fullerton, as he requested, which were delivered early in September and he, himself, indicated during our meeting at Meech Lake that he would be interested in participating. I am now told at this point that there may be a conflict in the dates. Frankly, I find this kind of procedure and performance quite unacceptable and suspect that it is simply a reflection of the incompetence and insensitivity of his staff and also perhaps a certain hostility of his staff towards me or towards my office.

"Recently, while I have maintained my admiration for the man in terms of his intellectual capacity, his chairmanship of meetings, etc. I am singularly struck by the flaws which run so clearly through his character once the charisma and mystery is swept away. He appears to lack imagination and he seems clearly devoid of really gut feelings except when they concern a passionate dislike for someone who has 'cut his throat.' The number of the latter seems to grow exponentially whether it be premiers or businessmen. This is, I suspect, a result of carrying too much baggage over too many years to the point where it is almost impossible to liberate himself from history. The lessons of history which we do not like to see repeated can often become a prison and that is where the PM currently finds himself.

"In economic matters generally, whether they be fiscal, monetary or otherwise, he is good at the macro level because he understands it. At the micro level he is devoid of understanding the issues which motivate private investors. He again is quite insensitive and has no understanding or grasp of the motivations of normal mortals. It is indeed sad because he could be so good. But he has become testy and, I believe, too impatient ever to undergo a real learning experience at this stage in his life.

"He is determined to rely upon his analytical equipment rather than a knowledge base and if he can destroy or wound an argument which he doesn't like with a quick logical thrust he would rather do so than have to wrestle with the fundamental merits of his adversary's position.

"I recognize that these are sad commentaries but alas they are true beyond doubt. He is older than we recognize and time has left its marks. He is an extremely self-centred, self-reliant man and cares little for the inconvenience of others if it in any way interferes with his own pursuits. At the same time he is extremely loyal to friends and trusted advisers . . ."

As it turned out, Trudeau did speak at the conference but, to our surprise, not with the text we had prepared upon his request. Instead of dealing with the challenges and the opportunities technology presents, his remarks focussed almost entirely upon the protection of workers, only one of many key issues. The social democrats in the Prime Minister's Office had struck again.

Winston Churchill's description of Russia as a "riddle wrapped in a mystery inside an enigma" would also be an apt way of describing Pierre Elliott Trudeau. He has as many facets as a well-cut diamond. Some we know. Others we suspect but do not see. He constantly surprises, disappoints, delights and angers.

I mentioned Trudeau's proclivity for confusing names. During the election campaign in 1979, he visited the riding of Port Neuf, a seat contested by Rolland Dion, who subsequently became my Parliamentary Secretary. At the end of a rousing speech on the merits of the candidate, Trudeau exclaimed ". . . and that is why I want you to support my old friend, Léon Dion."

There followed an embarrassing silence, especially for Rolland Dion. Any flattery offered by being confused with one of Quebec's eminent constitutional authorities was entirely lost on him.

Trudeau's penchant for forgetting extends beyond peoples' names. In June of 1978, on the eve of St. Jean Baptiste Day, he joined the citizenry of Beaupré to celebrate the town's 50th anniversary. After the banquet he addressed the crowd, ending with the exhortation "vive les gens de Beauport."

The gaffes Trudeau committed with respect to names are all the more interesting because of the man's prodigious memory. He never takes notes and prides himself on remembering every detail of significant events. It is with great satisfaction that he recalls the circumstances of a particular adventure. This is only exceeded by his satisfaction in correcting someone else's recollection of the same event.

While forgetful of names that may be inconsequential to him, his mental filing cabinet is impressive. For example, in January of 1977 he spoke at the Chateau Frontenac to the Quebec Chamber of Commerce. Jean-Marie Cloutier introduced the Prime Minister in a self-deprecating manner, declaring himself to be a simple *inconnu* (unknown). Trudeau graciously responded by saying Mr. Cloutier would never be *inconnu* as far as he was concerned.

Much later the same Mr. Cloutier came to Ottawa as part of a delegation from Quebec City to meet United States Vice-President Walter Mondale. Trudeau immediately identified him, much to Cloutier's surprise and delight.

Trudeau remembers what he wants to remember.

Trudeau always protected his loyal troops. He never hesitated to rise during Question Period to defend the actions of a minister or a member, and he did so with an inquisitorial saber that quickly disemboweled the question, and sometimes the ego, of the questionner.

Shortly after my arrival in the House of Commons in the autumn of 1978, Bryce Mackasey was named chairman of Air Canada. The appointment met with immediate and almost universal criticism. The Conservative opposition was quick to jump on the issue. On December 15, David MacDonald, then Member from Egmont, in questioning the Prime Minister suggested that Trudeau had "probably downgraded both the independence and objectivity, and possibly the efficiency of Air Canada in view of Mr. Mackasey."[8]

Watching from the back bench I wondered how Trudeau would handle this sticky patronage issue.

He rose: "Mr. Speaker, I did note that he (MacDonald) used the word 'downgrading' in association with the appointment of a former Cabinet minister to the chairmanship of the board of Air Canada. I do not remember the honourable member opposite saying to the Honourable Bryce Mackasey, when he was a minister or present in the House, that he was not an honourable man or was not an intelligent or capable man. Therefore, I can only conclude that in the mind of the Honourable Member, a man who has served his country well in the House of Commons is not competent to serve his country well in other pursuits. This is not the view of the government."

On another occasion, I vividly remember how he came to my defence in the Liberal caucus. While Cabinet communications are subject to the 30-year secrecy rule, there is no similar prescription for caucus. I trust my colleagues will forgive me for providing this small glimpse of Trudeau in this environment.

After my appointment as President of the Treasury Board, Bill McWhinney, then a Deputy Secretary of the Board, and now Executive Vice-President of the Canadian International Development Agency (CIDA), came to see me. Bill is a giant of a man possessed of great intelligence and no less a sense of humour.

"We have an outstanding woman candidate for the TAP program," he said. (TAP was the acronym for the Temporary

Assignment Pool, a kind of SWAT squad of about 40 extremely capable, and frequently brilliant, bureaucrats under the jurisdiction of the Treasury Board, assigned on a temporary basis to various other departments as challenging projects arose.)

Never having been consulted previously on appointments to TAP, I asked Bill why he was seeking my approval.

"There are some political considerations," he answered. "You see, this particular candidate is Pierrette Alain Lucas, a former candidate for the Progressive Conservative Party in the Verdun riding (in Quebec) in the 1977 by-election. Since you have responsibility for the TAP program, you might get some flak if she is hired."

I was thunderstruck. Pierrette Alain and I had dated many years before during our bachelor days and she was a friend of long standing. She had also been a friend of Trudeau's. Her intelligence, bilingualism and wit made her a superb candidate for the TAP program. We were also trying to increase the number of women in the bureaucracy. There remained only the political problem.

"Bill, had it not been for this political question, would you have hired her on the basis of her credentials?"

"Absolutely," he answered.

"Then do it," I replied.

More than a year later, Pierrette's name surfaced in an *Ottawa Citizen* column entitled "Bureaucrats," where mention was made of her appointment to a senior post in the PCO. Sure enough, some members of the caucus were up in arms. I was forewarned that the matter would be raised by Jacques Olivier, Chairman of the Quebec caucus.

The next day Jacques Olivier rose in national caucus and addressed the Prime Minister in the strongest terms regarding the appointment. He stressed the naivety of "some ministers" who did not appreciate how demoralizing it was to loyal troops that a defeated Conservative should receive better treatment from the government than a defeated Liberal.

As he spoke I jotted down notes that I would use in rebuttal. I was about to rise when Trudeau stood up. He was an unexpected but welcome ally.

He advised the caucus that he had personally verified the record of Pierrette Lucas' employment by the federal government. Furthermore, he added, her qualifications were impeccable: She had been approved by the Public Service Commission and, in keeping with the neutrality of the Public Service, it was quite appropriate that she should have been hired as a TAP officer. She progressed from there, he explained, on the strength of her own talents and abilities.

Trudeau then challenged caucus members to justify the denial of employment to someone like Pierrette Lucas, a capable, bilingual women, who would clearly make a solid contribution. Finally, after a lengthy pause he added:

"Besides, Pierrette has been, one might say, a friend of the family for many years."

That final touch, delivered in a tone rife with ambiguity, brought an admiring titter from the caucus. The question was never raised again. It was as if the mere raising of the question of Pierrette Lucas had been an invasion of Prime Ministerial privacy. It was a class act and there were many more like it.

Trudeau's joy in being with children is genuine. It is not exaggerated. He shows patience and generosity not associated with his public persona. Visiting with us in Nova Scotia, he delighted in taking everyone's children swimming. They numbered not less than eight and sometimes more. He would supervise them, instruct them and entertain them by the hour. That would be followed by a game of "kick the can" where he did not pretend to have expertise. In fact, his competitive instincts made him less of a success there than in the pool. Not venturing far enough from the can to round up the others, he was soon dubbed "base-sticker" by the kids. It's a game where to win, you have to gamble.

Whatever the children did, he joined in, not out of a sense of duty, but with a youthful exuberance seldom seen in a young parent, let alone a senior citizen.

Pierre Trudeau is as combative physically as he is intellectually. An incident on Gold River, Nova Scotia, in the summer of 1979, will always be inscribed vividly in my memory.

Heather, Pierre and I had taken eight small children, including his three boys, and two of our girls, and a babysitter to a swimming hole on a beautiful stretch of river near Chester. The spot was deep in a gorge below white water and could only be reached from the road by a long, steep, winding trail through heavy spruce growth.

103

Unfortunately, a gang of local toughs, reminiscent of the low life depicted in the film *Deliverance*, had decided that Gold River was a good location for an afternoon drunk. When we passed three of them on the trail swigging sherry from a bottle, they recognized Trudeau and followed us down to the swimming hole. Trudeau and the children had worn swimming suits so they plunged right into the river. Heather, who had planned to change in the bushes, was now having second thoughts. Two of the toughs sauntered over to her and, nodding in my direction, loudly asked:

"That guy his bodyguard?"

Heather quite liked that illusion and did nothing to change his mind.

Observing the whole scene from a large rock a short distance along the shore, I suddenly realized that the one they called Tarcy was sending his companions downstream to invite the rest of the gang to join him for some anticipated action. They soon appeared, walking, wading and paddling upstream in rubber inner tubes, carrying beer and sherry bottles. They were drunk, swaggering and loud. I knew we were in for trouble.

Trudeau and the others were oblivious to the gang's arrival. I summoned them from the water and asked Heather to take the children up the trail to the minibus as quickly as possible. Pierre lingered to tie the shoelaces of one of his boys and I stayed with him. That's when Tarcy made his move.

He sauntered up to us, a dozen drunken backers not far behind.

"You're Trudeau, ain't ya?"

Trudeau acknowledged his identity.

"What would happen if I just punched you out right now?" asked Tarcy, moving toward Trudeau. He now stood between us and the trail back to our vehicle.

Trudeau's eyes narrowed. With jaw set, he stepped up to Tarcy and put his closed fist under the bully's nose. With clear blue eyes fixed on Tarcy's bleary ones, Canada's fifteenth Prime Minister threatened through clenched teeth:

"Just you try it . . ."

Tarcy was somewhat taken aback at this and Trudeau moved unhurriedly past him onto the trail, his son Justin in hand and me close behind.

Murder Point, Nova Scotia, 1979. Left to right are: *Alexander Watt, Sacha Trudeau, Rachel Johnston, all supported by Pierre Trudeau. (Barbara Collins).*

top: *Author with American space shuttle commander Paul Weitz and P.E.T., Parliament Buildings, 1983.*

above: *Author and P.E.T. talk with students from Selwyn House School, Montreal, 1983.*

top: *Liberal Caucus, Mont Gabriel, 1978. Marc Lalonde, author, P.E.T.*

left: *With Trudeau at memorial service for Frank Scott. Winter 1985.*

Author, Heather and Prime Minister Trudeau campaigning in Montreal during the 1978 by-election. (Marc Pouliot)

Children present home-made birthday cards to Prime Minister, 1978.

The challenge had been so direct I was sure Tarcy and his gang would soon recover their wits and charge after us. Trudeau, however, seemed unconcerned and simply observed to me that we now had the high ground on a narrow trail and could easily handle a gang of drunks one by one. I sensed he would have almost welcomed the opportunity.

Trudeau is no bluffer. We came within a hair of a fight, the outcome of which I prefer not to contemplate, but Pierre had won the day.

Whether it is in Cabinet, at a First Ministers' Conference, at an international summit or on a lonely stretch of river bank miles from nowhere, Trudeau will not back down or run away from a fight.

Trudeau also has a dispassionate capacity for self-assessment. He knows his own strengths and uses them skilfully, although he did admit after the Gold River incident that he should remember he is in his sixties. He also knows his weaknesses, seldom exposing them to adversaries. Above all, even after sixteen years as Canada's Prime Minister there is not a trace of pompous self-importance. I doubt that many tread the corridors of power and leave, as he did, seemingly untouched and unchanged by the praise, prestige, privilege and, in Trudeau's case, international acclaim often bordering on adulation. Many in public life are captured by their own press clippings and the flirtation with power which does not belong to them but for which they are merely custodians of the public trust. But not Trudeau. Like Harry Truman, he remembers who he is and where he came from.

On the international stage Trudeau transferred his capacity for rigorous self-assessment to the country itself. He knew Canada's measure in the international community and the effective roles it could play in the East-West dialogue as well as in the North-South dialogue. He never oversold Canada's position. As a result, our country emerged from Trudeau's stewardship widely respected around the globe. Canadians who travel abroad quickly realize that.

In the international arena, Trudeau also sought to impose obligations on his political counterparts, beseeching them to abandon the carefully prepared positions of the bureaucrats, especially the military ones, and to speak on behalf of the people they represented. His efforts were to little avail, with the exception of the May 1983 Williamsburg Economic Summit where he successfully brought about the drafting of a communiqué on the spot. Commenting at the press conference following those meetings Trudeau said:

"Here, the communiqué was written overnight, as it were, and the declaration on disarmament, which Canada had brought as an idea to the summit, was practically written from scratch during the discussion we had on the subject. In that sense I think it is very successful. It permitted leaders to express divergent views and it gave them the time to seek reconciliation of those divergent views."

It is that same process that Trudeau sought to achieve at First Ministers' conferences, in consultations with labour and business and later, on his peace mission.

Trudeau recognized that dialogue must be established between politicians acting as their own spokepersons. In his view, leaving strategic decisions to military "pipsqueaks" and nuclear accountants on both sides is to abandon political responsibility and edge the world closer to nuclear holocaust. The problem is that most political leaders are too intellectually insecure to assume that responsibility. The collective bureaucratic opinion, the product of many brains thought to be more informed than those of political leaders, provides comforting assurance for such politicians. Trudeau never required that security blanket.

Trudeau's detractors are many, his supporters legion. In truth, it will be years before the full impact of his contributions can be understood.

I summarized my own feelings at the Liberal leadership convention in these words:

"I see the Prime Minister sitting here on the 16th anniversary of the magic of his election to the leadership of this party.

"What a Canadian!"

His outstanding character personifies the striking contrast of this nation. He is warm. He is cold. He is wild. He is serene. But, above all, he is honest with himself and with others. These qualities we treasure because they reflect our national character.

"Pierre Elliott Trudeau, par la noblesse de sa pensée, par

son sens de l'histoire et de la réalité du monde d'aujourd'hui, aura donné au Canada l'importance qui s'accordait véritablement a sa grandeur."[9]

Unless he tells his own story, we shall continue to have an obscure picture of the man himself. Even then, he may prefer to perpetuate the mystery and leave historians with the question: "Who was Pierre Elliott Trudeau?"

VII

Lessons for Losers

*"As it turned out, not only was the Party un-
prepared for an election, there followed one of
the worst organized and most poorly orchestrated election campaigns in the country's
history."*

The year 1984, despite its Orwellian overtones, will be
etched in the memories of Canadians for other reasons, many
of them unforeseen.

The resignation of Pierre Elliott Trudeau as Prime Minister brought mixed feelings of melancholy, nostalgia and expectation. Soon afterwards, the leadership race, which ended in
the coronation of John Turner, provided excitement and the
opportunity for Liberals to gather in the cathartic atmosphere
of their first leadership convention since 1968. The election
campaign, followed by massive Liberal defeat brought despair,
insecurity and, for some, bitterness. It was a memorable year
in Canadian political history.

For many months before his walk under the snowflakes,
there was speculation, public and private, about Pierre
Trudeau's future as leader of the Liberal Party. In fact, the
issue had been doggedly pursued by the media since the 1980
election. Among Liberals, unity and loyalty held sway; only
the mavericks dared publicly denounce the leader or question
his authority. Exchanges about the need for change erupted
almost exclusively in the privacy of back rooms. Trudeau's
leadership was not questioned by Liberals in public. The respect with which he was held made that unthinkable.

Only the Trudeau-haters believed he coveted power for its own sake, and that holding onto office was the full extent of his interest. They were hopelessly ignorant of the full measure of the man. Those who knew him better understood that he would sense when the time had come for him to leave.

Toward the end, the Party was in disarray, approaching disintegration. Grass roots workers were dispirited, riding executives demoralized and even caucus members disenchanted. While his personal popularity remained high, Trudeau's authority in the Party was fading. Well into his last term his intentions were a puzzle to most members of the Party. Jim Coutts, Keith Davey and others were pressing him to stay. If he had done so, I am sure the Party would have held at least eighty seats in the 1984 election, most of them in Quebec.

But I always felt that Trudeau meant what he said in resuming the leadership for the 1980 election, that it would be his last mandate; that he knew to take the Party into another election would be a mistake both for himself and for the country. Had the 1980-1984 Parliament, both Government and Opposition, been returned in the same proportions in a 1984 election, I believe it would have been a tragedy. The painful East-West split would have been reinforced; the country could not have tolerated another four years of regionally unbalanced representation in Parliament, with Quebec dominating the caucus and the Government and the western provinces feeling they had no voice. The strains on Confederation would have been too great.

Considering the mood of the country, a true national mandate for Trudeau seemed impossible. I am sure he was aware of the pros and cons of his remaining or leaving better than anyone else. As a senior Deputy Minister once said to me at the height of the acrimonious constitutional debate: "Pierre Trudeau will make whatever concessions the situation demands because he is a very wise man."

By Christmas 1983 Trudeau had said nothing publicly. If he had disclosed his intentions privately, it was not to me. There had been hints in conversations over many months which could be taken either way. He probably enjoyed keeping people speculating and off balance, especially the media. Political tactics and the management of government dictated silence.

118

Some say he knew the Party would be defeated. He could lead the Party to defeat and then turn it over to a successor with a fresh mandate to rebuild, unencumbered by the stigma of defeat. Alternatively, he could resign before an election. I think that Trudeau was too competitive for the first scenario to have been appealing.

So we come to that fateful February 28th walk under the snowflakes, and Trudeau's announcement the next day that he would resign. The leadership campaign was on: the right decision at the right time. A full year remained in the Liberal mandate leaving Trudeau's successor many options as to when to call the next election.

Would Donald Macdonald run? Would John Turner run?

Macdonald said no. Back in 1979, although a leadership campaign did not have time to develop following Trudeau's first resignation, Turner had announced that he would not be a candidate. Would he change his mind?

Late in 1983 when John and I had a private dinner at Bigliardi's Restaurant in Toronto, it was clear that he was keeping his options open. Should he decide to run, his reason would be his sense of obligation to save the Liberal Party, considering himself to be one of the few, if not the only person, in a position to do so. A year later when I read the *Maclean's* interview by Peter Newman I was reminded that his comments to me were almost exactly as quoted:

"If one has been given the benefits of a good education, health and talent, and the ability to participate in public life, then I believe one has a duty to do it."[1]

I explained my position, adding that I would likely run when the leadership opened whether he ran or not. John accepted that.

Turner was troubled by Trudeau's silence. Undue delay, he felt, would make it impossible for a new leader to turn around public opinion before an election. When Trudeau's resignation finally came I was one of the few who believed John would not join the race. Having backed off in 1979 when Liberals were ahead in the polls, why would he now come in when the Party's popularity was down and defeat was almost certain?

In the end, six Cabinet ministers and John Turner entered the race. Most of the ministers closest to Trudeau and strongest in his administration openly supported Turner. Perhaps they believed he was the most electable candidate because, not only had he distanced himself from Trudeau, he was viewed as anti-Trudeau. Further, he had no recent record to defend.

The day Trudeau resigned I was in Montreal for a meeting with Blair Williams at his Concordia University office. I had come to discuss the Party leadership and to give a speech to students at the McGill Law Faculty. Maria Lang, president of the Young Liberals at McGill and Otto's and Adrian's daughter had organized the gathering. Just as I was about to speak she took me aside:

"We have just heard Trudeau has announced his resignation. He said he decided after a walk in the snow."

I was astounded, not by the news but by the timing. Late the previous afternoon I had met with Trudeau privately in his office to discuss a specific dossier and had detected no sign of his impending decision. Maybe it was the snowflakes after all.

Imagine my conflicting emotions! The career of the man I most respected as a politician was over. But for me, was this to be the beginning of a great new challenge?

Eight days later I declared my candidacy. Was I ready? One is never really ready for a decision of this magnitude that can radically change a career or even lead to insolvency. My wife Heather, David McNaughton, Rick Anderson and other key advisers all urged me to be the first to declare my intentions to run. In all likelihood some other candidates would have higher profiles but, by being the first, I could pick up immediate media coverage undiluted by their presence. It seemed logical.

We began with a press conference in the Commonwealth Room of Parliament. Heather and I both answered questions but, in retrospect, I now realize we little knew what lay ahead. My statement on that occasion, underlining the need for coherence in facing challenges of the future, became a guide throughout our three-month campaign. I emphasized the notion that issues and ideas should play a central role in any leadership race and singled out a number for special consideration:

- to capture the benefits of exciting new technologies while managing the changes and dislocations they would create;
- to revitalize our education and training systems to respond to developing needs;
- to secure for Canadians equal access to opportunities in a non-discriminatory society;
- to maximize opportunities for all Canadians to realize their full potential;
- to satisfy Canadians that government is not their adversary but, rather, is a powerful instrument to assist them in accomplishing their objectives;
- to insist that all levels of government co-operate in serving the needs of Canadians; and
- to build upon Trudeau's bold and vital peace initiative, never ceasing in our efforts to halt the insane stock piling of armaments around the world.

That night after the press conference Mike Robinson and I flew to Toronto where I was Barbara Frum's first guest on her "Race for the Rose" series for CBC's *The Journal*. The campaign was launched and the strategy of being first in the race seemed to be working.

The next thirteen weeks were a blur of frenetic nationwide activity: speeches, coffee parties, chartered flights, Sunday brunches, policy conferences in Saskatoon, Halifax, Montreal, Vancouver and Toronto. We chased delegates across the country over mountains, lakes and prairies, in fair weather and foul, and when not on the road, we manned the phoncs. It was tiring, exhilarating, stimulating and expensive, leaving me at the end with a campaign debt approaching $300,000.

My travelling companion was usually Elizabeth Coburn, a remarkable young woman from London, Ontario, perfectly bilingual, with several years of experience in the Quebec City office of the Liberal Party and in Ottawa. She was chatty, as her friends will attest, perceptive and, above all, full of good humour and advice.

Whether in small towns or in big cities, in the East or the West, I was consistently impressed by the quality of the Canadian Liberals I met. Questions were thoughtful and comments illuminating. They stimulated my resolve to run a policy-rooted campaign. Issues of education, income support, the impact of technology, world trade, peace, and a host of other national and international level concerns were probed. Discussions were almost never sidetracked onto purely local issues.

One amusing feature of this kind of campaign gradually came to light as I discovered how important it can be for a candidate to have family connections in all regions of the country. Jean Chrétien's huge family seemed to supply him with an endless stream of western cousins. John Turner's origins were established in five separate places concurrently: New Brunswick, Montreal, Ottawa, Toronto, Winnipeg and Vancouver. Then in Brandon, Manitoba, he pointed out that it had been the birthplace of his father-in-law, David Kilgour.

I began to scrounge around among relatives and ancestors to see what I could find.

For a start, I was born in the Ottawa Valley, lived in Quebec and was married to a Nova Scotian. This covered three provinces and enabled my supporters to tout me variously as an Ottawa Valley boy, a Quebecer or as "Nova Scotia's favourite son-in-law" as the situation demanded.

This latter entitlement was further consolidated in Cape Breton when I mentioned my late uncle, J. P. MacMillan, from Lake Ainslie, the first superintendent of Cape Breton's magnificent national park opened in the 1930s. When Don MacDougall added "and Allan MacEachen didn't get him the job," it brought the house down.

I was able to counter Turner's Brandon origins by pointing to my mother-in-law's birth in Winnipeg.

Then there were rumours of distant Johnston cousins in Saskatchewan where my grandfather had lived for a short time in 1904. There were Johnston connections in Alberta and British Columbia who could be established through my father who had resided in Comox and Victoria for many years prior to his death in 1982.

This left only three provinces in addition to the Yukon and the Northwest Territories where I had no family connections.

The so-called policy sessions were well chaired by Paul Martin, Jr. but the policy content was minimal. Neither the presentations by leadership candidates nor the question and answer periods did much to clarify where candidates stood. The dominant strategy seemed to be to play it safe and avoid broaching controversial subjects. In the hope of winning supporters over the long haul, each tried to be the candidate to offend the fewest people by the time of the convention.

Several weeks into the campaign I began to attract some media attention, earning the label "ideas man" for my strong stands on a variety of issues, including calling for the government to sell Petro-Canada's retail gas outlets and promoting the idea of a guaranteed minimum income for all Canadians. To be honest, however, I do not know how much of the interest in my campaign was simply a response to my black eye. That celebrated shiner became a trademark and a source of increasing intrigue as the campaign progressed. How did it happen? The real story never emerged during the campaign and the mystery has persisted to this day. Now is a time for truth.

Brian Nelson, now a star anchor-man in Florida on Ted Turner's all news network, was the communications expert on my campaign. He and I had left the CKAC radio station in Montreal following a lunch hour interview with Pierre Pascau. As we were getting into our rented car, somehow I managed to slam the door in such a fashion that it caught my glasses and drove them into my right eye socket. How I managed that freak feat I'll never know (but it perhaps explains why campaign managers are so anxious that candidates not be permitted to let themselves in and out of cars).

The pain made me want to scream. In seconds a swelling the size of a golf ball appeared. My immediate concern was for the semi-final doubles tennis match I was to play that afternoon with Jack Spencer against Ron Kay and Eric Klinkoff. Brian was horror stricken, thinking about upcoming media events. He kept saying "my God, my God . . ." He ran to a restaurant and returned with ice which I held tightly against the swelling until I reached home. I took a pain killer, increased the ice and lay down until my tennis match.

Arriving at the Montreal Indoor Tennis Club on Côte-des-Neiges, I was met by a phalanx of media who had somehow heard about my involvement in the match. The old staid establishment was crawling with journalists. The staff and patrons were neither accustomed to nor much amused by the attention. The ice had done its job and the swelling of my eye had subsided. The discoloration that was to stay with me for weeks had not yet appeared. But after the media left, a few games into the first set, there it was, a lovely black eye. I appeared that evening at my next function sporting one of the world's great shiners. Members of the media assumed I had been hit in the eye during the match. Who was I to deny them this much better notion? Although we had lost the match, I had attracted unexpected media attention. The record will show that I never claimed it happened during the match.

The cause of the black eye remained the best kept secret since a still unidentified MP found himself locked outside his Parliamentary office with nothing between himself and the public gaze but a small towel.

As the campaign progressed, many Canadians began to associate themselves with our message because it addressed vital issues. Some, including my campaign chairman David McNaughton, had at first been cynical about the whole leadership selection process to the point of not intending to participate.

We forged a team from East to West, albeit with a number of weaknesses, notably in Quebec where the struggle between Turner and Chrétien forces dominated the field. But three Quebec caucus members, David Berger, Claude-André Lachance and Raymond Savard, eventually came on board. Guy St. Pierre a former Quebec Cabinet minister helped round out our Quebec team.

Members of the media were generally positive but coverage of our campaign was consistently overshadowed by the attention being paid to Turner and Chrétien where the great showdown was seen to be taking place.

Ten weeks into my campaign I was encouraged when Jim Fleming, former Minister of State for Multiculturalism, Senator Gil Molgat former National President of the Liberal Party of Canada, and Professor Blair Williams, a former National Director of the Party, all three of whom have been prominently involved in the reform movement within the Party, joined my team.

In the joint endorsement released May 23, 1984, these three thoughtful supporters were critical of the leading leadership contenders for "not challenging Canadians with ideas and reform sufficient to our time or to the future of Canada," and accused them of believing "that simply changing the style or image of the leader is good enough." They argued that Liberals

124

should "demand more from the men who would be leader" and select a candidate "who is most attuned in terms of approach . . . and best able to involve the membership of the Liberal Party in the revitalization of Canadian liberalism."

They stressed the importance of having "a third option offering substance in this contest for the Liberal leadership" and urged others who agreed to join them in supporting me.

I believed that the Party must have a better reason for wanting to stay in office than merely relishing power. Similarly, I felt it was important for leadership candidates to state their reasons for being in the race and give delegates something substantial upon which to base their choices. This is what I tried to do throughout my campaign. Simply covetting the keys to 24 Sussex Drive was not enough. By inference, my remarks were considered a rebuke to Turner and Chrétien.

I felt Turner was running on 1975 issues. His long absence from Ottawa had created a generation gap. In politics, nine years is a generation, especially during that period of oil shocks, stagflation, recession and technological change. He appeared to ignore the intervening years, dissociating himself from Trudeau's initiatives on the NEP, the Constitution and management of the economy. I strongly agreed with his emphasis on controlling the public debt and sound fiscal management and said so.

Chrétien seemed to be arguing that he had earned the leadership. He reminded delegates of his critical role in the Constitution debates, his many portfolios over the years and his love for Canada. All of this was true but I felt he avoided current issues and future policies. As a veiled shot at Turner, he reminded us repeatedly that his commitment to the Liberal Party was "a lifelong commitment." Being warm, sensitive and charismatic, Chrétien soon, and deservedly, became the sentimental favourite in the race. He also had a good liberal reform issue on his side. When he first entered the race, a number of Liberals were outspoken about the requirement, based on "long Party tradition" to alternate the leadership from francophone to anglophone. Chrétien argued successfully that it is high time we stopped worrying about what language is being spoken and started listening to what is being said, accepting people at face value regardless of their language or ethnic origin. This debate was significant and worthwhile.

It was the media who proclaimed Turner the Party's saviour in its hour of need and anointed him victor at an early date. According to them, because of his nine-year absence from Ottawa, he was the only candidate who was untainted by the Liberal government's arrogant mismanagement of the country. As if to reinforce that image, Turner quickly drew around him a number of advisers who had also retired from active Liberal politics. Dangerous as that appeared to the rest of us, supporters swarmed to him in droves because he looked like the winner. Momentum was on his side and the forces in play were self-reinforcing.

The media also conferred upon John Turner the dubious distinction of being the most like Brian Mulroney. From this they concluded he would be best able to keep the vote that would otherwise go to Mulroney. Chargex versus MasterCard, some pundits observed. No doubt responding to this analysis and compounding the faultiness of the logic in doing so, delegates by the score admitted they had decided to vote for Turner, even though he was not their own personal choice, because they believed he alone could stave off a Conservative victory. My campaign advisers and I were convinced that, confronted with a "Turner Liberal no policy" campaign and "new broom Mulroney," the electorate would go for change. We were proved right.

With victory pre-ordained, it did not matter that Turner ran an unimaginative leadership campaign, lacking in policy content, but not in funds. The theme of his campaign was simple: Win with John Turner; experience, trust, confidence.

During the too long, too expensive and exhausting leadership race, I was gratified that the media characterized our campaign as innovative and thoughtful. I always tried to put policy over polish, content over appearance.

As Friday night drew near when we would address the delegates and a national television audience, the tension mounted. We drew fifth place. Only Turner and Chrétien would follow. My speech went well and I felt good about it. It was the time and place for reinforcing impressions created over the previous three months. I spoke to the key issues raised by so many of my supporters during the campaign:

"Those who are involved with me in my campaign are tired of the old refrain that the world is a hostile, competitive environment, that we must peer beyond our borders wary and trembling in collective insecurity."

"Not at all!" I continued. "The future I see is one overflowing with opportunities in a world that is starving for Canadian initiative, innovation, services, products, and especially that sanity that Canada can bring to the nuclear arms debate . . .

"Too many Canadians are worried about our country's future. They see our resources, our skilled and energetic people, and so much else, and they wonder. They wonder why things aren't working out better, why we keep missing the brass ring when we have so much going for us . . .

"We can turn our worries about technolgical change into opportunities . . .

"We can turn Parliament into a modern legislative forum that earns the respect and support of Canadians."

I listed other challenges and added that we could accomplish none of this simply by tinkering with existing programs or seeking refuge in going back to yesterday's solutions. "The Liberal way," I said, "has always been to use dramatic initiatives to find solutions to new problems . . ."

While we felt momentum building, it was too late. We knew that only a particular combination on the first ballot could bring us victory from third position. Everyone except the two front runners claimed third spot but our analysis seemed to confirm that we had it. If we could attract 400-500 votes on the first ballot with Turner at 1,400 and Chrétien at 1,000 we would have a chance. As it turned out, Turner won 1,593 putting him beyond reach. The outcome was certain. Turner would win no matter what the rest did. My own 278 delegates were fairly evenly divided between Turner and Chrétien as their second choice.

The movement to Chrétien between the first and second ballots tugged hard at my own delegate strength. I was under strong pressure to join. Jean and his supporters invaded our section to plead with me. For me, the choice was clear and I think Jean accepted it. I would stay on for the second ballot. This left the delegates with three choices—better for the Party than the complete polarization which would have resulted if I had dropped out leaving no bridge between the two first runners. Most of my delegates rejected expediency on the second ballot and stuck with me on principle. We held with 192 votes.

Defeat is never fun. The meaning of Jim Grant's homily delivered on the occasion of my first political victory, "winning sure beats losing," took on a whole new dimension as it played and replayed inside my head. I was terribly disappointed. The compliments about the campaign we had run did little to overcome a sense of lost opportunity. Then when I began to realize the magnitude of my campaign debts, I despaired. Raising $300,000 for a candidate who had lost did not look easy.

Before long, however, friends and supporters began making plans for fundraising events to help retire the debt. They knew the task would not be easy, especially since contributions to leadership campaigns are not tax deductible. Once more, Jim Grant spearheaded the effort. Colleagues like David Smith who had worked for Turner helped organize a roast in Toronto. Bob Rae of the NDP roasted me until I was well done. Geills Turner, John's wife, and his sister Brenda Norris shared that same platform in St. Lawrence Hall in Toronto to help me out of debt.

In Ottawa, John Crosbie, Charles Lynch, Jean Chrétien, Gerry Regan, NDP House Leader Ian Deans and, again, Brenda Norris, joined forces, to raise more funds.

But the most celebrated event took place at the Maison Alcan in Montreal. To add another dimension to the traditional cocktail party or roast, the organizers decided I should play the piano. As a spoof it was promoted as a piano recital by Donald Johnston. Everything was donated: space, bar, sandwiches and glasses. When the appointed time arrived, I dutifully obeyed the organizers, made my appearance in a white suit, white tennis shoes, straw hat and rhinestone glasses à la Elton John. I did my best to give a few piano renditions that bore absolutely no resemblance to a witty program prepared by Graham Watt which included:

"Brother, Can You Spare 2 Million 500 Thousand Dimes!" by D. Johnston;
"No, No, They Can't Take That Away From Me!" by B. Mackasey and C. Dupras;
"God Bless America," by B. Mulroney;
"Second Hand Rose," by J.N. Turner;
"Boldfinger," by P.E. Trudeau, and
"The Green, Green, Grass of Home," by R. Hatfield.

Because it was rumoured that both Trudeau and Turner

would be present, the national media came in droves. My piano playing, which lasted only a few minutes, was completely upstaged by the presence of these two former Prime Ministers and the associated swarm of cameras, microphones and lights.

To the credit of those who organized the evening, it was a great success as a fundraising event. Sadly for my campaign debts, the City of Montreal advised us that my piano concert justified a levy of amusement tax of up to $8,000. I thought the *Globe and Mail* editorial on February 8, 1985 summed the matter up very well:

TINKLING THE IVORIES

Ever since former Liberal justice minister Donald Johnston played the piano at a fundraising gathering, his critics have been raving. Some of them still are—asserting that Mr. Johnston owes the City of Montreal $8,000 in entertainment tax. Mr. Johnston, attempting to scramble out from under a heavy debt burden after his $900,000 bid for the federal party leadership, says his audience showed up for charitable reasons, not for his musical abilities.

We understand how difficult it must have been to make such an admission, even for one who claims no more than amateur standing (or sitting) at the keyboard, but we are prepared to accept the protestation at face value. Mr. Johnston faces a cruel dilemma as he prepares to beat back the voracious municipal tax collectors. Will he be forced to call upon the testimony of his guests, who included former prime ministers John Turner and Pierre Trudeau, for evidence that whatever Mr. Johnston contributed to that evening, it was not entertainment?

There is no indication that any of the 400 people present for the fundraiser fled the hall with their hands over their ears to exclude Mr. Johnston's maltreatment of Richard Rodgers; but neither did this seem to be the kind of situation in which they would demand their money back because Mr. Johnston hit the occasional clinker.

If he had told funny stories instead of playing, would the tax collectors still have tried to collect $8,000, offered a discount for jokes that fell flat, or ignored the proceedings entirely because not a note of music was heard? From the Globe and Mail's account of the event in the issue of Nov. 21, 1984: "Mr. Johnston played the piano and said a few words, but the presence of Mr. Turner and Mr. Trudeau was the focus of attention."

Now *that's* entertainment.

Pierre Trudeau has offered to defend me against the charge because, as he put it, "I was not amused." John Turner insists on appearing as a witness because he believes that any tax levied on the quality of my playing would be a gross miscarriage of musical justice. It could be an interesting day in Court.

In all, the 1984 Liberal leadership convention was a political failure compared with the one in 1968. Trudeau's nomination as leader had brought with it a serious commitment to change. All members of the Party had confidence that he would stand for nothing short of radical change. He was a man for a new era.

In 1984 the Liberal Party changed leaders but did not refurbish its image. Turner tried to camouflage the Party's exhaustion, its paucity of ideas and principles. He spoke of a new Liberal Party, but there was no supporting evidence. Something was seriously wrong at the party level.

The convention had done more than exhaust the participants and drain their coffers. It had left the Party with a painful division between Turner and Chrétien supporters that would take a long time to heal. This rift was reinforced by the absurd little drama shortly after Turner's victory was announced. In her introduction of Jean Chrétien, Liberal Party President Iona Campagnolo referred warmly to him as "second in the vote but first in our hearts!" She probably expressed the sentiments of a majority of those present but, to an already divided audience, it did not seem an appropriate comment if unity was an objective.

A few minutes later, after Chrétien's gracious remarks in defeat and his request that everyone at the convention make the vote for Turner unanimous, a second event occurred which subsequently influenced numerous Liberals. All of the defeated candidates were at the back of the stage in a wide semi-circle. Pierre Trudeau was there too. When Rémi Bujold invited him to come to the microphone to speak, Trudeau did not. He took a single step forward, raised one hand in a wave, and smiled enigmatically while the roar of the crowd first built in anticipation and then died away in confusion. Our leader of sixteen years, by this simple non-action, legitimatized the notion of holding back support from Turner. In the critical

130

months that followed, many other Liberals did the same.

While Turner, as the new leader, must bear ultimate responsibility for declaring a general election in the summer of 1984, he was hardly familiar enough with the Party apparatus to rely on his own judgement. Some ministers felt the election should be delayed. Jean Chrétien was strongly of this view. He believed that such a delay would permit Turner to raise his profile, especially during the planned visits of Queen Elizabeth and Pope John Paul II.

From where I sat it seemed we should make sure the Party was ready for an election before taking the leap. By that I meant money, policy, candidates and organization. Those of us who had just emerged from the leadership contest did not have much stomach for another campaign. In the judgement of some senior ministers, the Party would only be ready once an election was called. That view prevailed. Buoyed by the temporary surge of popular support engendered by the leadership campaign and the judgement of senior Cabinet ministers and key advisers who felt the time was right, Turner called the election. As it turned out, not only was the Party unprepared for an election, there followed one of the worst organized and most poorly orchestrated election campaigns in the country's history.

Political scientists and political pundits will pick over the results of the Tory landslide on September 4, 1984, for many years. The impact of the television debates, the bum-patting, the spilled coffee and confusion over Turner's position on language rights in Quebec and Manitoba, will all find their places in the history of that election campaign. Blame will also be assigned to the patronage appointments, especially that of Bryce Mackasey as Ambassador to Portugal.

These incidents combined to play a significant role in the Liberal defeat. They could not be offset by imaginative policy options because none existed. Individual candidates were left to fly solo for the most part, in many cases doing their best to stay non-committal in controversial areas where no clear direction had been indicated by the Party. In fact nothing seemed to be working right. As the campaign advanced and the Tory tidal wave began to reveal itself, many of our star candidates had to withdraw from the national context and stick to home base to try to save their own ridings.

At the outset, we believed that minimal losses in Quebec would be offset by Turner gains elsewhere. Mulroney, although perfectly bilingual and a Quebec native, was thought to have too much hostile conservative baggage to be acceptable to the French-Canadian voter. Initially it looked as though he was in trouble even in his own riding, Manicouagan, running against the young and popular incumbent, André Maltais. When it was suggested that as many as a dozen seats in the province might swing Conservative, Liberal MPs, myself among them, laughed. When newspaper polls suggested that certain Quebec ministers were at risk, we looked upon them with detached disbelief.

Gradually, the strength of the blue wave made itself felt in Quebec. My own riding of St. Henri-Westmount was judged to be a Liberal haven so I was called upon to campaign with individual candidates in ridings all over the country, mostly outside of Quebec, visiting 35 ridings in the space of four weeks. But so strong was the movement of public opinion to the Tories that my own margin was reduced to 4,000 votes against a virtually unknown Conservative candidate who had no profile in the constitutency. Had the Tories targetted my riding with a high profile candidate, the outcome might have been different and I could have found myself writing these chapters from my Montreal law office.

Pierre Trudeau always argued that Quebec voters are among the most astute, never wanting to be on the wrong side of a national election. Unlike their western counterparts, they believe that federal goods and services are likely to go where government has support. So they argue there is a benefit, measurable in real terms, in being represented by an MP of the government in power. When it became clear that Mulroney was going to win, Quebec voters had no trouble whatsoever changing their allegiance.

And what of the much vaunted Quebec big red machine? It did not exist. What we did see was the importance of Pierre Elliott Trudeau, not only to Quebec voters, but voters elsewhere as well. In the minds of voters, Pierre Elliott Trudeau was the Liberal Party and when he went, so did it. The ghost of the Laurier phenomenon had returned to haunt us. The lessons of history had been forgotten.

Despite all the polls, as election day approached few of us suspected that we would sustain such an overwhelming rejection by Canadian voters. The only good news election night was John Turner's victory in Vancouver Quadra. His gracious and articulate nationally televised comments in accepting our Party's defeat was a character lesson for losers.

VIII

The Laurier Legacy

"The Laurier legacy is not the property of the Liberal Party. It belongs to all Canadians who identify with his principles of liberalism ... The political party which best reflects those principles in its actions, policies and in the minds of Canadians will form our national government."

If I had a dollar for every time the question has been asked "Why are you a Liberal?" I would have a tidy sum of money.

What attracts anyone to a political party? Often it is simply people. Trudeau was a lightning rod that attracted a new generation to the Liberal Party. For these Canadians, Trudeaumania was enough reason to be Liberal.

Others are attracted by power and reward. Separating the power mongers and the patronage seekers from the dedicated is a chronic problem of political parties. This process is easier following defeat when hard work rather than a place at the public trough is the only reward. When the beast is dead, parasites migrate to another warm body.

Still others are party loyalists because they grew up in a particular tradition. For them, political allegiance is much like religion. When I visit Prince Edward Island, I sense that tradition is still alive. In P.E.I. it is said that a mixed marriage is one between a Liberal and a Conservative!

In my case, I joined the Liberal Party because of Pierre Trudeau. Working with him from within seemed more productive than complaining from without. But I remain because of liberalism, and the people who share its principles. I see those as faith in the individual, compassion for the weak and

135

oppressed, tolerance toward others as individuals or groups, equal opportunity for all, and reform, namely to strive constantly to improve the quality of life of Canadians and all mankind.

The importance of the individual and the drive for reform can be traced through nearly 200 years of developing liberalism from as early as Adam Smith, David Ricardo, John Stuart Mill and others. The other principles, especially tolerance, have strong Canadian roots.

Laurier was the architect of Canadian liberalism. He espoused these principles and managed to bring liberals to the Liberal Party where they have remained for most of this century. I would argue that non-doctrinaire, pragmatic, common sense liberalism finds much greater support in Canada today than during the Laurier period.

Indeed, Canada is a country of liberal-thinking people. The principles of faith in the individual, compassion, tolerance, opportunity and reform are widely shared by people who move their votes freely amongst the three major parties.

But I believe Canada's is a special liberalism. The principle of tolerance has flourished in Canada. Ours is a rich liberal legacy created by forces not present in the world of Smith, Malthus, Ricardo, and Mill. Ethnic, cultural and religious differences combined with regional disparities have forged that special liberalism. Canada is a nation of ethnic minorities, aboriginal peoples, European immigrants, and increasing numbers from the Pacific Rim and the Far East. Dominating the mix is the official bilingual and bicultural phenomenon and the determination of Quebec to preserve the French portion of its linguistic and cultural heritage. Taken together with our geographical diversity and economic disparities, this describes a nation that could only survive if a majority of its people were tolerant of each other in good times and willing to share with each other in tough times. As a result, Canadians are more pragmatic, more tolerant and less ideological than most peoples. Moreover, religious and racial intolerance, once widespread in this country, have diminished substantially.

Sir Wilfrid Laurier and Sir John A. Macdonald before him stand in the history of Canada as statesmen far above the din of today's partisan politics. If Macdonald was Canada's Washington then certainly Laurier was its Lincoln. Canadians of all political affiliations must recognize the contribution of Macdonald to nation building and of Laurier in bringing Canada to the world stage and forging the alliance between French and English, Catholic and Protestant.

Laurier had that insatiable appetite for reform, a key characteristic of the liberal. As early as 1877, nearly twenty years before becoming Prime Minister, he said:

> "For my part, I am a liberal. I am one of those who think that everywhere, in human things, there are abuses to be reformed, new horizons to be opened up, and new forces to be developed... We only reach the goal we have set for ourselves to discover new horizons opening up which we had not before even suspected. We rush on toward them and those horizons, explored in their turn, reveal to us others which lead us on ever further and further."[1]

The Laurier legacy is not the property of the Liberal Party. It belongs to all Canadians who identify with his principles of liberalism. What Canadian would not embrace his philosophy which he shared with young Canadians in 1919 shortly before his death:

> "As for you who stand today on the threshold of life, with a long horizon open before you for a long career of usefulness to your native land, if you will permit me, after a long life, I shall remind you that already many problems rise before you; problems of race division, problems of creed differences, problems of economic conflict, problems of national duty and national aspiration. Let me tell you that for the solution of these problems you have a safe guide, an unfailing light, if you remember that faith is better than doubt and love is better than hate.

> "Banish doubt and hate from your life. Let your souls be ever open to the promptings of faith and the gentle influence of brotherly love. Be adamant against the haughty, be gentle and kind to the weak. Let your aim and purpose, in good report or ill, in victory or defeat, be so to live, so to strive, so to serve as to do your part to raise ever higher the standard of life and of living."[2]

The political party which best reflects those principles in its actions, policies and in the minds of Canadians will form our national government.

Canadian Liberals have wandered from these principles. Venturing onto the treacherous terrain of dogma, the liberal and Liberal Party have parted company.

In the Liberal Party we have not paid sufficient attention to Mark Twain's observation that "the radical of one century is the conservative of the next." In our age of exponential change, centuries shrink to decades. Important policies of the 1960s lost relevance in the 1970s and became obsolete in the 1980s, but some Liberals still cling to them, treating them like dogma and forgetting the principles upon which they were based.

Take the notion of universality. In its origin, universality was to protect the dignity of the individual from the humiliation of "means testing." Besides, we could afford it. So, family allowance cheques and old age security cheques go to the wealthy and the poor alike. Now the country is in a financial straight jacket and poor Canadians are slipping further and further under the waves of poverty. But many still cling to outdated programs in the name of universality; once a policy, it is now dogma. Despite declared intentions to move away from universality,[3] prejudice has increasingly won over argument and political expediency has displaced principle.

By 1984 the successful marriage Laurier had created between liberals and the Liberal Party had unravelled. Liberal support had been reduced to a social democratic coalition. The election results of 1984 were startling proof of that, leaving Liberals stunned. With only 40 seats in the House of Commons, a large debt and little public support, where were we to start picking up the pieces?

Like survivors of a natural disaster, we banded together, initially in small groups, to assess the damage and evaluate the future. Out of the confusion and general dismay the re-building process began to unfold. There were far more questions than answers: Would John Turner stay? Would the NDP supplant the Liberals as the official Opposition? Would the Liberals be forced into a coalition of the left? Was this the beginning of extreme left-right polarization in Canada which would eventually see the Liberal Party go the way of its British counterpart and some provincial Liberal Parties?

We now know the answers to these questions. The Liberal Party has regained support at a surprising pace but it is not clear to Canadians where it stands on many of the critical issues of the day. The confusion sown by *ad hoc* policies and the rudderless election campaign of 1984 remains. Which political party now best reflects liberal principles? Carrying as they do the vested interests of organized labour, the NDP can never do so. In the 1984 election campaign, the Tories sounded like Liberals. But subsequent actions such as the proposed de-indexation of Old Age Security demonstrate they are not.

During my cross country campaigning in 1984 I was told time and again that neither the Conservatives nor the Liberals met the approval of voters. For me that meant that neither party met the expectations of liberals. It was a matter of choosing the lesser of two evils. It will be sad for Canada if only the same choice is available next time with neither major party offering voters a vision for the country and its future.

Looking over these comments, I imagine you may be ready to throw open the window and scream out in anguish. The current political choices may not give you that warm glowing feeling that all is well and that you can live your life and go about your business unconcerned about the state of the nation.

What should make us exceedingly happy is that we live in a democracy where the ordinary citizen can do more than be frustrated. In some countries even screaming is out of the question. But in Canada, the opportunities for direct political involvement abound.

You may or may not make it to the Cabinet table. But you can certainly influence the choice of candidates, the choice of party leaders and, if the Parliamentary system is reformed, you will be able to help make policy. Why don't you do it? Is anything else more important? If it is, then stop complaining. Too many Canadians carp about their politicians, seldom recognizing the ability, sacrifice and dedication of so many of all parties at all levels of government.

Get involved in the political process. That is step one in taking action!

PART TWO

TAKING ACTION

IX

Rapids of Change

"Suddenly we have found ourselves in white water, accelerating through the rapids of change with rocks and danger all about... And where are our skilled people, our voyageurs? We have forgotten them, our most precious resource, while we plundered nature's bounty."

For most of its existence Canada has prospered from the riches of nature. Beginning with a vigorous fur trade, then lumber, mineral resources, fish, agricultural products and energy, Canada has ridden the strong currents of demand created by the needs of others. God's legacy has provided us with great wealth and one of the highest standards of living in the world.*

It has also made us complacent, looking always to our storehouse of natural riches for our future; seldom to our people.

As schoolchildren we marvelled at our inventory of riches. Never do I recall any teacher telling us how many universities, engineers, scientists, artists, Canada had. We knew we had a big rich country of which we were proud. Even as a student of economic geography in France at the University of Grenoble, I remember how I basked in the reflected glory of statistics our professor recited about Canada, especially our incomparable hydro resources. Again, our people were never mentioned.

And so, like a happy relaxed Sunday canoeist, we have been content to be swept along by the strong friendly river of

*Note: Statistical data relevant to this chapter may be found under note 1 in the *Notes* at the back of the book.

demand for riches from our storehouse, seldom needing to put a paddle in the water either to move ahead or change direction.

Other nations looked at us with envy as they hit violent white water. They were devastated by war and economic upheaval. But they emerged tougher, experienced and more productive while Canada drifted on in the friendly current, smug and secure.

Suddenly we have found ourselves in white water, accelerating through the rapids of change with rocks and danger all about. We hurtle towards them, glancing off some, banging hard into others. We rode out the recession but the damage was great. The mounting deficits weigh us down. Even skilled paddlers may not be able to manoeuvre our debt-ladened canoe through the rapids lying in wait. And where are our skilled people, our voyageurs? We have forgotten them, our most precious resource, while we plundered nature's bounty. Only they can bring us safely through these rapids of change.

There will be no more strong friendly currents to propel us safely through tranquil waters. The river has changed. There is only white water where people skills, not money, not resources, can navigate a safe and prosperous passage.

Technology and the information society have diminished the importance of our resource wealth. Our comparative advantage in resources has paled beside that of the Japanese and Swiss in skilled people. Our resource exports are meeting tough competition from new low cost suppliers and technology is reducing the demand for many of our minerals. Ceramics and composites are pushing some traditional metal applications into the distant past. And new fast-growing trees may displace our pulp and paper exports.

Even our health in grain exports will slowly fail as China continues to increase its production. Make no mistake, Mikhail Gorbachev will apply radical surgery to Russia's agricultural sector to make it self-sufficient. What will that do to our prairie economies? And while we wax enthusiastic about the Pacific Rim, watch Russia grab our resource markets as the BAM project[2] opens up the wealth of eastern Siberia.

Yes, we risk swamping in this treacherous white water unless we man our canoe with innovative people who can patch our vessel and set it on a safe course.

Are our people ready for the task? Are there enough of them? If current birth, death, immigration and emigration patterns hold, our population will reach thirty million people by 2021 and then begin a gradual decline. By that time our post-war "baby boomers" will be reaching old age and the elderly will represent 23 per cent of the population, more than double the present level. The canoe will certainly be in experienced hands.

But we must also assure ourselves of a continuous supply of young well-trained people. Sadly, it is our youth who have been hardest hit by the recession with over 430,000 unemployed representing 16.9 per cent of that age group (15 to 24 years old).

Then there are the working poor, mostly single parent women drawn into work to eke out a living to support a young family. Men still benefit from higher wages for like work. The wage gap persists. We also have unemployed workers, displaced by robots, who are too old for effective retraining and too young for pension entitlement, public or private.

If we accept that skilled people will make the difference and bring Canada safely through the turbulent rapids, surely education is the answer. Indeed, it is the highest priority. Is it improving? Why do less than two-thirds of our eighteen-year-olds graduate from high school? Before my research, I thought it would be closer to 95 per cent. It is gratifying at least to find that more women are in our universities. Are enough of them in science and engineering? And why are we graduating fewer people from universities? Do we know whether our basic education is responding to the needs of society today? And what of our unskilled unemployed, can they benefit from life-long learning outside the formal education structure?

As we career headlong into more rapids, will our educational system give us the skills to guide us through, or will we be trapped in a souse hole of mediocrity, while our skilled competitors make their way beyond the white water into a glorious future at our expense.

145

Our success in the past depended on capital—capital to build harbours, canals, railroads, roads to our resources—capital to open mines, build smelters, pulp and paper plants, sawmills, rail cars, ships and barges; in other words, capital to build our canoe. We still need that capital, not only for the canoe but for the technology that will make us more productive.

There are problems. Not enough Canadians own our businesses. Many Canadian businesses remain undercapitalized. Our real interest rates are too high making debt more attractive than equity. We have seen a revolt of the savers. They will never allow themselves to be ripped off as they were in the past. We must find other sources of capital for our entrepreneurs and small and medium sized businesses.

While our resource base is of less importance than before, it remains a great asset contributing 14.2 per cent to our GDP (Gross Domestic Product) in 1982. Yet our forests and agricultural wealth, both renewable resources, are in jeopardy.[3]

Yes, the waters ahead are treacherous indeed. But it seems that the currents and rocks that could destroy our canoe are largely of our own creation.

Yes, capital provides us with the best canoe. It is laden with great natural riches that most of our competitors do not possess.

Yes, only people of great skill can bring it safely through the rapids of change. Our entire future lies with our people; with their sense of security; with their education; their innovation, creativity and productivity. The fiscal and regulatory environment must support them. The institutional framework beginning with Parliament itself must give them the tools to do the job.

Unfortunately, what we want to accomplish may escape us if we do not come to grips with the security and health of the international environment. Even then we must face up to one overriding constraint, namely, the state of our own public sector finance and the impediments it is creating to flexible, innovative public sector planning.

If we do the right things quickly, the rapids of change will not swamp us nor leave us wallowing in a souse hole; they will propel us forward to an exciting and properous future.

X

Global Imperative

"One evening while sitting in my den in Montreal watching a television documentary on the East-West confrontation, my daughter Kristina, then fifteen, turned to me and asked: 'Daddy, do we really have a future?'"

Lester B. Pearson was awarded the Nobel Peace Prize in 1957 for his proposal, as Canada's Minister of External Affairs, that the United Nations form an emergency military force to supervise a cease fire during the Suez Canal crisis.

Pierre Elliott Trudeau, well known for his "citizen of the world" perspective, made efforts as Prime Minister of Canada to draw less developed countries into the mainstream of international deliberations. He was also recognized all over the world for his innovative strategy of suffocation[1] to achieve nuclear disarmament, for his leadership toward multilateral free trade at economic summits in recent years, and for his international peace initiative in 1983-1984.

While Canada contains only about one-half of one per cent of the world's population, through these leaders we have engaged actively in world survival debates. We must build on that legacy. We are all in this together and Canada has much to contribute. Men like Mike Pearson and Pierre Trudeau have shown us the way.

Three challenges on which our lives depend face us:
1. The East-West arms build-up and the nuclear threat.
2. Raising the standards of living of the Third World, the so-called North-South issue.
3. Saving the environment we breathe, eat and live in.

147

All three are intimately related. The resolution of the North-South challenge and the complexity of international trade relationships are very much the product of the costly East-West arms build-up. Until a climate of trust and mutual support exists there is little hope for action on the environmental front.

When Jeanne Sauvé, then Speaker of the House of Commons, invited me to participate in a Parliamentary delegation to the Soviet Union in August of 1983, I leapt at the opportunity. There were many reasons but the first was that I knew from previous experience that travelling with Jeanne and her husband, Maurice, is a delightful experience.

In 1982 I had visited Algeria as the government representative in a delegation which included the Sauvés and the House Leaders of the opposition parties, Ian Deans of the NDP and Erik Nielsen, a PC, later Deputy Prime Minister. My wife Heather, Ian's wife June and Erik's daughter Roxanne completed the delegation. Notwithstanding our political differences, we all got along extremely well, learning much and, I hope, offering our hosts a good impression of Canadian parliamentary democracy.

Jeanne Sauvé is a wonderful spokesperson for Canada, spontaneously giving articulate speeches in French and English, tempered and spiced with her ever-present sense of humour which the twinkle in her eyes betrays. This latter trait was certainly put to the test in Algeria when we informed her that, as leader of the delegation, she would be offered the eyeballs of the lamb being roasted at our desert picnic. Etiquette and diplomacy dictated that she accept this culinary token of esteem. At least that's what we advised her, supported by the counsel of our ambassador, Louis Delvoie. Jeanne's reaction was a delight to watch.

Another reason for being interested in the trip to the Soviet Union was more serious. Growing up during World War II and being a teenager during the darkest days of the Cold War had lulled me into acceptance of the East-West struggle. We had learned to live with the bomb. One evening while sitting in my den watching a television documentary on the East-West confrontation, my daughter Kristina, then fifteen, turned to me and asked: "Daddy, do we really have a future?"

I was stunned. Her question was one that I had put aside for too long. There I was, an elected representative of the people, a Cabinet minister in the Canadian government, seized with the same sense of helplessness as any other citizen, and just as incapable of assuring my daughter of a secure future. Surely there was something I could do about it.

The first step seemed to be a better understanding of the Soviets. Jeanne's invitation was timely.

We exchanged views on the East-West threat with senior officials, including Mikhail Gorbachev. He had a special interest in Canada because of his recent trip to examine the Canadian farming sector as Minister of Agriculture. He spoke warmly, almost affectionately, of Eugene Whelan, who had accompanied him on much of his trip and entertained him at the family home in Windsor. A famous Whelan Stetson hung in the Kremlin.

The fear of nuclear annihilation was present at all levels of contact in the Soviet Union. A woman selling stamps in the Hotel Leningrad grabbed my hand saying:

"You Canadians are friends with the Americans. Please do what you can to stop war between us." I assured her I would do what I could.

"You see," she went on, "my daughter just had a baby and I am so afraid."

Yes, the Russians do love their children too.[2]

The day we left the U.S.S.R. is a day that will be engraved in our memories for many years to come. It was September 1, 1983. Korean Air Lines civilian flight 007 had strayed into Soviet air space and was destroyed by Soviet fighter planes. All 269 people aboard were killed in the brutal attack. A sense of outrage swept the Western world. Retaliation was on the minds of many in the wake of this heinous crime. Would any response to the Soviet Union be adequate to express what our nation felt?

Shortly after the travesty I watched a U.S. television program which assessed the sentiments of Americans through the eyes of senior journalists. I thought the best description came from an editor who said the people in his community were caught up in a sense of helpless rage. Those words, "helpless rage," summed up for me the feelings of many of us in Canada. But why helpless?

Western nations are sovereign states; we have a network of relationships with the Soviet Union; we have military power and economic sanctions to bring to bear. Why this sense of helplessness? The answer is so clear that the question is rhetorical. Our helplessness is based on the reality that the world is teetering on the brink of nuclear annihilation. A knee-jerk response of a kind that might have satisfied those who wished to punish the Soviet Union could have thrust us all over that brink. Fortunately, the response was measured and responsible.

Just as the U.S.A. is capable of blowing civilization off the face of this planet, so is the U.S.S.R. And yet it appears gripped with a sense of paranoia, curious in a nation of such enormous power. Imbued with an ideology supporting a totalitarian system which feels itself to be constantly threatened, the Soviet Union is one of the most unfathomable adversaries that any nation or group of nations has faced in the history of civilized man. Our sense of helplessness persists because we, as Western nations, do not have a coherent view of how to deal with this beleaguered giant.

At the same time, our sense of helpless rage has forced many of us to realize we must find a way of co-existing with the Soviet Union. Knowing that we cannot simply give vent to our fury, by responding in kind, we are driven to other approaches. We have learned that embargoes on grain or other products not only hurt us, they also fail to deliver any message of significance to the Soviet people.

No issue preoccupies me as much as the challenge of disarmament. It is not simply an issue of the day, it is the issue of our time. The importance of arresting the arms race penetrates the consciousness of new layers of world society daily. The same is true of Canadians, especially our youth. Unemployment, inflation, interest rates and provincial-federal conflicts all pale against the importance of removing the threat of nuclear war.

Another reality is the permanence of our relationship with the Soviet Union. The communist system is likely to be with us for a long time. Common sense should tell us that we must actively manage our relations to the ultimate advantage of mankind, the most important objective being to defuse the prospect of nuclear war. This requires perseverance and patience; there is no quick fix.

I am convinced that the Soviets fear a nuclear war at least as much as we do. They have endured a turbulent history of invasions through many centuries. Twenty million Soviets died in World War II defending Mother Russia and repelling the German invasion. The effects of that massacre of ten per cent of Russia's population are everywhere to be seen in today's Soviet Union. The challenge they met in World War II is at once a source of pride and a reminder of tragic loss. Few Soviet families were untouched by the barbarism of Nazi Germany. Part of the legacy is an abiding fear of another war, especially a nuclear war which cannot be won.

There are other factors that would argue strongly against military confrontation from the Soviet perspective. Under a rigid totalitarian regime, and a state-imposed planned economy, the Soviets have risen from the ruins of World War II and are anxious to hold on to what they have. Whether it be a twelfth century mosque in Samarkand, or the Summer Palace of Peter The Great, they have devoted vast sums of scarce capital to preserve and restore their heritage. This dedication to preserving their pre-revolutionary past is hardly compatible with plans to engage in a conflict that would reduce everything to ash.

Soviet authorities hold to the ideology of Lenin with religious fervour. His injunction that "to dissent is heretical, to question unacceptable" is as inescapable as is his graven image. The Soviets have attempted to isolate their society from influences that might erode the Lenin religion. This psychology is reminiscent of that which brought us the Spanish Inquisition and appears to be at the root of the human rights problem in the Soviet Union. Each dissenter, including anyone wishing to leave the Soviet Union, is viewed as a loose thread capable of starting the unravelling process.

Surely, after sixty-eight years, Soviet-style communism does not pose an ideological threat to us. On the other hand, while Soviets are proud of their accomplishments, I suspect their confidence has been shaken by the superiority of the Western industrialized world in terms of productivity, technological development and social progress.

151

How, then, do we explain the military juggernaut? Why are the Soviets steadily amassing the greatest military machine the world has ever seen? Why aren't those resources being devoted to public housing, economic infrastructure, consumer goods or social purposes?

I believe the answer is to be found in the deep-rooted belief Soviets have that the West intends to preside over the destruction of Soviet communism. They see the Western military alliance, fueled by a military-industrial complex, as ready and willing to use every means at its disposal to destabilize the U.S.S.R. Ironically this is a mirror image of the scene we in the West paint of the U.S.S.R.

There is no doubt that statements by the U.S. administration in the early 1980s on the possibility that a "limited" nuclear war might be winnable frightened Soviets at the highest levels of government to the point where a nuclear confrontation is viewed by them as something the United States might be prepared to undertake. Discussions at all levels in the Soviet Union during my visit turned quickly to the subject of peace and the necessity of disarmament. As Gorbachev said to us, "Time is running out."

The Soviet Union appears to be anxious to establish wider contacts with the West, which would be to its technical and economic advantage. At the same time it is trying to seal itself off from Western ideas which could undermine its ideological foundation.

How, then, should we in the West conduct our relations with the Soviet Union?

First, we must demonstrate to the Soviet Union that, rather than seeking to destroy or destabilize it, we are prepared to engage in friendly competition, however much we may deplore the Soviet system of government. Evolution, not revolution, will ultimately move the Soviets closer to us. Bellicose rhetoric has no role to play in this approach.

Second, we must establish contacts in areas of mutual interest and maximize the exchange of people: politicians, bureaucrats, professionals and business representatives, athletes, students, scientists, artists and tourists. There is much more to be gained from such exchanges than the mere acquisition of technical information and its companion economic advantages. It is the surest way of bringing about mutual understanding and a weakening of the hermetic seal that separates us.

Third, we must pursue disarmament with specific proposals. That is why Trudeau's suffocation proposal made good sense. With "suffocation" in place, the nuclear arsenals would gradually become obsolete. That is the importance of the nuclear freeze option. But this is unlikely to happen unless a sense of trust can be established between the superpowers. I see a role for Canada in this process, provided our approach is even-handed, and provided we do not become simply another mouthpiece for Washington's policies. Trudeau was singularly successful in that role.

Many Canadians are making creative contributions to this debate. The establishment of the Canadian Institute for International Peace and Security coordinate and focus these efforts. Geoffrey Pearson, son of the former Prime Minister and once our Ambassador to Moscow, is heading this institution.

International peace can only follow international trust. It is a long process. The first steps may have been taken by the 1985 Geneva meetings between Reagan and Gorbachev. Patience and perseverance must be our watch words, as Mao Tse Tung taught in his parable about the foolish old man who removed the mountains. The old man and his sons set out to dig up the mountains blocking their view. To those who considered him foolish he said, "When I die, my sons will carry on; when they die, there will be my grandsons, and then their sons and grandsons, and so on to infinity. High as they are, the mountains cannot grow any higher and with every bit we dig, they will be that much lower. Why can't we clear them away?"

The wall of distrust between East and West is like those mountains. Each positive contact made with the Soviets strengthens the bonds between our cultures and weakens the barriers that separate us.

My own experience during my trip to the U.S.S.R. in 1983 suggested to me that Canada did enjoy an extraordinary amount of good will from the Soviets, due largely to the respect earned by Pierre Trudeau.

During an official lunch at the Kremlin I found myself sitting with Georgi Arbatov, member of the Central Committee and adviser to the Politburo on North American affairs. He expressed Soviet appreciation of Canada's readiness to adopt independent stands on matters of principle despite our close friendship with the United States.

The Soviets are realists on the subject of our U.S. connection. Arbatov, for example, admitted that it is only natural to expect that a country such as the U.S. which buys seventy per cent of our exports would enjoy a close and privileged relationship with us.

However, there could be an honest broker role for Canada to play in establishing more trust between the superpowers. The Soviets sense that we understand them better than the Americans do and may be able to convey their message to the U.S. Administration. Any role Canada might play as intermediary will be seriously jeopardized if they think we are becoming mere sycophants of Washington.

Before Trudeau left the world arena in 1984, he tried to get the debate out of the hands of bureaucrats and technocrats and into the hands of politicians, an endeavour which must be carried forward. At the end of his peace initiative, Trudeau summarized the following ten points of general agreement which he believed to be a starting point for a broader East-West consensus:

- nuclear war cannot be won;
- nuclear war must never be fought;
- the risk of accidental war or surprise attack must be eliminated;
- the dangers inherent in destabilizing weapons must be recognized;
- improved techniques of crisis management are needed;
- the consequences of being the first to use force are awesome;
- security must be increased while costs are reduced;
- horizontal proliferation (the spread of nuclear weapons to other countries) must be avoided;
- the East and West each have legitimate security interests; and
- strategies for security cannot be based on the assumed political or economic collapse of another nation.

As the superpowers are presumably agreed on these ten points of common interest, what is preventing us from putting an end to the nuclear nightmare?

It is not going to be easy or quick. We must survive the short-term madness in order to build a durable long-term peace. We will need to develop the kind of patience and perseverance not usually associated with Western societies as we build upon Trudeau's ten points of East-West consensus. But it is well worth it because it will permit us to create a safer world for our children and for our children's children. We will be moving one step closer to the late John Lennon's dream:

"Imagine all the people
living life in peace.
You may say I'm a dreamer
but I'm not the only one.
I hope some day you'll join us
and the world will be as one."

The most insidious threat to peace on Earth is the disparity between the wealthy and the poor. Trudeau addressed this issue in his North-South dialogue. The North-South challenge and the issue of international trade are inseparable. International charity through transferring ever-increasing amounts of aid money to the less developed countries does not get to the root of the problem. The challenge is analogous to our attempts to develop the poorest regions of Canada. In many cases these attempts have increased dependency and widened the very economic disparities they are trying to eliminate.

The solutions, both in the case of domestic and international disparities lie in building structures based on comparative advantage. Less developed countries must have access to opportunities which offer them a permanent basis for economic growth and development. They need technology, know-how, capital and trade opportunities.

Prosperity for all nations is fundamental to managing the world's population. As Gérard Piel recently pointed out, all of the world's nations which have undergone industrial revolutions have also moved toward near-zero population growth rates while the rest of the world is experiencing population explosions.[3]

Piel estimates that world-wide zero population growth by

the year 2000 would give us a maximum world population of eight billion in the year 2025. That would be approximately twice the current population and, in his opinion, would not be likely to create major problems for our resources.

If the world does not achieve zero population growth until the year 2075, seventy-five years behind schedule, the population would reach twenty billion by the end of the next century. The world's capacity to sustain civilization as we know it would then, I believe, be in jeopardy. In Piel's words: "At twenty billion, however, there are good reasons to be concerned that the logistical task of meeting human needs would require the acceptance of a harshly disciplined, highly centralized world order ... a world which we must hope our grandchildren will not live to see."

Overpopulation of the planet would cause world chaos. We are on that road. History has shown us the solution. Population growth rates always drop as the standard of living is raised. Aside from humanitarian considerations, it is easy to see that our own self-interest lies in bringing prosperity to the Third World. Their birth rates will inevitably fall; the capacity of the Earth to support future generations will be ensured.

This brings me to the subject of international trade.

Trade, a critical element of the global imperative, is closely linked with the East-West arms build-up, the North-South challenge, and domestic economic issues. Those linkages are well described by Robert Reich.[4] He argues that neither American conservatives nor American liberals are in tune with the times. It is a hauntingly familiar theme.

Reich starts with the colossal American arms build-up. Since 1981, real defence spending in the U.S. has increased by thirty per cent. In 1986 alone they will spend nearly $300 billion on defence. This stock-piling of weapons has been accomplished mainly through deficit spending. To finance those deficits, the U.S. has had to increase its interest rates to attract foreign capital. The influx of this capital, principally European and Canadian, has in turn increased the value of the U.S. dollar relative to other currencies causing products manufactured in the U.S. to be more expensive than equivalent products imported from elsewhere. As a result, U.S. domestic markets have become vulnerable to import penetration, the trade deficit has grown steadily (reaching $148 billion in 1985), and the demand for protective measures including tariffs, quotas and countervail has increased.

This line of reasoning leads to the conclusion that the U.S. arms build-up and the U.S. deficit it causes are together bringing about a net reduction of world trade and, at the same time, siphoning off large quantities of investment capital. The impact on less developed and newly industrialized nations is nothing short of devastating.

Some of these countries, such as Brazil, have enormous foreign debts which cripple their economies. Each increase in the U.S. interest rate has a profound effect on the capacity of these indebted nations to service their foreign loans. Add to this the current protectionist tendency of the United States to import less from these same countries, and we have an impossible situation. How can Brazil and others in the same situation raise the money needed to pay back the loans?

This whole scenario, from arms build-up to economic slumps, causes serious problems for Canada and other industrialized nations.

While Canada has been a major beneficiary of the increased U.S. demand for imports, we have had to defend our currency by increasing our own interest rates. Those increases have had a dampening effect on economic recovery. The same forces have been at work in Europe where the economy experienced an even more serious downturn.

Now the Americans have legislated the deficit out of existence at the end of five years. If accomplished, will we see dramatic deflation? Or will the deficit be eliminated by a massive reduction in defence spending, the only sensible option if further economic upheaval is to be avoided.

As for our own trade policy, some Canadians suggest that we should continue expanding as many foreign markets as possible, especially in the United States, perhaps under a comprehensive trade agreement, while maintaining quotas and other protective devices to ensure continuing employment in our soft sectors. With approximately thirty per cent of our GNP (gross national product) dependent on exports and with a partial dependence on outdated, low productivity sectors such as clothing and footwear manufacture, they argue that Canada

157

cannot afford to do otherwise. While Third World exporters would suffer as a result of such a Canadian strategy, enriched aid packages could maintain our image as friend and supporter of poor nations. Politically seductive perhaps, but I do not like this approach as I look at the longer perspective.

Providing financial aid and technology to less developed countries will not increase their standards of living unless they can sell their products to us and to other Western markets.

As one of the major trading nations of the world, and the largest trading partner of the United States, it is up to Canada to take the lead in arresting and reversing the constriction of international trade arteries induced by the U.S. defence-fiscal-monetary policies.

I believe that the East-West confrontation can be managed. There is no alternative. In contrast, the North-South challenge is a sleeping time bomb.

Up to the present we have failed to share our success, our wealth and our know-how with the impoverished Third World. How much longer can developed nations go on ignoring that we are all part of a global village?

Western myopia was brought home to me during a 1982 ministerial session at Davos. We had spent several hours in collective hand wringing over the fearful prospect of reaching a ten per cent rate of unemployment amongst industrialized nations. Our Indian colleague, Narain Datt Tiwari, had remained silent. As the session was brought to a close he said:

"Gentlemen, when you say there will be ten per cent unemployment, doesn't that mean ninety per cent of your people will have jobs?"

As I recall, the comment was greeted with silence, tinged no doubt with a little shame. India's GNP per capita in 1982 was only $260 (U.S.). The GNP per capita in Canada that year was $11,320.[5]

There are many pitfalls involved in trying to make direct comparisons of this type among societies that differ so markedly in geography, expectations and costs of living. But we do know that the gap between the per capita GNP of industrialized countries and developing nations is widening. From $4,600 (U.S.) in 1955, it had increased to $9,880 in 1980 with the percentage of humanity in developing nations moving from 68.1 per cent to 73.5 per cent over the same period.[6]

No one really knows what magic combination of ingredients launches a nation on a pathway that permits it to improve the standard of living of its citizens. For example, what conditions caused Japan to move from being a developing country in 1955 to a major industrial power in 1980? Is there anything the wealthier nations can do to help less developed nations repeat the Japanese experience besides opening up our markets to their products?

Aid programs are important but they should place much more emphasis on education than in the past. For example, more scholarship funding to students from the Third World at Canadian Universities is something I would like to see happen. With world class universities able to welcome students who speak French or English, we are especially well suited for such programs. Not only do foreign students enrich our university communities, they also cement long-term relationships between themselves and Canadians.

For those who think this would be a one-way drain on resources, nothing could be further from the truth. The lasting bonds created would encourage those students to turn to Canada in years to come for goods, services and expertise. As Canadians, we have much to give and much to gain.

The biosphere is in peril. One by one, as particular environmental problems reach crisis proportions in one country or another, nations begin the slow process of getting into gear to attack the problem. Polluters are often not all located within the boundaries of the country suffering their effects. International discussions become deadlocked trying to agree on how to partition blame.

The world has just seen the tip of this iceberg. Countless time bombs lie ticking around us, about to explode and destroy us all. The ozone layer is being depleted, the greenhouse effect threatens to heat us up, our tropical rain forests are disappearing, the deserts are growing, our water and air are accumulating poisons. The potential impacts are almost beyond imagination. Another ice age may come, polar caps may melt, huge sections of low-lying land may be flooded, plant and animal species may disappear, farmlands may no longer bring forth their bounty and good health may become a thing of the past, impossible to attain at any price.

What are we Canadians to do? Made poor by the recession of the early 1980s, spending on the environment is seen by many as a luxury. Critical programs to monitor, protect or clean up our world often land on the chopping block in the name of spending restraint. While each cut may, in fact, reduce the dollar value of the government's deficit, it is time we recognized that, as surely as we live and breathe, a massive environmental deficit is being created in its place.

For example, Europe and Canada have begun to lose jobs, exports and profit as a result of forest depletion. It will cost billions of dollars to attempt to clean up the hundreds of waste disposal sites across North America that are beginning to leak their poisons into the water supply.

The world's environmental deficit is out of control. This deficit, and the additions to it, are unfortunately much less visible than financial deficits; much easier to ignore. Nonetheless, someone someday will have to pay the cost.

My home is in Montreal, a great vibrant metropolis on an island at the confluence of two of the world's great rivers, the St. Lawrence and the Ottawa. Surrounded by lakes, beaches, smaller islands, rapids and inlets, the area should be paradise for fishing, sailing, swimming, canoeing and all manner of water sports. But the waterways are sewers, polluted through years of thoughtless abuse. The historic Lachine Canal is condemned even for boating, so high is the pollution level. What a disgrace.

Yes, the place to begin our assault on pollution is in everyone's own back yard. Public action is necessary but individuals can do much in prevention and cure. Look at the members of Trout Unlimited,[7] a group of volunteer conservationists and fishing enthusiasts. They got together and restored rivers all over North America where the delicate trout again thrives.

In the mid 1960s Lake Erie was considered a dead lake. The fish had all but disappeared and algae was taking over. Today, after two decades of co-operative action between Canada and the United States the lake is once again abounding in life.[8] No, we do not have to accept the *status quo*. Seemingly hopeless situations can be turned around by political and individual will.

When someone tells me that it is impossible to introduce laws to protect the environment without working too great a hardship on the business community, I say: "Nonsense."

As Charles Caccia, former Environment Minister, says: "the ecologically sensible and economically sensible thing to do is to prevent the problems from occurring in the first place . . . environmental constraints faced by one industry turn out to be the entrepreneurial opportunity seized by another."[9] I agree with him.

This is much more than an economic issue. All of our bodies, without exception, require clean air to breathe and pure water to drink. It should not be difficult to develop co-operative action and demand it from our governments. It is so fundamental to human survival that arguments to the contrary are laughable. *Any government that fails to put the environment at the top of its priorities should be thrown out of office at the first opportunity.*

Our future is intertwined with the future of all nations. A flare-up in East-West relations could lead to a cataclysmic holocaust and the end of human life on Earth. Stifling less developed countries could lead to the eruption of North-South conflict and major disruption of world financial systems. What threatens life on this planet most is the lack of international political will to recognize and solve environmental problems.

Pearson put us on the world stage teaching Canadians in the process how essential a supporting role can be. Remember there are no small parts, only small actors. And that means our *own* role, not one produced and directed by Washington.

XI

Fiscal Imperative

"Deficits are much like a fever. While symptomatic of an underlying disease, the fever itself can be fatal when it rises uncontrollably. We are near that point."

The young student was about eleven years of age. He had come with his class from Westmount Park Elementary School to visit Parliament. We set up a committee room to receive them and after a short address to my young constituents I asked if there were any questions. The boy's hand shot up:

"What are you going to do about the deficit, Mr. Johnston?"

Yes, indeed . . . nearly every Canadian has heard about the deficit problem. Much of the debate is emotional, less of it factual. We must expose both the myths and the realities so that informed action can be taken.

The deficit, or more precisely the national debt, presents problems and opportunities. The problems arise from the enormous drain on government revenues necessary to pay interest on our public debt. The opportunities are created by the necessity of governments making hard choices as to what must be cut to fund urgent priorities. Experience shows that when revenues are available as they were in the 1960s and early 1970s, governments only add new programs. They do not scrap old ones. It's a difficult habit to break.

Fiscal constraints of the kind now facing governments at all levels mean that cuts must be made in some programs to support new initiatives. The alternative of simply adding to the

163

public debt is not acceptable. A few figures make the point. Ten years ago the gross public debt of the government of Canada was $59.4 billion. Five years later it had doubled to $120.3 billion. At the end of 1985-86, estimates place it around $265 billion, representing a net increase of over $200 billion in ten years.

The deficit of each year must be met with borrowed money which adds to the national debt. Interest must be paid on that debt, and as these numbers suggest, that interest cost has been increasing at an incredible rate. In the year 1984-85, the interest paid on the national debt reached $22.3 billion. In 1985-86 it will rise to $26 billion. If the trend continues, simple arithmetic demonstrates that within another ten years the government could owe more interest on its debt than it receives as tax revenues.[1] "Borrowing from Peter to pay Paul" would become the basis of public finance.

It doesn't work for individuals and it doesn't work for governments.

One of the most serious outcomes of carrying a large national debt is that it makes a nation highly vulnerable to sudden interest rate increases. Dramatic increases in interest payments tie up financial resources which could otherwise be used for programs to soften the impact of recessions and stimulate economic recovery. Therefore, a large national debt will severely limit government flexibility at precisely the time it is most needed.

Canada had room to increase the deficit during our last recession. Jobs were created and much hardship avoided. But what room is left if we hit another economic downturn? Where could further stimulus come from?

Think of the room for deficit spending as a cache of food for emergencies. When the emergency passes, replenish the cache. If a series of emergencies were to deplete the cache, no one would survive.

I want sound fiscal management. I want a national commitment to the reduction of deficits. The mounting public debt must be brought under control as quickly as possible. It must be reduced. This is my fiscal imperative.

How did Canada get itself into this predicament, this financial straight jacket?

The Throne Speech of April 14, 1980 said: "My government will reduce the federal deficit in a planned and orderly manner, but not to the exclusion of other objectives such as reducing unemployment and promoting industrial growth."

Finance Ministers Allan MacEachen and Marc Lalonde both raised the problem of the deficit in each budget speech as the spectre of soaring deficits and a growing national debt appeared in the early 1980s. They emphasized the importance of controlling the deficit and reducing it in a measured way without disrupting the fundamental social infrastructure through knee-jerk cuts.

Despite these expressions of intention, the deficit rose from $13 billion in 1980 to over $30 billion in 1983-84. Both ministers wanted to follow through on their intentions. This was not mere political rhetoric. And that is why the deficit problem is so frightening. It was like chasing a runaway horse. Neither MacEachen nor Lalonde could get it back into the corral. The last time I looked, Michael Wilson was in hot pursuit but further from the corral than either of his predecessors.

The mounting deficits of the early 1980s are not the result of new spending initiatives nor of a deliberate program to circulate Canadian savings through public borrowings. They were the product of program structures put in place over many years in periods of strong economic performance. For example, unemployment insurance and welfare programs (sometimes referred to in economic jargon as "automatic stabilizers") were triggered by a downturn in the economy to cushion the effects of unemployment.

The early 1980s brought us the worst recession since the 1930s. With such programs in place, public expenditures quickly rose. The 1980s also brought us the new phenomenon of stagflation—record high inflation and no economic growth. That, I think, was the main problem. Government expenditures indexed to the rate of inflation while tax revenues were de-indexed (as they were in the early 1970s), forced the government to borrow more every year to close the widening gap between its revenues and its expenditures. The deficit and the national debt ballooned.

The wisdom of de-indexing tax revenues while indexing transfer programs can be questioned with the benefit of hindsight. But when these measures were introduced they were widely acclaimed by people who today wring their hands about the mounting public debt.

I fear that more and more will be said about the problem while less and less is done.

Politicians motivated by the desire to win votes at the next election will succumb to the "what have you done for me lately" syndrome. Political resistance to doing the right thing about deficits will be nourished by a handful of economists matched by polls which have consistently shown that the deficit problem registers low on the Richter scale of public opinion. For the majority of politicians, that fact alone is enough to hoist the deficit issue on to the shoulders of a future generation of politicians and taxpayers.

Even Brian Mulroney, with 211 seats in the House of Commons following the 1984 election, was too easily spooked by public opinion polls and, despite a lot of talk, did not take action on the public debt.

The deficit must not be an ideological issue. Just as in a business, there are times when it is advantageous to spend more than is taken in and other times when it is harmful. It depends upon the economic circumstances of the day. Some of the questions I ask are:

1. Is the increase in the deficit intended to create economic activity during a period of economic decline when low private sector investment is anticipated?

2. To what extent is the deficit being used to finance the economic infrastructure of the country, such as building roads, ports, schools, hospitals, educating people and doing research, all activities which ultimately will contribute to the standard of living and the quality of life of the population by increasing the efficiency and productivity of the economy?

3. Is the deficit being incurred deliberately at reasonable interest rates to absorb savings in excess of capital market requirements, thereby easing the burden of taxation?

4. Is the deficit cyclical or structural? That is, how much will it decline in a period of medium to strong economic performance?

There is an analogy to be drawn between the fiscal constraints that face a family and those of governments. Family expenditures frequently exceed revenues when a major purchase such as a house or a car is made, or when financing children's education. When funds are borrowed for such purposes, some belt tightening takes place and the loan is repaid over a period of time. If not, the family is obliged to sell assets and take other steps which would normally reduce its standard of living.

Public sector borrowing is similar, except that governments have the option of continuing to borrow, re-finance and tax to maintain and service a large public debt whether it is incurred for consumption or productive investment. Unfortunately, the part of our debt in such investments is small.

One example of the investment approach is the Special Recovery Capital Projects introduced in Lalonde's 1983 budget. This was intended to put savings of Canadians to work to produce economic infrastructure such as research institutes, roads, dams, and airports. Unlike some government job creation programs which rely on make-work jobs for their success, these projects were part of existing long-term plans to promote economic development. Nearly all the projects were already on the drawing board. The time-frame was simply moved forward to fill the vacuum created by the slump in private sector investment in capital projects during the economic downturn.

In marked contrast to this kind of productive investment, most of the current deficit converts the savings of Canadians to consumption, expenditures that create no enduring asset of value. In other words, it is non-productive spending, running the country into debt to pay current program operating expenses. It is as if instead of putting an addition on the house, you elect to have an expensive Florida vacation.

There are four strategies governments may use in a variety of combinations to tackle a serious debt problem:

1. increase taxes;
2. cut expenditures;
3. increase economic growth;
4. monetize the debt, that is, print more money without any increase in economic activity.

The way out of our dilemma is to find the right combination of the first three options so as to minimize expenditures and increase revenues, not through thoughtless cuts or onerous taxes, but through growth. Major tax increases are counterproductive. They are likely to decrease demand, decrease production, decrease jobs and decrease government revenues.

The fourth approach has found favour with governments throughout history although it is not the one I would choose for Canada. The government simply prints money. This causes immediate devaluation of the domestic currency with a corresponding increase in the rate of inflation and a fall in the standard of living. The very existence of this option is of great concern to money lenders. As a result, in times of high deficits, lenders insist on interest rates far above the rate of inflation (high real interest rates) to protect themselves against the inflation that would ensue if the government resorted to printing money. The high interest rates in turn exert a dampening effect on economic growth, consumer spending and entrepreneurial activity.

Not everyone agrees that the deficit must be reduced, however. There are competing views that have political appeal but are economically unsound; rationalizations which defer tough decision-making. For example, the NDP appears to argue that government should increase the deficit to create short-term jobs. Short-term jobs simply to provide a form of unemployment insurance is not what Canada needs. There is a better use for tax dollars, especially now that the recession has passed.

Others argue that the structural element of the deficit is quite modest and that economic growth will by itself reduce the deficit. That opinion has been undermined by recent economic performance. In 1984 we experienced 4.8 per cent real growth, strong by any standards, and yet Finance Minister Wilson himself was puzzled by the failure of this growth to relieve unemployment. Despite continued strong growth in 1985, high unemployment remained and the deficit persisted. I believe the reason for this anomaly is that the growth we have witnessed is not broadly based. There are major disparities among growth rates in different regions.[2] So, in the case of Canada's current economic recovery, the Kennedy view that a rising tide lifts all boats does not apply. But it will if growth is broadly distributed and is focussed on the areas where most new jobs will be created: small and medium sized businesses.

Finally, there is another dangerous myth that must be dealt with. Some people are of the opinion that the size of our national debt is not important since more than 90 per cent of it is owed to Canadians.[3] In other words, the increasing interest burden is simply money being paid to ourselves. While it is true that the debt is now largely held domestically, there has been a trend to increased holdings by foreigners. Even at current levels that would mean close to two billion dollars annually flowing out of the country in interest payments.

More significantly, the interest paid on public debt goes to Canadians who can afford to save. As a result, Canadians who receive the interest payments will be under no pressure to use this money to purchase goods and services the way low income Canadians would. Even the most ardent believers of the "trickle down" theory would have difficulty in defending the economic benefits of distributing over one-third of our federal tax revenues to people whose incomes permit them to buy government bonds.

Yet, as the national debt grows, the federal government increasingly becomes a tax collector who then redistributes the gathered wealth as interest to the few who can afford to lend money to the government. This procedure is a long way from the idea of redistributing a portion of the wealth to those who are most in need. The only way to turn it around is to reduce the amount of interest paid each year and that, among other things, means reducing the deficit.

The immediate challenge is to arrest the growth of the deficit; the next, to reverse the trend. The government should present a realistic deficit reduction program with specific targets for each of the next five years. Without such detailed planning, any proposal becomes no more effective than wishful thinking.

So what do we do? What is the right combination of increased taxes and expenditure cuts that will protect the needy and not dampen economic growth? In the long run, it is only growth that can solve the problem. From my first-hand acquaintance with government programs, I know there is not room for huge expenditure cuts without a major backlash. But there can be and must be cuts. More important, there can be major reallocations of funds to priority areas that will create growth.

Here is my eight-point program to reduce the deficit:

1. The government must explain why the deficit has to be reduced. A broad consensus must be built as it was around the Trudeau government 6 & 5 program. Canadians are willing to make personal sacrifices if they understand the importance of the cause, the government's strategy and if they believe the approach is fair.

2. The government must make cuts in government programs. The Nielsen Task Force has reviewed and reported on nearly 1,000 government programs. Private sector volunteers have devoted much time and effort to the exercise. Because they have the benefit of outside analysis, those reviews should form the basis of the government's own cutting exercise. To have credibility, they should be published with all supporting documentation. Without seeing the results of the Task Force's work, it is impossible to estimate the size of the recommended savings but I would anticipate annual savings of several billion dollars.

3. The government must be rigorous in keeping inflation under control *because* the interest on the public debt is the fastest growing component of public expenditure. The lower the inflation rate, the lower the interest rate. We are already benefiting from low inflation but it can be improved. More important, it must be held in check.

4. The government must abandon industrial support programs not already committed and resist corporate bailouts unless there is a clear cost/benefit to public finance.

5. Tax revenues must be temporarily increased in a manner that is fair and understandable. (Tax reform is discussed in Chapter XIII.) It may be that a value added tax with credits for those at the low end of the income scale is the best approach, focussed as it would be on consumption rather than investment.

6. There should be no *new* government programs except those suggested in the following chapters.

7. The government must also be perceived as exercising restraint. If Canadians are to tighten belts in a war against deficits, they must have leadership from the Prime Minister and his Cabinet. They must behave as responsible statesmen placing all public spending under tight control, not as opportunists taking advantage of high living at taxpayers' expense.

8. And what of targets? Do we need them? I value targets because people rally to them. The 6 & 5 program is a good example. It is hard to know if a war is being won when victory is not defined. The target I suggest is a deficit reduction through cuts of 10 per cent per year with up to one billion dollars directed to New Productive Investment (NPI) as certified by the Auditor General. NPI would be a defined category restricted to education, training and research and development. It would extend to supporting infrastructure such as a national communications network. Having defined the categories, the Auditor General would monitor the expenditures, classify them and report his findings to Parliament through the Public Accounts Committee. The committee would be expected to provide direction for meeting any shortfall in deficit reduction targets the next year.

   Even without increased taxes and more revenues the 10 per cent annual cut would reduce our deficit to $19 billion by 1991-1992. With maximum NPI allowance it would be reduced to only $24 billion. However, the $5 billion difference would have been invested in laying the groundwork for future productivity. The incentive to reallocate monies to NPI is important. If the approach works, it should be extended beyond 1992 until the wild horse is securely back in the corral.

A final word of caution for those fiscal conservatives who see deficit reduction as an end in itself. Deficits are a symptom, not a cause of economic malaise.[4] We must get at the disease itself. Otherwise it will remain after the deficit is gone. Deficits are much like a fever. While symptomatic of an underlying disease, the fever itself can be fatal when it rises uncontrollably. We are near that point.

XII

An End to Welfare

"We must stop thinking of social programs as welfare or government handouts and recognize them as fundamental to the prosperity of society as a whole."

In the blinding snow, Kate almost missed the dark green garbage bag leaning against the lamp post. Her fingers, numbed by the subzero temperature, fumbled with its wire collar. It finally gave way and spilled its contents onto the frozen sidewalk. Clutching a few gnawed chicken bones and a stale bun, she moved on. Only three blocks to go.

There would be no welfare cheque for several days, her only income since her unemployment insurance ran out over a year ago. Kate had been displaced by a word processor. Too old for retraining her boss said, too young for Old Age Security, Kate had joined the jobless. She was fighting for survival in Canada, one of the wealthiest countries in the history of mankind.

Over 250,000 Montrealers are believed to live on incomes that are less than 60 per cent of the poverty line. It is also estimated that 3,000 to 4,000 homeless women like Kate live on the streets of Montreal.[1]

Does everyone need a job? For most Canadians that would be a rhetorical question. To earn a livelihood through employment has been our guiding ethic for generations. Besides, how else could income be distributed short of creating more and more welfare recipients like Kate?

It is that work ethic that has permitted successive genera-

173

tions of Canadians to produce and accumulate wealth far beyond the dreams of our ancestors. Most of them toiled in the fields and forests from dawn to dusk just to eke out a living. Mere subsistence was their concern.

Today jobs remain the single most important vehicle for distributing our national income. So important are they that, incredibly, some even resist automation simply to preserve tedious, mindless factory jobs better accomplished by a robot. The threatened worker sees no other source of adequate income.

We also pump scarce tax dollars into obsolete industries like Sydney Steel in Cape Breton so that employment levels are maintained. This is disguised welfare of a costly kind.

Nonetheless, in time, irresistible economic forces will prevail; obsolete plants will either modernize or close. The miracles of technology will one day eliminate millions of jobs now filled by Canadians. What will happen to them? Will there always be alternative employment? Will jobs continue to be the basis of income distribution? Or will there be more and more Kates?

The issues engender conflicts. Some authoritative voices say there will be less jobs and the challenge will be finding new techniques to distribute wealth. Others disagree saying that jobs will be there.[2]

Are publicly-financed income support programs simply welfare handouts to the indolent or do they serve a much greater need in our society?

Sadly, too many Canadians see all payments of public funds to individuals as welfare or as rip-offs. Celebrated abuses, especially of unemployment insurance, have reinforced those perceptions. Yet, ensuring the income security, pride and self-esteem of our most important asset, people, is much more important to our economy today than fire insurance on plants and equipment. Physical capital and financial capital are easier to find and easier to replace than human capital.

Just as a healthy environment is not in conflict with economic development and job creation, a revitalized social security program should be part and parcel of our economic development. We must stop thinking of social programs as welfare or government handouts and recognize them as fundamental to the prosperity of society as a whole.

How? I would like to change perceptions of our income support systems; I want them recognized as a critical ingredient of economic growth. Many think they are too generous already. By international standards, we expend less in this area than the average for OECD (Organization for Economic Cooperation and Development) countries. Does that simply mean we need to spend more money?

The answer is a resounding no.

There are too many holes appearing in our patchwork quilt of income support programs to be satisfied with their present design. Some of these became painfully obvious during the recession of the early 1980s. How many of us knew unemployed Canadians who had exhausted their unemployment insurance entitlements and experienced the humiliation of accepting public welfare?

Remember the rule: once a program is created the government becomes a political hostage to it. Our current income support systems prove the rule. Instead of scrapping and rebuilding the whole system in a coherent fashion, we have propped up, patched and bandaged. As a result, at the federal level alone, we have not less than 15 support programs. Each carries its own bureaucratic burden and a degree of complexity and regulation which is bewildering. Layered upon these are the equally disjointed, duplicative and bureaucratically costly income assistance programs of the provinces and municipalities.

Could any reasonable person conclude that this menu of support measures would not be improved through rationalization and simplification?

And this is not all. We must also add to the list the provisions of the Income Tax Act designed to accomplish similar objectives (for example, family support through dependent deductions and the child tax credits). This morass leads to an inescapable conclusion: there must be a better way; a way that is simpler, cheaper, more equitable, and more effective.

We need a rationalization of the plethora of complex income support programs that litter the federal, provincial and municipal sectors. We know they are inadequate in design and funding; we know that resources available are not being used to maximum advantage in helping Canadians in need; we know they can be better structured to help people improve their skills and re-integrate into the work force, to serve more as trampolines than as safety nets. We also know that while they have served the country well, they are no longer in tune with Canadian needs.

The deficiencies in our system were identified many years ago. In April of 1973 when Marc Lalonde was the Minister of National Health and Welfare, he published a working paper on social security in Canada, popularly known as the Orange Paper.[3] The circumstances of the Canadian social security system described in that document are as valid today as they were then. If anything, events not even contemplated at that time have reinforced them. Technological unemployment and stagflation, are but two. Furthermore, at the time the Orange Paper was drafted, the Leontief thesis of high productivity with fewer jobs would have been perceived by most as sheer fantasy. Now many serious observers regard this scenario as an imminent reality.

Without expanding on each of the deficiencies in our support programs noted by the Orange Paper in 1973, consider the following:

1. Full employment is a simplistic and erroneous notion and program designs cannot be based on it.

2. Employment does not always yield adequate income. In some families, particularly those with single working mothers, overall earned incomes are sometimes totally inadequate.

3. In many cases there is no incentive to get off social assistance and return to the workforce.

4. Because of the confusion of various programs there are differing levels of assistance for families with the same needs.

5. There is a lack of co-ordination of the elements in Canada's income security system. We are faced with a "patchwork quilt" of programs.

At piano in Keltic Lodge, Ingonish, Nova Scotia, 1981 with Allan MacEachen and Jim Fleming.

*In 1983, we signed the first economic
development agreements (ERDA) with
the premiers of seven provinces.
P.E.I. signing not illustrated*

top: *Premier Hatfield, New Brunswick.
Romeo Leblanc is with me. Fredericton,
1983.*

left: *Premier Buchanan, Nova Scotia,
Halifax, 1983.*

right: *Frank Miller, Ontario, Queen's Park,
1983.*

left: *Grant Devine, Saskatchewan. The Hon. Eric Berntson is in the background.*

middle: *Manitoba. From left to right are: Samuel Uskiw, Howard Pawley, Wilson Parasiuk, author, Eugene Kostyra, Lloyd Axworthy, David Smith, Michael Decter and Mrs. Jean Edmonds.*

bottom: *Premier Peckford, St. John's, Newfoundland, 1983.*

left: *Conservatives Flora Macdonald and Joe Clark with Auditor General Jim Macdonell at party we organized upon Jim's retirement.*

middle: *Author, Chairman of the MUC Pierre Desmarais, Mayor Jean Drapeau, Chairman of the City's Executive Committee Yvon Lamarre and Vice-President of the National Research Council Maurice Brossard at sod-turning ceremony for the Biotechnology Institute, Montreal 1983.*

top left: *With Secretary of Commerce Malcolm Baldrige in Washington, D.C. discussing economic prospects for Canada and the U.S.*

right: *Ambassador Joseph Stanford and author at wreath-laying at the Yad Vashem Memorial for Holocaust Victims, Israel 1981.*

180

Author showing great form, Curling Bonspiel, Renfrew, Ontario 1981.

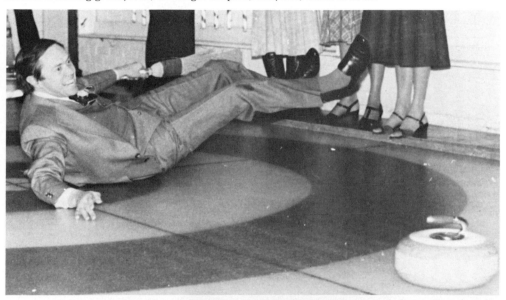

right: *Debating a point
with William Buckley, Jr.
Montreal 1983.*

left: *With Governor General, former speaker Jeanne Sauvé at Auditor General Jim Macdonell's farewell party.*

below: *Monique Bégin at meeting in St. Henri.*

Author with Producer Harold Greenberg and Senator Leo Kolber at the Senator's Montreal home, 1985.

Announcing Canada's first astronaut, Marc Garneau. March 1984.

We reach agreement with Public Service Alliance. From left to right are: *Jack Manion of the Treasury Board, author, president of the PSA Andy Stewart and president of the CLC Denis McDermott. Ottawa, 1980 (Canapress Photo)*

top: *Chance meeting with Brian Mulroney at Halifax Airport — he is there to campaign in Central Nova, I on my way to Murder Point, 1983 (Canapress Photo)*

left: *Author "puttering around in the country" spring, 1983, Sutton, Quebec.*

The Orange paper argued that it was particularly difficult for people in need to deal with the maze of authorities they must face:

"At the federal level there is the Department of National Health and Welfare, the Manpower and Immigration Department and the Unemployment Insurance Commission—and rarely are these agencies located in the same buildings. At the Provincial level there is the Provincial Department of Welfare, the Workmen's Compensation Board and, sometimes, Manpower or Training departments. And at the municipal level there are the municipal welfare offices and many voluntary agencies. Somehow the poor citizen is expected to co-ordinate all of these bureaucracies if he is to resolve the problems with which he is confronted—a degree of co-ordination which even the governments themselves have been unable to achieve."

Familiar? In the intervening years since 1973 what have we done to reform this outrageous situation? It would appear to me that the Orange Paper was well ahead of its time. While 1973 is recent history, the economic and social changes which have reshaped Western industrial society in the intervening years push it into the distant past.

If a massive reform of our income support programs was important in 1973, it is critical today.

We have seen the incredible array of disruptive forces that have invaded our lives since the early 1970s. Escalating energy costs, galloping inflation, low and even negative economic growth, skyrocketing interest rates, the technological revolution, huge unemployment, all combine to leave helpless victims bobbing up and down in their wake. Who are the victims?

We see throngs of unemployed youth despairing of finding a decent job with the skills they possess. They need income support and training.

We see more and more single, divorced and widowed women unemployed prior to pension entitlement. They need income support and, in some cases, training.

We see laid-off older workers, often heads of households, rendered superfluous by technological innovation; sometimes replaced by a steel collared worker, a robot; sometimes the victim of industrial "downsizing." They need income support and sometimes retraining, especially if an early retirement program is not available.

185

We see the working poor, usually single parent families headed by women, struggling in low paying jobs to support a young family.

We see farmers faced with crop failures, drought and falling prices, their meagre incomes sapped by mortgage interest payments. We see fishermen in the same predicament.

We see the small business proprietor, his company bankrupt along with thousands like it in a nation-wide recession, forced to go on welfare to feed his family because, despite years of hard work, the system says he is not eligible for unemployment insurance.

We see the middle-aged executive, with children still in high school or college, his job made redundant through corporate merger; life savings gone in a flash in an effort to maintain the family while searching in vain for re-employment in a world of recently qualified MBAs.

We also see working Canadians living under a cloud of anxiety, expecting each day to receive a pink slip telling them that they too are joining the ranks of the unemployed. Against this background, is it surprising that many are suspicious of technological innovation, robots and automation? They see jobs as the only way to participate in the fruits of a productive economy. Therefore, there are strong pressures to resist the introduction of new technologies. Arguments about the benefits Canada will receive from new technologies do not impress people whose jobs are to be taken by robots. Canadians must be assured of personal income security before they can be expected to accept change. The complex array of federal, provincial and municipal programs that now exist are incoherent, inequitable and do not meet the needs of those victims I have just described.

The time has come in this country for a comprehensive income support system (CISS, pronounced "kiss").[4] The overall purpose of the CISS would be to replace the confusion of tax deductions, allowances, Canada Assistance Plan Payments and Unemployment Insurance benefits which currently characterize our system. The plan would ensure efficiency and provide assurance that all those in need are cared for.

CISS would require federal-provincial co-operation. Once in place, it could provide Canadians with a "leading edge" income support system which would self-improve as the economy develops and expands. This would be accomplished by indexing it to economic growth instead of to the cost of living. It would address all the needs referred to above while providing a means of participating in the growth of the economy without holding a paying job in the conventional sense. CISS would carry the additional benefit of reducing bureaucratic overload. I believe better benefits could be delivered to Canadians at less cost.

I expect criticism. Lalonde's Orange Paper and the Macdonald Commission got it. But provoking the debate is important. I want to arouse Canadians to action. We must not embrace the *status quo*, defending programs which have long outlived their design. We have to take care of Kate and many thousands of Canadians who are being left behind. The inadequacies of the current system force us to evaluate new approaches.

Critics usually hang their hats on one or more of the following arguments:

- First, we cannot afford it;

- Second, income assistance has an associated social stigma unless the program is made universal;

- Third, it will create an even greater class of welfare bums and be subject to massive abuse.

On the issue of money, the program initially would be managed within existing levels, currently in excess of $60 billion per year.[5] Not only can we afford it, it is an investment in our people that we must make if we are to stimulate a strong growing economy.

With regard to stigma, there would be none. The days of justifying need before a welfare officer would be gone forever. The system would operate universally through the tax system, cutting in to provide support the moment income falls below a prescribed level.

Finally, there should be no disincentive to seek a job. That must be part of the program design. At lower income levels a substantial part of CISS should be retained even when other income from employment is received.

The issue of abuses was raised in the Orange Paper and, though they existed, they were considered minor. With our complicated and inequitable tax system nurturing the growth of a cash underground economy, they are probably increasing.

The overall design of a new model which meets the criteria set forth above will be much debated. The CISS I am advancing would be delivered through the mechanism of the income tax system. The approach would be similar to the existing refundable child tax credit. In broad terms, the plan would draw upon the combined resources of existing federal and provincial support programs. Changes in the income tax system could parallel the introduction of such a program, changes that would simplify the tax system while providing a simple efficient mechanism for the delivery of CISS benefits.

Many models can be designed. My preference would be one that combines all support programs and makes maximum benefits available to low income groups—those below a credible poverty line. Entitlement would fade out quickly as income increases. How quickly depends upon the amount of CISS that can be retained compatible with an incentive to find work.

In summary, the new comprehensive income support system would:

1. provide a sense of security for those removed from the workforce through age or infirmity;

2. protect those who fear unemployment, whether through technological change or otherwise, while providing an incentive to re-enter the workforce because it would not all be taxed back;

3. supplement the income of those in the workforce whose incomes are inadequate to meet their family circumstances;

4. provide an incentive and a mechanism for those who wish to upgrade their skills;

5. consolidate all income support programs, federal and provincial, including those for the elderly and retired.

6. be simple in design and administration to eliminate the staggering bureaucratic costs of the programs which now exist; and

7. not be means tested.

A central recommendation of the Macdonald Commissioners is the creation of a universal income support program (UISP).[6] Their goals, which correspond closely to those of the Orange Paper and my own thinking, may be summarized as follows: better matching of benefits to needs; more appropriate incentives for Canadians to participate in work, training or education; simplification of the system so that it becomes easier for Canadians to comprehend; appropriate integration of tax, income transfer and social systems; ease of administration; provision for the personal dignity of the individual; and rapid responsiveness to changes in situations.

The Commissioners illustrate their criticism of the existing complex web of social program delivery systems by an assessment of fiscal provisions for dependent children. The combination of child tax exemptions, refundable child tax credits and the universal family allowances is so complex that families have difficulty understanding their overall impact. A major component, the tax exemption, is strongly regressive in effect. The area is a model of incoherence and confusion.

In an overall assessment, the Commissioners point out that the income security system in Canada is ineffective, too complex, creates work disincentives, is inequitable and must be changed: "The issue is not whether reform is necessary, but rather how deep and rapid that reform must be."

Many "deficit cutting" Canadians will be disappointed that the Commissioners concluded, as I have, that the restructuring of the system should not have as its principle objective a reduction in cost. It should be a reallocation of existing resources.

The Report offers two options for their UISP. In the first, the personal income tax exemption would be eliminated, adding money to the program. In the second, the personal exemption would remain, reducing the benefit package.

Under these proposals a family of four with no other income would receive $9,180 or $7,000 from federal sources alone. If the provinces participate, the amounts could increase to $13,000 and $11,500 depending upon the option selected. These options were designed to be illustrative.

It is important to open the debate immediately and establish a national consensus in favour of radical reform with a CISS scheme being the ultimate objective. I believe it should be integrated with a complete overhaul of the personal income tax system, leading to the simplified tax option discussed in Chapter XIII.

While our work in this area is only beginning, the Macdonald Commission has given important impetus to us. The efficiencies, coherence, equity and contribution to human resource development that CISS would provide are incalculable. The most significant benefit of all would be economic freedom: the freedom to make career choices, the freedom to live in economic security. The unhappy plight of Kate and the many thousands like her would be gone forever.

XIII

Who Pays the Piper?

"We have created a tax jungle where very little light penetrates. Successive governments have made it worse..."

Do you know how much tax you really pay? We are all familiar with public clamouring to get corporations to pay higher taxes. The New Democratic Party (NDP) feeds itself on that perception. Would you be surprised to discover that you and your neighbours are the ones who pay that tax?

What most people feel sure of is that the tax system is unfair. They also know it is hopelessly complex and that it takes them many hours and often paid consultants to figure it out.

We tried tax reform in 1971. It was a disaster. The system is more inequitable, complex and incoherent than ever. The need for a fair and sensible tax system is so desperate that it makes me angry when I think about it. Canadians from coast to coast feel the same. They know how unfair it is. Some are seen as getting a free ride or ripping off others who are hard working. There are too many people who cycle in and out of jobs just long enough to become eligible for another holiday on Unemployment Insurance benefits (UI); too many participate in the underground economy, dealing in cash, reporting only small parts of their incomes and paying little or no tax; some upper income people arrange their financial affairs, with the help of expensive accountants and tax lawyers, so that they pay little or no tax. Even where these moves are legally justi-

191

fied, often encouraged by government, they undermine the integrity of the system. Remember, not only must justice be done, it must be seen to be done. Finding ways to save money through tax avoidance schemes is now as important as making money through productive economic activity. It is ridiculous.

In order for Canadians to judge a tax system as fair, they must first be able to understand it. This is now an impossibility. We must overhaul our tax system to make it fair, equitable, simple and compatible with our economic needs. In considering how this should be done, let us examine the goals of a well-designed tax system and how corporate taxes and other charges are really hidden ways of taxing all consumers. Then I will describe the current sources of government revenue and propose immediate and practical means for improving our tax system.

In 1967 the Carter Commissioners described the kind of tax system they perceived Canadians as wanting in the following terms:

> "A tax system can be judged from different points of view. Is the system fair? Does it contribute as much as possible to the growth and stability of the economy? Are the rights and liberty of the individual protected? Does it help strengthen the federation?

> "These questions reflect, not only the many facets of taxation, but also what we believe to be the principal objective that Canadians wish to realize through their tax system. They want equity, more goods and services, full employment without inflation, a free society and a strong, independent federation."[1]

Unfortunately, the 1971 reform of our tax system in response to the Carter Commission was a horrendous failure because it rejected the basic recommendations for reform and introduced specific measures in a complex and incoherent manner. After the tax bill was adopted, federal Ministers of Finance tried to make adjustments to bring it up to scratch. By the end of 1976 when I completed the last revisions to the third edition of my book on tax reform, approximately 800 amendments had been introduced to overcome the complex, illogical and inequitable tax law that had been enacted in the guise of reform.

Recent proposals in the United States are designed to shift the tax burden to the corporate sector and away from individuals.[2] (While that might be a politically popular move, it is in fact regressive.) Should the U.S. proposals be adopted, New York residents earning $35,000 could pay $3,000 less tax than Ontario taxpayers. Such a difference would exert a strong pressure on Canadians to move south.

But comparisons of the tax burden between the United States and Canada ignore the benefits of public services such as education and health. Anyone who has compared the costs of university education on both sides of the border knows that. And heaven forbid that you take sick and need hospital care in the United States without special insurance coverage! Nevertheless, only if our total package of tax and services is roughly competitive with that of the United States will we avoid a drain of human capital. U.S. corporations and universities will buy as much of our talent as possible, especially in the emerging new scientific disciplines. From professional athletes to nuclear physicists, talent is cheaper to buy than to create. The threat to Canada could become very serious.

On the subject of corporate taxes, there is a widely held misconception that our troubles would be over if government would just tax profitable companies more heavily. I strongly disagree.

First of all, companies are free to move. As soon as the tax burden becomes too great when compared with other places, they will. Second and more important is the fact that corporate taxes are simply a cost of doing business which is passed on to those who buy the products or services of the corporation. Higher corporate taxes may also be paid by limiting wage increases of employees or by reducing returns to shareholders. In other words, the corporation does not pay the tax. It just passes it on to consumers, employees and investors. As such, it can be as regressive as sales taxes, putting the same burden on low and high income earners.

Expense accounts are another example of not knowing who is really picking up the tab. Businessmen and women lunch at elegant restaurants and pass on the bill as deductible business expenses. About 50 per cent comes out of the pocket of the grateful taxpayer; the balance is absorbed by clients, customers, shareholders, partners or employees. Again, we do not know who. Is it equitable that only those who can "pass the buck" can afford to dine in these restaurants whose prices are inflated by the very existence of expense accounts? Expense accounts have become such a major element of our business culture that the system is hard to unwind. These examples illustrate that *the buck always stops with the individual who cannot pass it on.*

In an ideal world, hidden taxes passed on through corporations or the "sharing" of expense accounts would not exist. On the other hand, to suggest something as radical as eliminating corporate taxes and expense accounts tomorrow would be foolish. Only comprehensive tax reform dealing with all aspects at once can avoid throwing the system off balance. I admit that a painful and complex transition period would be required.

The first step in determining what should be done about our tax system is to understand government sources of revenues under the current system.[3] Total government revenue is made up of taxes on income, on consumption, and on capital, as well as certain non-tax revenue.

Income taxes from individuals account for 28 per cent of tax revenues. While progressive in theory, they do not tax wealth and hence tend to perpetuate and even widen the gap between those with assets and others. The system is rife with anomalies and inequities. Corporate income taxes are not progressive but they only account for 8 per cent of revenues.

Let me cite one example of how our personal income tax system favours those with assets. Let us suppose we have two individuals with $50,000 income and $25,000 in the bank. One has no other assets; the other has a $100,000 stock portfolio. Each decides to buy a $100,000 home and prepares to arrange a $75,000 mortgage at 10 per cent interest. Now interest on money borrowed to buy a home is not deductible for tax purposes. Interest on money to buy stocks, on the other hand, is fully deductible. So, our fortunate owner of a stock portfolio sells $75,000 of securities, combines this with his $25,000 savings and purchases the home with cash. Then a mortgage on the house is used as security to borrow $75,000 to repurchase the very securities just sold. The annual $7,500 interest on this loan becomes fully deductible against the $50,000 income, a major tax saving because he now pays tax on $42,500.

The other individual does not have that option. The mortgage was taken out to acquire a home, not securities. Hence, not one cent of the interest is deductible. Other things being equal, this person will pay tax on $7,500 more income than the one with the $100,000 stock portfolio. Does this not widen the gap between those with wealth and those without?

Second to income taxes as a source of revenue are sales taxes and other consumption taxes amounting to 15.5 per cent of revenues. One could include user fees on services such as bridges and airports. Such taxes and user fees are regressive, that is, they absorb a larger proportion of the income of low income consumers. This would also be true of a value added tax, an initiative the current government is considering, unless compensated by credits for low income Canadians. User fees are likely to increase. They tax the person who directly receives the benefit.

Taxes on capital are levied mainly at the provincial and local level but these include federal taxes at death on unrealized capital gains. Municipal property taxes are applied irrespective of ability to pay and, except for private residences, they are passed on to tenants. By far the largest source of municipal revenues, they account for nearly 8 per cent of total government revenues. They are also regressive. Commercial tenants pass them on to customers, shareholders and so on.

"Non-tax" revenue accounts for about 23 per cent of government revenue. Three-quarters of this is collected at the provincial level, largely because of oil and gas provincial royalty revenues in western Canada.

Another component is revenue from lotteries, an issue my conscience does not permit me to ignore. Lotteries came into being because governments found them an attractive way to help fill the shortfall between revenues and expenditures. In Canada, they were initially wrapped in the flag, being in support of such supposed worthwhile endeavours as the Montreal 1976 Olympics.

Resorting to lotteries as a source of public financing suggests we have lost control over our fiscal integrity. The spectre of Canadians who are barely able to afford essentials going out and squandering welfare payments in the vain hope of becoming instant millionaires, is a blight on our society. Public lotteries should be done away with.

Having looked at the current sources of government revenues and keeping in mind our goals for a tax system which is simple, efficient and fair, what can be done?

First, the number of tax brackets in the personal income tax system could be reduced. In fact, if we were to introduce a comprehensive income support system at the same time, a single tax rate could be applied to all incomes ("flat" tax)[4] with the CISS payment in the form of a negative tax at the low income end and a surtax on income above a certain level (for example, $35,000). This combination could maintain the progressive element of income tax.

Second, CISS would replace a whole series of programs and tax adjustments. We could dispense with personal exemptions and a host of other deductions including unemployment insurance, child care expenses and so on.

Third, full integration of corporate tax between companies and shareholders would make the tax system correspond to economic reality. It would also eliminate the need for partial dividend tax credits and simplify calculations.

We have created a tax jungle in which it is easy to get lost and where very little light penetrates. Successive governments have made it worse. Now the government proposes an Alternative Minimum Tax. Complex and counterproductive it will spawn a whole new generation of tax avoidance techniques. If the basic system were working, everyone would be paying his or her fair share. There would be no need for a minimum tax proposal. For heaven's sake, why not do the obvious and sensible thing for a change?

With the right changes, there is no reason why most people could not fill out their own tax returns in several hours; no need for fiscal experts.

In the long term, the simplest and fairest tax system for Canada may be one based on taxing consumption instead of income. I know it doesn't sound progressive, but it could be. Tax would be applied on the amount remaining after gross income is reduced by a large basic exemption (the progressive element) and savings and investment. Any savings withdrawn for consumption during the year would also be taxed.[5]

Certainly the transition from a tax system based mostly on income to one on consumption would be disruptive. After all, personal and business financial planning is designed with our existing income tax system in mind. It would require careful preparation to avoid major shocks. When I look at it, it reminds me of what happens to your family when you change all the wiring and plumbing in your house at the same time. You would like to move out and come back when the work is finished, the debris removed and the furniture replaced. It is great when life returns to normal and everything is working. That is why the improvements of a tax system based on consumption should be evaluated. But for the time being, we have to get along with our old wiring and plumbing upgraded as much as possible.

My proposal for simplification of taxation on the business and corporate side is guided by the idea that the extent of government subsidy, through tax expenditures or direct grants, should be minimized so as not to distort the market place nor create unnecessary dependence on public money. This would also lead to greater neutrality in the corporate tax system, meaning corporations in the same economic circumstances should pay the same tax.

This proposal will stimulate further debate between the capital-intensive manufacturing sectors (for whom accelerated depreciation and other tax expenditures have enhanced competitiveness) and the new wave of less capital-intensive manufacturing and service industries. The conflicts can be resolved while still introducing neutrality.

On that score, I believe our grant programs, notably the Industrial Regional Development Program (IRDP), the biggest industrial subsidy program, destroyed neutrality. Bigger grants go to companies in weaker economic regions. Communities next door to each other can get different amounts based *only* on geographic location. Such programs cater to economic weaknesses rather than economic strengths, often placing regions and communities in competition and conflict. The IRDP was a substantial step toward simplicity because it consolidated many grant programs. It was also a step in the wrong direction. In the domestic market sector those grant programs should be scrapped. Why should taxpayers' dollars be used to give one Canadian business a competitive edge over another?

I have two proposals in the area of increasing the supply

of capital to the business world, particularly attractive to the small business sector. First, we need incentives to encourage pension funds and Registered Retirement Savings Plans to invest in small and medium sized Canadian businesses.

To their credit, the Conservative government produced mechanisms for that purpose in the 1985 budget. Unfortunately, the proposals were insufficient, having as a centrepiece an increase in the 10 per cent foreign property allowance for pension funds of $3 for every $1 invested in Canadian business. While superficially attractive, the proposal has many pitfalls, a major one being suddenly too much money for too few opportunities. Many undeserving projects may get funding simply to release funds for foreign investment. Besides, the proposals are unduly complex. I do not have all the answers. I wish I did. Much more work is necessary. But a preliminary move should be to open up Canadian limited partnerships to pension funds. At the moment they are considered foreign property. The proposals for Registered Retirement Savings Plans are more practical because the plans are smaller.

Second, we need to modify our capital gains tax. The $500,000 lifetime exemption introduced in 1985 is complex, unfair and counter-productive. Instead, I suggest Canadians be entitled to sell Canadian capital assets without paying tax on the gain, provided the proceeds are reinvested in an active Canadian business within a defined period, say six months. In this way, capital would roll from one productive investment to another with tax becoming due either upon death or when amounts are withdrawn for personal consumption or to make ineligible investments such as real estate or foreign properties.

This approach could apply to foreign holdings as well if they are sold within a prescribed period of time, provided the proceeds of disposition are reinvested in active Canadian businesses. Would it not be good for our economy and our dollar if Canadians were to bring home their capital from off-shore trusts and other foreign investments and put it to work here?

Entrepreneurs like this idea. It would incite them to move capital from opportunity to opportunity and it would discourage investment in raw land, paintings, jewellery and other hedges against inflation. It should encourage business investment. It could not be decried as unfair because, ultimately, taxes would be paid on the gain. In the interim, the capital

198

would be working to create economic growth for Canada and jobs for Canadians.

Unfortunately, our determination to achieve a neutral fiscal system is eroded when dealing with some capital-intensive industries oriented primarily to international markets. It is here that support for adjustment purposes may indeed have a role to play in the manner of the Canadian Industrial Renewal Board approach. Other countries may bid for the establishment of new major manufacturing concerns and, once again, (where there can be substantial spinoff benefits for our small and medium-sized business sector and a likely increase in Canadian exports) there is a role for well focussed government intervention. The competitive international environment is such that some measure of public support is necessary to offset the subsidies offered elsewhere. However, I would much prefer support through incentives such as tax holidays than through grants. Place the onus for success and profits on management. Those who see such tax holidays and grants as the same are mistaken. The grant comes out of the taxpayer's pocket regardless of the success or failure of the project. Taxes are foregone only if the project *is* successful and more taxes will be collected in future.

The combination of a fair and neutral fiscal system, improved access to pension fund capital and roll-over provisions for capital gains would provide a strongly market-oriented industrial strategy for Canada.

Tax reform on its own is not enough. The regulatory framework must also be brought up to date. For example, some municipalities still have by-laws governing the watering of horses at public troughs. Our regulations, federal, provincial and municipal, have evolved chronologically in an uncoordinated way. Thus many have survived far beyond their useful lives. If the watering trough example is a ridiculous exaggeration at least it is harmless, but consider if you will the Crow rates for grain transportation established by law in 1897:

In 1983, because this law had never been amended in almost a century, grain from the Prairie Provinces was still carried by the railways for half a cent per ton per mile. Coal, on the other hand, cost five times as much to ship (2.52 cents), fresh fruit was eleven times more expensive (5.42 cents), automobile freight rates (8.07 cents) were sixteen times that of grain. Perhaps this will explain why the Crow had to go.

Apart from red tape, cost and inefficiencies, some programs create enormous distortions in the operation of markets. For example, taxi medallions in some cities cost tens of thousands of dollars. That investment by the taxi owner has to be recovered from the paying public. It increases taxi fares and is inflationary. That is true of all public licences that have a market value. Our Economic Council has reached alarming conclusions in that regard estimating that supply marketing boards of agricultural products cost Canadian consumers hundreds of millions of dollars per year.[6]

As President of the Treasury Board, I was asked by the Prime Minister to look into regulatory reform. For me that did not mean knee-jerk deregulation. We need better regulation. Sometimes we need more, not less. At that time and to this day, I believe there are two basic guidelines that lead in the right direction:

1. Before regulatory programs are introduced they should be subjected to a cost-benefit analysis so that legislators and the general public know who is bearing the cost, what the cost is, who derives the benefit and what the benefit is; and

2. All regulatory programs should be subject to periodic review and evaluation so that they can be terminated, modified or continued. Many are long overdue for such a process.

In other words, regulations are essential in many areas, especially to protect the environment. But they often live on long past the time when they have served their purpose. The kind of monitoring I propose would ensure that they die a timely death.

The Conservative government was elected in 1984 with a massive mandate for change and reform. Taxation should be a first priority. So far the signs are discouraging, especially the budget of May 1985 and the proposed minimum tax.

Prime Minister Mulroney has spoken many times of creating an environment of confidence and certainty. He is right. Long-term business planning, explosive entrepreneurial activity and the jobs these activities create, depend upon it. And the most crucial component for building this confidence is a stable tax and regulatory environment.

Just as we want clean air, pure water, and an end to acid rain, we also want a clean tax and regulatory environment. But right now it is as polluted as our natural environment. Its pollutants are complexity, inequity, incoherence and even stupidities. Even worse, it is unstable. Taxpayers never know when or how the rules are going to change. Long-term planning becomes more and more difficult.

The clean-up of both environments must be top priorities.

XIV

Why Replace Robots?

"Today we need all the brainpower we can get. We cannot afford to squander it by using people for mindless jobs better left to sophisticated machines."

Give a man a fish and he'll feed himself for a day. Teach him how to fish and he'll feed himself for a lifetime.

This well-worn adage is supposed to be the guiding principle of foreign aid. If we have not been successful in teaching others how to fish, at least we should teach ourselves. Without well-educated peoples we have nowhere to go but down. Parents know that the most important investment they can make is in the education of their children. If we know that as parents, why on earth don't we insist that our governments respond?

Let us suppose that we have introduced a comprehensive income support system (CISS) and that our tax and regulatory system is equitable and efficient. Low income people would no longer be economically trapped or robbed of their dignity by the welfare system; they would be supported by CISS.

Unfortunately, Canada has its share of prisoners of earlier prejudice who view income support as a sort of suspended animation state for those who either do not have a job or are unable to work—a way to sustain them, keep them treading water, so to speak—perhaps even akin to the U.S. system of paying farmers not to grow crops, paying people to do nothing. So our first challenge is to change that thinking. With over twenty-five million people in Canada and know-how playing the most important role in economic development, the "people investment" has to be our first priority.

Years ago basic education consisted of reading, writing and arithmetic with a few added frills from history, literature and classical science. These were viewed as adequate preparation for a successful career and, by and large, they were. We believed so firmly that education was valuable to society as a whole that we made it universal, free and compulsory up to the age of sixteen.

Today, the three Rs approach falls far short of preparing a person to compete in and contribute to the world. For example, rapid access to vast quantities of information stored in computers has become a critical tool in many fields from agriculture to medicine and retail business and has the potential of improving the quality of our lives immensely in years to come. Our students must be able to use these computers and the information they contain. They also need to learn *how to learn* so they will be up to the task of adapting to new technologies throughout their lives.

Another change we need to make has to do with our preconceptions about brainpower. The stereotype of manual labourers using their hands while their bosses use their brains has been firmly cemented into our culture. Even today in many obsolete manufacturing facilities, a handful of managers and designers do all the thinking for a manufacturing plant employing hundreds. Each step is designed to be "fool-proof." Innovation is seldom expected from the mere workers. They are the robots of the smoke-stack economy. But today we need all the brainpower we can get. We cannot afford to squander it by using people for mindless jobs better left to sophisticated machines.

We will also squander that resource if we do not extend the employee's interest beyond the weekly paycheck. Modern day studies show us that we need workers at all levels who take a proprietary interest in the job they are doing. Shared management and employee participation in brainstorming sessions to improve products or develop markets are experiments which have been highly successful. A well trained, motivated, workforce is unbeatable where quality of product is concerned. More and more it is quality that wins markets.

Thinking as a pursuit, the idea of refining our ability to think throughout our years, both within the educational system and without, needs to gain credibility in our culture.

Reliable statistics tell us that unemployment rates go down as the level of education goes up. In 1981, for example, Canadians with high school diplomas or the equivalent had unemployment rates 72 per cent higher than those with more education.[1] At the same time, despite the presence of 1.25 million unemployed people in this country, two different kinds of jobs go unfilled: some requiring special skills such as tool making, engineering or computer know-how and others which offer minimum wage for work requiring few skills. Training could produce the people to fill the former; only changes in motivation could affect the latter. The notion of starting at the lowest rung of the ladder and working your way up seems to have been lost.

When I reflect on the problems of our society—poverty, attitudes of discrimination, racial intolerance, inequality, poor productivity, crime, broken families, weak industrial sectors— and when I reflect further on the opportunities we have missed and others we are likely to squander, and when I look at the great things we have achieved, I find one common denominator: good education. We suffer in its absence; we prosper in its presence.

That is why society's most important investment is in the education of its people. It has been true of all great civilizations. The most successful peoples have always been the best educated. Look at the Japanese. They have heeded that lesson of history. Others are quickly waking up to it, spurred into action by the Japanese success. Alas, Canada is slow to react.

As usual, the Canadian people are ahead of our governments. When I travelled the country during the 1984 leadership campaign, education issues were raised at every stop. Parents know that the world is changing and only good education and training can provide adaptability. They are right.

Their concerns are rooted in a growing awareness that many of today's jobs require new skills (such as mathematics and computer science) and that the educational system is not preparing students for those jobs. Are those concerns justified? Indeed, we may have an educational crisis on our hands of which most Canadians are not aware.

It would be reasonable to assume that nearly everyone in the country would stay in school long enough to graduate from high school. What is disturbing is that little progress is being made in increasing the number of high school graduates. Why do so many of our young people not see a basic education as a good investment in their own futures? Has our education system moved with the times? Does it equip our students to deal with the world of the 1980s and beyond?

More and more educators at the post-secondary level are emphasizing the need for better education in primary and secondary schools as a prerequisite for substantial upgrading at the post-secondary level. They receive a semi-finished product from the secondary school system and can only work with that material. It is trite to say that one cannot make a silk purse from a sow's ear. Yet that may become the impossible challenge of our universities.

A few years ago a report prepared in the United States by the National Commission on Excellence and Education entitled "A Nation at Risk"[2] rocked the country by illustrating how inadequate U.S. educational systems were when compared with those of other nations, especially Japan.

In Britain, there is growing concern that the curriculum content is not equipping children with skills and attitudes to science that are relevant in today's world. "A chasm has opened up over the past century between the world of education and the world of work."[3]

But in Canada, we do not even have a means of determining what the quality of our educational system is.[4] In a recent report, Claude Forget recommends the creation of a national institute to tell us what is happening in our education system. Is it up to scratch? Until information of this kind becomes available, we can only speculate on the state of our primary and secondary schools. The following are a number of my own concerns:

Is education at the primary and secondary school level as relevant as it should be? Do our educators themselves understand today's needs and opportunities? Do school teachers have the skills to teach the new disciplines? In my day, our physics teachers had not come to grips with Einstein's theory of relativity, some 45 years after it had been postulated. Are our teachers up to date?

What of our physical plant and equipment in the school systems? We know it has become obsolete at the university level. I suspect it is worse in our schools.

Do children have the opportunity to exploit their potential? The average Canadian student spends 180 days in school per year, whereas the average Japanese student spends 240. In Elizabethan England, school children attended classes from early morning until late at night.[5]

Do comparable educational standards exist across Canada or are some regions and communities falling far behind?

Has the unionization of teachers had a deleterious effect on the education system by creating rigidities, making it difficult to remove incompetent personnel while reducing working hours, homework and extra curricular activities?

Why is the private school option becoming more attractive to affluent parents? Will we see a society with two educational streams, one from a well-financed, up-to-date private school system, and another from an under-financed, inadequate public school system? Would that not perpetuate economic disparity and unequal opportunity?

As a parent, I want to know the answers to these questions, fast. I also want to know them as a Canadian worried about this country's future.

No one seems able to supply these answers. The data base available at the national level is totally inadequate to permit evaluation of primary and secondary school education in Canada.[6]

How could anything be more important? The primary and secondary schools are the very foundation of our entire educational pyramid upon which all else depends. Finding out how strong that foundation is and strengthening it where required is clearly an urgent national priority.

With our educational foundation solid and secure, the future of our universities will also be assured—provided we maintain their excellence and relevance. Most of the debate about Canadian education has focussed on the financing of university education. That is an important but narrow issue.

For example, the Bovey Commission[7] recently reported that modernizing and increasing the accessibility of Ontario's universities would require an additional $91 million per year. According to the Commissioners, a high quality, broadly accessible system is "a critical element in restoring growth and competitive vigour to the economy and society" because we live in "an increasingly knowledge-based society and international economy."

They recommend that student fees gradually increase until they reach 25 per cent of basic operating income. At the same time, to ensure access by all, they want to gear loan plans to income.

The current federal funding mechanism through block transfers to provinces is seriously flawed.[8] Almost all provinces spend less per student now than in 1977.

The Macdonald Commission recommends terminating the block transfers of funds for education to the provinces and substituting a voucher system whereby the students would receive the funding directly. This would put pressure on the universities to respond to the needs of students and would ensure that federal dollars earmarked for education would reach their target. Working within existing funding limits, there is the possibility of providing different levels of funding through vouchers for under-graduate and post-graduate students in amounts of approximately $1,500 and $7,000 respectively. If no distinction were to be made between under-graduates and graduates, the average payment would be $1,850.

The challenge for educators goes far beyond our primary and secondary schools, our universities and colleges. Canada has vast reservoirs of untapped talent—people who for one reason or another, sociological, cultural, financial—have not had access to adequate training. Many of the 1.25 million unemployed are in this category. Add to this homemakers who have dedicated themselves to raising a family, older people whose family responsibilities took them away from school early, people in the workforce who need retraining, and people who have had limited access to training because of geographical or cultural isolation or physical or mental abnormalities.

Canada needs a far-reaching flexible network of educational facilities to encourage the continued pursuit of knowledge by all Canadians. This education network could include community based volunteer organizations, educational institutions, the media, libraries and the work place. Programs on a wide range of subjects including new technologies and their application in contemporary society could be delivered in communities of all sizes across the country. New technology itself, such as cable television, is an excellent educational vehicle.

Flexibility will be the key to success. Programs and associated services such as child care facilities, transportation and income support should be tailored to specific needs to assure truly universal access.

Removal of the road blocks to training and education will release many from the ghettos of dead-end careers. For example, the 51.2 per cent of working women employed in the clerical and service sectors[9] could up-grade their skills to accommodate innovations made possible by computer and telecommunications applications. This training, in turn, would open doors to new careers.

Access to education has another more subtle side. Cultural biases about "men's" work and "women's" work, or what is appropriate behaviour for an elderly person or a person with a handicap, all play a role in the choices we make. Educational institutions are in a unique position to help eradicate these traditional stereotypes and create a culture in which people at any age or stage would feel free to choose careers and educational directions on the basis of their own abilities and interests with no regard for some perceived society norms.

We must create awareness among educators at all levels of the importance of this challenge. The current trends in the case of women are positive. More women than ever before have entered careers previously reserved for men.[10] These trends need to be reinforced.

Half of all Canadian brains belong to women. It is hard to believe that women have had to fight to achieve equal rights. It is incredible that Canadian women have only been permitted to vote in federal elections since 1921. Now that women's rights are entrenched in our Constitution, the difficulty comes in moving from the acceptance of equal rights to the reality of equal opportunity. I want the key to that to be education, not just of women, but of society as a whole. Affirmative action and equal opportunity programs have an important role to play during this period of transition, but they must not become permanent fixtures.

How will we know when the transition is complete? For me the answer is simple: when Canadian women and men have equal opportunities of occupying positions in the power structure of Canada, we will have reached our goal. Then women will be properly represented in all law-making and policy-formulating bodies. Questions of wage gaps and struggles for equal pay will disappear because women will share in decisions that determine wages.

Over the years my wife and I have agonized over decisions about our own children's education. As a product of the public school system I held a bias against private schools. We tried public schools, but a combination of teacher strikes and lack of homework soon made us change our minds. All four of our girls ended up in private schools. My conversations with parents, educators, students and employers across Canada bring home the urgency of improving our public educational system.

The time to take action is now. Educators and government officials at both provincial and federal levels must not guard their jurisdictions so jealously. Let the common good prevail.

I propose we establish a National Task Force on education made up of educators and representatives of provincial and federal governments, industry and labour. Let it address these propositions:

1. A national institute should be established to gather data and evaluate the primary and secondary schools, public and private across Canada. It should offer comparisons with the circumstances in other countries.[11]

2. Minimum national standards should be created to help families transfer from one region to another and to remove regional disadvantages arising from pockets of lower quality education.

3. The role of the federal government in financing post-secondary education and post-graduate research should be examined. The innovative ideas of the Bovey, Johnson and Macdonald Commissions would make a good starting point for these studies.

210

4. Public financing of student costs should be evaluated. What level of funding should be provided? Should support be through grants, loans or a combination of both? How could such support be integrated with CISS?[12]

5. The number of foreign students in Canadian universities should be increased.

We must speed the process of reaching a national consensus on the importance of upgrading education. The Task Force results would help. But the sooner we establish a national institute to gather information on all aspects of education, the sooner we will be able to correct defects and measure the effectiveness of new approaches to education.

By now, I hope you agree with me that the most important intervention and the most productive investment our government can make is to provide Canadians with the best education.

A citizenry with an appetite for education is the very cornerstone of a liberal society in which the good and bad lessons of history are known, tolerance and understanding are practiced, and respect for the dignity and freedom of the individual are cherished and protected.

We must match our unquestioned capacity to produce gadgets ranging from digital wrist watches to space vehicles with the production of brains that use this proven mechanical genius to serve people.

To find the best way of doing this, we need to apply the talents of a coach trying to perfect a student's tennis stroke. A coach can begin almost anywhere: foot position, weight transfer, grip, rotation of the body, eye contact, ball contact, or any number of other details. The mediocre coach will do just that. A good coach will narrow the focus somewhat, ignoring inadequacies that arise purely as a result of other problems. The mark of a great coach, however, is the ability to identify correctly the root cause of the weak stroke, knowing that one key adjustment will carry with it a multitude of others. That single adjustment is self-correcting for the whole stroke. I see one self-correcting concept which should provide assurance that our descendants will enjoy a quality of life not yet dreamed of: good education.

I am normally suspicious of politicians who profess to have "dreams" for their countries. But I do harbour one ambition: to help set this country on the road to having the best educated people in history; to make Canada the intellectual capital of the world. Everything else that is good for Canadians and for humanity, material and spiritual, will follow.

XV

Teaspoons or Steamshovels?

"If we continue to dissipate our limited financial resources as we have been doing, we will soon be like the forlorn motorist on an isolated road in winter with a dead battery."

In London during the great depression, two unemployed workers watched a steamshovel excavating for a large construction project. The steamshovel was a major technological breakthrough. One worker turned to the other and said bitterly: "There's enough work there for a thousand men with shovels."

A third chap, a few feet away, piped up: "Yes, or perhaps ten thousand with teaspoons!"

Let us suppose that before the arrival of this technological wonder, our men with shovels were receiving $5 per hour. The steamshovel and operator cost $250 per hour. Technology will save $4,750 per hour! To match the steamshovel, our workers would have to reduce their wages to 25 cents per hour, not an acceptable option.

Obviously, if the Japanese and the Americans are using steamshovels, we must too. However, what will happen to our 1,000 men with shovels? Where will they find work? They do not know how to operate the steamshovel. Nor have they been trained to manufacture, maintain or repair the steamshovel. They do not have the skills. They have become victims of technology. The fact that the steamshovel is able to generate the same output for $4,750 per hour less does not impress them. That benefit is going into someone else's pocket. They are frightened, jobless and resentful. Workers on other sites are fearful that they too will soon be replaced by steamshovels. For these workers, the very word "productivity" carries notions of unemployment and hardship.

Their fears are heightened by union leaders who know their membership will fall if the steamshovel arrives. Even the owner of the construction company would be pleased not to invest his capital in a steamshovel provided his competition does not get one. They may all join forces to erect trade barriers and keep all steamshovels out of the country. Familiar?

Our job is to remove the anxiety of those workers and enable them to participate in the new wealth generated by the steamshovel and face the future with security and confidence.

The radical reforms recommended in the previous chapters—a comprehensive income support system (CISS), simple and fair taxation, and higher quality education—together will help create that security and confidence. But more is required. Let us return for a moment to our symbolic steamshovel.

First, since the steamshovel will eliminate some jobs, do we need it at all? Second, will the steamshovel create more wealth? Third, will the steamshovel ultimately create more jobs or less jobs? Fourth, will the steamshovel provide opportunities for job creation in other areas unrelated to the construction site? And fifth, could the steamshovel contribute to the quality of life of all Canadians?

Let us take a brief look at each of these questions.

First, we need the steamshovel. Those who argue that we must keep those men at work with shovels should extend their thinking to the teaspoon scenario. Full employment at any cost?

The only way to maintain and increase the standard of living of Canadians is through a high wage, high productivity scenario. The alternative is the teaspoon approach: full employment using teaspoons. That approach is familiar to those who have visited the Soviet Union. The Soviets boast of full employment. When soldiers lug cement on mortar stretchers and sweep the streets with twig brooms as I saw in Moscow, full employment is easily attained. That is the teaspoon approach. For us, such an approach would mean an utter collapse in our standard of living. We would become the proverbial hewers of wood and drawers of water. That is simply not an acceptable alternative for Canadians.

Thus, a full employment strategy in *traditional* jobs with high wages is a recipe for disaster. Other countries with low standards of living can keep the shovels or teaspoons and pay workers 25 cents an hour. We must pay $5 an hour. In a labour intensive industry, how could we ever make our product competitive? Either we invest in the steamshovel and help our workers adjust or we accept the advice of those who want full employment at any cost. Indeed, it could be accomplished through artificial job creation either directly by governments or indirectly through subsidies to inefficient industries; it could also be brought about by high tariffs or other forms of protectionism. In both cases, jobs will be saved for a few at the expense of society as a whole. Instead of some workers suffering a lot, we spread the pain. Neither result is acceptable. The challenge is to see that no one suffers.

Second, the steamshovel will create more wealth because it increases our productivity and our capacity to compete here and abroad.

The word productivity enjoys wide currency in western industrialized nations. Canada is no exception. Here it is paraded about by economists and others as the answer to most of the problems that beset us. Better productivity is often touted as a passport to lower inflation, an expanding economy and a higher standard of living for all Canadians. There is truth in this but the subject is more complex than many realize.

Many things contribute to productivity besides labour. Capital, materials and energy are examples. Recently some experts have begun to call the whole package Total Factor Productivity (TFP).[1] TFP is an important concept. It does not provide easy answers to sources of productivity because it still leaves analysts with the task of determining what weight various factors should be given with respect to each industry. But it destroys the popular myth that workers are to blame for poor productivity. This myth exists only because statistics we see relate to output per worker employed. While the workforce is extraordinarily important as an element of TFP, it is becoming less so. It is easy to see that in an agricultural economy

215

human hands tilled the land, sowed and harvested the crops and marketed the produce. The role of labour was paramount. As capital and technology became significant in the industrial economy, workers' inputs diminished. This trend has accelerated in our post industrial knowledge based economy. So, the issue of worker output is less significant today than it has ever been. Workers are sensitive to the fact that, in the public's mind, they are considered to be one of the productivity problems. With few exceptions, they are not.

There is also confusion about the rate of productivity improvement on the one hand, and absolute productivity on the other. If productivity increases by 4 per cent one year and 3 per cent the next, for example, productivity on an absolute scale would have increased by 7 per cent. The annual rate of productivity growth, on the other hand, would have decreased by 1 per cent between the first year and the second.

In the post-1973 period, Canada has not done well in improving the *rate* of productivity increase.[2] But in terms of *absolute* productivity, on a scale where the United States is number one at 100, Canada ranked fourth in 1982 at 92.3 per cent. While nearly 8 per cent behind the U.S., we were almost 20 per cent ahead of Japan. Contrary to much popular belief, we remain a highly productive country. The reason I cite these numbers is to emphasize that we are not out of this game; we have done well, and we have an opportunity to overtake countries that have outperformed us recently in productivity gains.

However, these numbers do camouflage the fact that on a sector by sector basis, especially in the manufacturing sector, we are now outperformed substantially by some other countries. Japan overtook us in the manufacturing sector in 1981. It is our high productivity in natural resource exploitation, agriculture, and other primary sectors which has enabled us to maintain a relatively high level of absolute productivity.

Finally, we must realize that the productivity slowdown from 1974 to 1981 was an international phenomenon. It was shared to varying degrees by all of the western industrialized countries. It emerged during the growth slowdown which occurred following the simultaneous expansion of industrial economies, oil price increases and the rapid acceleration of inflation in the 1970s. Attempts have been made to relate the productivity slowdown to all of these developments, as well as to a host of other phenomena.[3] But investment in technology, the steamshovel, is clearly a critical element in re-igniting productivity growth.

For productivity in 1984 and beyond, the onus will fall on capital and management. Our capital must be invested in steamshovels, not shovels nor teaspoons, and the operations of the steamshovel must be managed to minimize unnecessary excavation.

Third, does the steamshovel create more jobs or less?

Answer: more. When the owner of the construction company decides to invest his savings in that steamshovel he unleashes a chain of economic activity. He borrows money from his bankers; he obtains a variety of insurance policies; the machine is designed and manufactured in large and small plants all over the country; the components are shipped to a major assembly facility; the machine and back-up parts are shipped to the construction site; fuel, oil and maintenance must be supplied. On and on it goes with jobs created at every stage, each one requiring more skills and being better paid than the men with shovels. As technology improves, fewer and fewer people are employed in the final manufacture of the steamshovel. Any job requiring a worker to simply "pick and place" gives way to a robot, our steel collared worker. Now someone must manufacture it. Someone must design software programs for its computer brain. Someone must service and repair it and so on.

What we see with our symbolic steamshovel is happening each day. Fewer and fewer people work in the big manufacturing assembly plants while more jobs are created in small business. When capital is invested to modernize textile mills, steel mills, automobile and appliance manufacturing concerns, productivity will increase and jobs will be eliminated. That is why the 500 largest corporations in the United States have lost over three million jobs in the 1980s.[4] That trend is evident in Canada and will not abate.

Jobs will be created in manufacturing, but not on the scale that existed in the past and definitely not in the traditional "smoke-stack" sectors. In manufacturing there will be a net job loss. What transpired in agriculture will happen in manufacturing. It has started and will probably accelerate. In the aftermath of World War II, 25 per cent of Canadian workers were on farms. Today, just over 4 per cent are employed on farms yet productivity in the agricultural sector has increased every year;[5] fewer people but more productivity, just like our steamshovel.

In the transformation of the agricultural economy, workers migrated into the large smoke-stack manufacturing sector. Thousands of unskilled production line jobs soaked up the unemployed agricultural workers. The migration must now be from the large smoke-stack industries into small and medium-sized business, especially in the service sector.

Most new jobs will come from the entrepreneurial genius of small business; some will also come from the explosive growth of mid-sized business, and indeed, some from large businesses able to overcome the bureaucratic lethargy inherent in large organizations and maintain the entrepreneurial spirit in a decentralized environment.[6]

But today more jobs are being created in the service sector than in the manufacturing sector. That trend is not likely to change. Small and medium-size companies in either sector are the source of most new employment.[7] Unlike the migration of agricultural workers to unskilled jobs in manufacturing, the new job opportunities in all sectors now require more skills.[8] That is the reason for the unhappy plight of our workers displaced by the steamshovel. The transition period from the steamshovel to other better jobs will be more difficult and longer than the transition from agriculture to the smoke-stack sector. That is why the concept of CISS and retraining have become so important.

Here is another widely held misconception: that *all* small business are job creators. In reality only a fraction of businesses create all the jobs in that sector.[9] What fraction? Between 12 per cent and 15 per cent. But what an important contribution those firms make. The vast majority of today's jobs are generated by small firms that are expanding and by medium-sized firms that step across the threshold of expansion.

It is fashionable to embrace simple notions supported by slogans. In his budget of May 1985, Finance Minister Wilson spoke of the 700,000 small businesses that would be encouraged to create jobs because of his encouragement. Nonsense! Many of those companies are tax shelters. Others are family-owned corner stores, flower shops and barbershops with no reason to expand. Only a handful are headed by entrepreneurs poised for growth, expansion and job creation.

The same is true of mid-sized firms. Again, only a few are likely to take off. There are probably large companies in similar circumstances. However, most have passed out of the hands of their entrepreneurial founders and management is more concerned with preserving market shares than embarking on bold new ventures. The inertia of the corporate bureaucracy has taken over.

It is also popular to believe that small hi-tech companies will be leading the way. However, we know from a recent study that a large number of rapidly growing businesses exist in traditional sectors such as "bicycles, donuts and textiles."[10] Creative entrepreneurs will always be there to build a better mousetrap. All they need is the right environment.

The same study identifies several features which are characteristic of successful enterprises: (1) they create and develop a small market niche, not seeking to penetrate huge markets; (2) they produce high-quality products at premium prices; (3) they provide top-quality service; (4) the entrepreneurial spirit of employees is encouraged (with an average employee holding of close to 30 per cent of company stock); and (5) the leaders in these companies never cease their search for improvement, being eternally dissatisfied with the performance and products of their companies.

Our own Science Council did some useful work in this area in 1982.[11] Its study points out that Canadian policy has focussed heavily upon small and large firms while essentially ignoring the needs and potential of those mid-sized businesses which stand on the threshold of robust international expansion. The latter have reached the stage of development where management systems are solidly in place. They have progressed beyond the entrepreneurial management style. Moreover, they have found a market share, usually through innovation, carving out a small piece of a market sometimes to the point of monopoly. They are called "threshold" because they are on the doorstep of a major leap forward in terms of expansion, profitability and job creation.

So the answer to our third question is that many thousands of jobs will be created by our steamshovel and all the

economic activity it will create in finance, insurance, manufacturing, maintenance and transportation. Moreover, entrepreneurs in small firms would design new tools to provide
more efficient maintenance and service as well as new financing arrangements to reduce costs. And if aggressive salesmen
succeed in finding export markets for our machine, all these
jobs will multiply many times over.

Fourth, the steamshovel does indeed provide jobs in other
areas. Remember, the productivity of our machine is creating
more wealth at the initial rate of $4,750 per hour. Let us as-
sume that this translates into profit for the construction company, with half going to the owner as a dividend and half to
the government in tax. The same thing is happening right
down the chain of economic activity the steamshovel has
created.

Those profits must be invested. Unless the monies are put
into foreign assets, the investment in Canada will create even
more jobs having nothing to do with the steamshovel. (That is
why I want to give Canadians an incentive to invest capital
here.)

But the government is also receiving more revenues because of our productive steamshovel. This brings us to the answer to our fifth question, namely, can this remarkable
machine contribute to the quality of life of all Canadians?

The answer is a resounding yes!

More government revenues will help to pay for the comprehensive income support system (CISS) for workers who
have put down their shovels and are being retrained for better
jobs and to those who cannot be retrained or who retire.

It would also be used to support broad based productivity
not measured nor measurable by our economists. For example, we could make our education system productive; we could
produce more highly qualified people capable of spawning
new wave industries; and we could produce trained technicians and skilled craftsmen.

We could produce the best possible environment for future generations. Examples would be rich forests and fertile
agricultural land. We could produce the best possible environment for the elderly, the infirm and the handicapped.

220

I could go on. The point is simple. Our prosperity in every way depends upon productivity of one kind or another. This is no revelation nor does it pretend to be. But it tells us that public policy must encourage and support broad-based productivity and the wealth generated by the steamshovel will make that possible.

We have seen where private sector jobs are likely to be created. There is a further role for government in permanent job creation. The quality of the environment and the quality of health care are areas that come to mind. They will be publicly financed and properly so. Most employees in such areas will be on the public payroll.

Where Canada must penetrate export markets and compete with imported goods or services, high conventional productivity is essential. But the importance of being competitive through better productivity need not apply across the board. There will be new occupations in the 1990s. One of them is "Geriatric Social Workers."[12] We may see as many as 70,000 well-paying jobs in that sector alone. Robots will never replace people as the purveyors of care to fellow citizens, be they the aged or the young in a day care centre. There should be employment opportunities for people trained to render these services—services which could markedly improve the quality of life of the young and the elderly, the infirm and the handicapped. Canadians familiar with the circumstances of many of our geriatric hospitals know the severe financial constraints under which so many establishments now operate. Staff is fully occupied with the essential services that must be provided, with no time available for prolonged human contact or mental therapy. To respond adequately to these needs, thousands of trained people must be made available. This would be a creative and efficient use of public funds.

Apart from the challenge of human care, there is the issue of our physical environment itself. Jobs created in this sector will enhance the quality of life and protect our economy and our environment. But we cannot expect to measure the productivity of this work in the conventional way.

Look at our forests, our water, and our soil.[13] Forestry accounts for at least one job in ten in this country and supports more than a quarter of our single-industry communities.

Canada faces a timber supply crisis brought about by a failure to replant cut areas. Our protection against fire, insects and disease is insufficient. Together they destroy trees at a rate equal to two-thirds of our annual harvest. We have fallen far behind our Scandinavian competition in protecting and enhancing this precious resource. I recommend a major public investment in our forestry sector that will bring 75,000 to 100,000 well-paying jobs over a twenty-year period.

Good employment opportunities could also be created by the manufacture of pollution control equipment and the expansion of our energy conservation goods and services. Look at insulation, control systems, heat exchangers and heating plants. We have good technology and opportunities abound.

Sadly, the National Research Council has abandoned alternate energy research. Among the casualties which had job creation potential were the "super window" providing extraordinary insulation. Even the very advanced wind energy research for which the Council is world renowned has been terminated.

Surely the conclusion leaps out at us. We must enhance productivity in all areas where we compete head on with other countries in our own market or abroad. In so doing, we will increase our wealth. That wealth will permit us to do more for our people and our environment. Economists can gauge our progress in productivity, but we must be the ones to measure improvements in the quality of life. When the two objectives coincide, then the system is working for us the way it should.

It looks to me like the steamshovel is a great investment. It is an investment in productivity, which means wealth, which means improved quality of life, which means more productivity. The circle is complete and ever-expanding, a kind of economic machine of perpetual motion. Where do we start?

Think of our economy as a car with a weak battery. There is just enough energy to get the engine started. Once going, the battery will quickly become fully charged. But the existing energy must be carefully husbanded so that the motor turns over and catches. How many of us have sat in sub-zero temperatures listening to a car starter strain, the battery getting weaker with each attempt. To have any hope of success, everything else must be turned off: lights, radio and heater. The same is true of our economy. If we continue to dissipate our limited financial resources as we have been doing, we will soon be like the forlorn motorist on an isolated road in winter with a dead battery. Some government programs must be turned off. More public resources must be invested in our people.

That is how Canada must start the car. But to get to our destination, we also have to get in gear after the car starts. At the moment, we see bursts of economic growth. The economic engine roars from time to time, but we do not appear to be moving ahead. It is like our steamshovel. It produces wealth, but what of wealth's application? Poverty increases, regional economic disparities persist, health care deteriorates, the environment suffers and unemployment remains high. So a roaring economic engine, that is, an efficient steamshovel, is not the whole answer.

First let's all change our attitudes in all sectors. Business must look beyond this year's bottom line. Labour must participate positively, not obstruct negatively. Educators must break with traditional thinking that is making our system less relevant. Politicians must become the people's instrument of change. We must look together in the same direction with a common set of objectives. We must insist that institutional machinery work for us, not against us.

We need the steamshovel but we also need public policy that ensures the increased wealth it produces is harnessed intelligently in the interests of all Canadians.

XVI

Getting in Gear

"We cannot allow this critical issue, this national challenge, to deteriorate into a fight between gung-ho free traders on the one hand and sovereignty protectors on the other. We risk being robbed of a great opportunity . . ."

During my political career I have been dubbed a right wing liberal, indeed a "blue grit." If those labels have been assigned because I have preached less government intervention in *business* activity, then I deserve them. The truth is, I am a strong advocate of interventionist government. None of the objectives I have described in previous chapters can be attained without substantial intervention. There is a major role for government. Some examples:

First, government must move to improve its productivity. Taxpayers deserve value for money. They want to know that the famous "white elephants" with which we are all too familiar are becoming an endangered species. Taxpayers must be satisfied that their hard-earned dollars are being well spent.

The capital demands on government are staggering; the resources limited. Research facilities, roads, harbours, power projects, airports, ferries, schools, hospitals and universities all must be built and maintained—the list is endless. Instead, governments use billions of dollars of your money to buy gas stations!

The question I put to Canadians is this: Is it not better for government to sell assets not serving a public purpose to the private sector? The freed-up capital could then be used for priorities that only the public sector can finance and which are now underfunded. That is being more productive with taxpayers' capital.

I suggested the sale of Petro-Canada service stations, but it could apply to any number of other assets of the government of Canada. I believe that governments, like corporations and individuals, must manage their assets more effectively to improve the productivity of scarce capital.

Productivity in the public sector means doing more with less for the people of Canada. That is what I believe we can do and, faced with the fiscal imperative, what we must do.

Second, the government must improve the fiscal and regulatory environment. If we want Canadians to buy a steamshovel, they must know what the tax bill will be on its purchase, operation and sale. They must also know what regulations will affect its use.

There seems to be a growing recognition that an employee's stake in the performance of the business will increase productivity. Gain sharing can take many forms. Stock ownership is my preference. Many such plans have been around for years. They are not yet widespread in Canada, however. They should be. Their importance cannot be exaggerated, especially as brain power replaces unskilled muscle power in almost every sector.[1]

Employers will see that gain sharing is to their advantage. Increased profits will result. They should be encouraged to introduce it by fiscal incentives. A tax incentive mechanism for that purpose could be easily designed; the greater percentage of per capita employee ownership or profit participation, the greater the tax incentive. Where we do have gain sharing plans, they tend to be used for executive compensation. They should involve employees at every level.

The more predictable the rewards and penalties for economic decisions are, the more productively-oriented towards the long term those decisions will be. Stable and predictable taxation would make a major contribution to improving productivity in Canada. We have not enjoyed a stable tax and regulatory environment for many years.

The government should also move to stop non-productive private sector activity. For example, there has been an increase of what is called "paper entrepreneurialism." Those who have been involved in finance and tax know that there has been too much emphasis placed on financial transactions, the rearranging of assets and other manoeuvres encouraged by an unduly complex government tax and incentive system. For example, more money is made by using our steamshovel as a tax shelter, selling it to passive investors and leasing it back, trading in units of its ownership, pushing it in and out of partnerships or taking it public, than by employing it to do productive work. Scores of auditors, lawyers and brokers are engaged in these pursuits with no tangible benefits being produced. There are now many urging a return to the basic business functions of investing, producing and selling. I am one of them.

The government must simplify taxation and regulation so that the incentive for creative tax and financing arrangements is reduced. Seen in this context, the simplification of taxation and incentive programs is not only good housekeeping, although good housekeeping is important, but a step towards enhanced productivity. We can then send all those bright tax lawyers and accountants back to more productive activities. Listen to economist Robert Reich describe the United States experience:

"The United States now has the highest percentage of obsolete plants, the lowest percentage of capital investment and the lowest growth in productivity and savings of any major industrial society.

"Simply put, the structure of our economy—its underlying organization, the incentives it offers—has discouraged long-term growth in favor of short-term paper profits. An ever-larger portion of our economic activity is focused on rearranging industrial assets rather than increasing them. Instead of enlarging the economic pie, we are busy reassigning the slices.

"The rearrangers are the accountants who manipulate tax laws and depreciation rules to produce glowing—or at least presentable—annual reports; they are the financiers who think up new varieties of debentures or new mutual funds; they are the consultants who plot acquisition campaigns and the lobbyists skilled at obtaining government subsidies; they are the corporate executives, trained in law and finance, who hire all of the above,

227

and the lawyers whose briefcases bulge with the statutes, opinions, depositions, interrogatories, motions and prospecti necessary to carry out their strategies.

"You hear less and less of the pie-enlargers—the engineers and inventors who create better products at less cost, and the entrepreneurs and workers who translate those ideas into new factories, new jobs, and ultimately into goods and services that people want to buy.

"By any number of measurements, including the total amount of money, effort and media attention devoted to each, the ratio of asset-rearrangers to asset-enlargers in our economy is running about 2 to 1."[2]

From personal professional experience I can testify that we have the same problem in this country. It is appalling. It cries out for reform.

In the previous chapter, we looked at the importance of entrepreneurs in the job creation process. They are the catalysts that marry capital and technology, often with explosive growth.

Public policy must enhance such marriages by providing them with capital and technology. Growth must be encouraged, not penalized by our tax system. The motivation of true entrepreneurs is to build. That is why we need changes to our tax treatment of capital gains.

Capital is also required to expand existing businesses and to help threshold firms leap forward. For too long they have been denied access to monies locked up in pension funds and Registered Retirement Savings Plans.

Third, government must provide the incentives and the mechanisms necessary to ensure that latest technologies are brought quickly to our traditional sectors: agriculture, mining, processing of resources, and manufacturing. All of these areas can become more productive through the application of new technologies. Of course many elements contribute to productivity—technology being perhaps the most important. We must replace the shovels with steamshovels. We have been incredibly slow in doing so.[3]

This is also true for new wave industries, creatures of the technological revolution: computer sciences, biotechnology, microelectronics, fibre optics and so on. The National Research Council should ensure the rapid diffusion of technology to Canadian industry. Many Canadian industries still don't use the steamshovel as many as five or ten years after its invention. Obviously government has more tools to facilitate the diffusion of technology than industry does.[4] To improve that information network, I recommend placing more science counsellors in other countries who can quickly identify and report upon technological breakthroughs and innovation that could benefit Canadian industry. Over 95 per cent of technology used in Canada is imported. Remember, the Japanese "miracle" was built on foreign technology.

Fourth, government actions could increase Canada's share of international trade.

No issue divides the regions of Canada as much as trade. So let's improve it. Some regions fear freer trade because they see a need to protect obsolete industries. They predict unemployment in their manufacturing sectors. Others, like British Columbia and Alberta, want freer trade to exploit further market opportunities, they being more dependent on exports than the other provinces.

The great trade debate is beginning, again. The opening salvos are being fired at the political level. The Macdonald Commission's recommendation on a comprehensive free trade agreement with the United States has focussed attention on the argument. The contribution was timely and will inject some sober reality into what might otherwise degenerate into a national mudslinging contest. Before looking at the merits of a comprehensive agreement with the United States, what are Canada's options?

In 1983 when I was Minister of State for Economic and Regional Development I told the Macdonald Commission that Canada must reject protectionism,[5] be outward looking and a global trader. What I believed then I am more firmly convinced of today.

Canada's interests lie in promoting freer trade through the General Agreement on Tariffs and Trade (GATT) and bilaterally with non-GATT members.

229

This global outlook is especially important because Canada's export markets are changing. New patterns of world demand and supply are emerging. Some traditional markets for Canadian produce have been decreasing. Only in North America has our market share remained fairly constant.[6]

Canada has opportunities in exciting new markets. For example, the People's Republic of China offers a potential market of one billion consumers. Official recognition by the Trudeau government in 1970 combined with the historic exploits of one of China's national heroes, Canadian Dr. Norman Bethune, have created a considerable reservoir of good will to our benefit. As a middle power we enjoy an image unhindered by political innuendo.

To get at that vast market, we must be aggressive in our trade efforts. But we must also allow Chinese products into Canada. In a recent commentary a Chinese professor said:

> "The issue of balancing bilateral trade between China and Canada now centres on joint efforts to open the Canadian market to Chinese goods . . . On the Canadian side, trade protectionism is a major barrier . . . As the export revenues of developing countries increase, they are able to import increased quantities of Canadian goods. The result will be increased employment in Canadian industries geared toward production for export . . . The new trade protectionism safeguards employment in one sector of the economy, but sacrifices opportunities in several other import-related sectors, creating a conflict of interest between economic sectors."[7]

The professor put his finger on the key issue of our internal debate. He could have added that those conflicting sectors are often in different regions.

China is a good example of a new market opportunity but there are many others. They will increase their importance as they increase their own wealth and purchasing power.

For example, in 1982 China's per capita GNP was $310 (U.S.) while Canada's was $11,320.[8] With only 25 million people, Canada's collective output would equal that of 912,908,000 Chinese, 90 per cent of the Chinese population. With greater disposable income, Canada's domestic consumer market is probably larger than China's. That will change quickly as China's GNP rises. In the meantime, China is a good market for Canadian products in transportation, energy, communications engineering and construction.

These numbers also place the importance of the United States market in perspective. With 232 million people and a per capita GNP of $13,160, that market represents the equivalent of nearly 10 billion Chinese consumers! That may be why fervent bilateralists see a comprehensive trade agreement with the United States as an end in itself. If such an agreement is a worthy objective, it must be viewed only as one piece of a much greater trade effort.

I see the major arguments for and against such an agreement as follows:

Those in favour of a comprehensive free trade agreement with the United States argue:

- that we need an agreement to secure our access to the United States markets because, even though three-quarters of our exports now go there, mounting protectionism in the United States Congress could seriously limit this access in future;

- that a free trade agreement will force adjustment on those Canadian industries that hide their inefficiencies behind tariff barriers at substantial cost to Canadian consumers;

- that a comprehensive free trade agreement would force removal of counterproductive interprovincial trade barriers;

- that such an agreement will lead to more economic activity and more jobs than in its absence;

- that a comprehensive free trade agreement will not compromise Canadian sovereignty; and

- that such an agreement would require removal of tariffs which have been the most important single irritant within our federation.

231

Not all those seeking the agreement support all of these arguments. For example, I know many who are less convinced about the incremental benefits of an agreement. They see it more as protecting the market position we already enjoy in the United States.

Those who oppose a free trade agreement argue:

- that it will cost us thousands of jobs in sectors where we will be unable to compete;

- that even efficient Canadian industries cannot gear up quickly enough to compete effectively with major United States companies who will use Canada as a dumping ground for excess capacity;

- that interprovincial trade barriers must be eliminated before we embark upon a free trade adventure;

- that many changes would be required in our social programs to satisfy the United States that we are on a level playing field and competing fairly;

- that the same kind of changes would have to be made in Canadian tax laws;

- that our cultural industries could be destroyed through nose-to-nose competition with United States counterparts; and

- that there would be a major assault on our sovereignty, our capacity to govern our affairs as an independent nation.

Unfortunately, in the emotionalism that has surrounded the debate, a polarization of views is developing. We cannot allow this critical issue, this national challenge, to deteriorate into a fight between free trading continentalists on the one hand and sovereignty protectors on the other. We risk being robbed of a great opportunity, not necessarily to become gung-ho free traders, but to examine the situation dispassionately and arrive at the best trade option for this country.

Sir Wilfrid Laurier advised Canadians of his day not to let prejudice stand in the way of argument. We risk doing just that on this issue. Objectivity becomes impaired when the heat of passion is turned up under each side of the debate. We must insist on a non-doctrinaire approach to trade issues and an answer to the pragmatic question: What is best for Canada?

Some might hope to base our decision on a balance sheet; the dollar advantages on one side, the disadvantages on the other. But what of the intangibles? Are there not Canadian values that cannot be expressed in terms of dollars? What of our cultural heritage, our relative independence and our pride in simply being Canadian? On the other hand, most would agree that such values can only be protected through economic strength. If our living standard were to slip significantly behind that of the United States, we would lose many of our most talented people.

So as a starting point at least, we must assess the tangibles. What will be the cost of a free trade agreement with the United States? What will be the financial benefits? We should know these numbers industry by industry, sector by sector, region by region.

But even in the absence of that data, there are irrefutable facts[9] of which all Canadians should be aware:

1. Approximately 30 per cent of Canada's gross national product comes from exports.

2. Approximately 75 per cent of those exports (representing 22.5 per cent of our GNP) go to the United States.

3. It is estimated that approximately 2.5 million Canadian jobs depend on trade with the United States.

4. Canada's reliance on the United States market, or if you like, its dependence on the United States market, increased from 59.8 per cent in 1954 to 76.3 per cent of exports in 1984.

5. Canada is the largest export market for the United States, accounting for 20 per cent of United States ex-

233

ports in 1983. However, since only 10 per cent of the gross domestic product of the United States is tied to exports, trade with Canada accounts for only 2 per cent of United States' GNP. (In other words, access to the United States market is much more significant for Canada than the Canadian market is to the United States. We should also recognize, however, that the United States depends upon a continuing supply of certain Canadian exports. This adds clout to our position at the bargaining table.)

6. For several years Canada has run a favourable trade balance with the United States making a substantial contribution to the current $150 billion United States trade deficit.

7. When the Tokyo Round tariff cuts are fully implemented in 1987, it is estimated that approximately 80 per cent of Canada's exports to the United States will be duty free; a further 15 per cent will enter at duties of 5 per cent or less and only 5 per cent will carry higher rates. On the other hand, Canadian tariffs in 1987 will, in many cases, be two and even three times higher than United States tariffs on similar manufactured products.

8. There is growing protectionist pressure in the United States so that as tariffs fall, non-tariff barriers move in to take their place. (Non-tariff barriers are techniques used by countries to discourage imports.) We have seen Canada's specialty steels, copper, the fisheries and soft wood lumber all threatened by such actions in the United States. The United States also invokes government procurement practices, agricultural quotas, product quality and safety standards that deny access to our products.

9. Finally, the Canadian tariffs on imports place unequal burdens on different regions of Canada. This disparity has been a major contributing factor to western alienation. Consider, for example, the Canadian West Foundation's estimate of the cost/benefit per capita of our

tariff structure on a regional basis on manufactured products: Western Canada, minus $57.17 per capita; Ontario, plus $56.00 per capita; Quebec, plus $9.21 per capita; and Atlantic Canada, minus $60.74 per capita. The difference between the West and Ontario is a full $133.17 per person, per year! No wonder we hear more voices in the Western and Atlantic regions supporting a comprehensive free trade agreement than in Ontario.

My own view is that a comprehensive free trade agreement with the United States would be an important asset for Canada provided specific sectors are excluded and an adequate period is allowed some industries to adjust. That transition period is necessary, not so much to adjust to lower tariffs, but because we have created a horrendous number of non-tariff barriers *within* Canada which impede the free movement of goods and services. Moving to freer trade could make such sectors vulnerable unless they are exempted temporarily or even permanently. Let us look at one simple example with which all beer drinkers are familiar: our breweries.

Canada has small brewing facilities scattered across this country because of provincial legislation. Economies of scale like those in the United States are unknown because beer cannot be transported interprovincially. As a result, a small brewery like Genesee in upper New York state with a 4.5 million barrel capacity is larger than any Canadian brewery. In Canada we have facilities with as little as 250,000 barrel capacity.

If our borders were opened to United States beer, what would happen to the Canadian industry? Producers in the United States would have two advantages in addition to their efficiency of scale. First, they are now operating at less than capacity and could immediately increase production without capital investment. Second, their costs for barley are only slightly more than half that of their Canadian competition who must buy barley from the Canadian Wheat Board at fixed prices.

Could we compete? Certainly not under present structures. Small breweries would have to close, large brewing facilities would have to be expanded, the cost of barley would have to be reduced and provinces would have to change their laws and regulations.

So, I say to those who believe that those who seek protection are simply trying to camouflage their own inefficiencies, the answer is not simple: sometimes yes, but also sometimes no.

Returning to the arguments which seem to divide the debaters, it is critical to find the common ground.

With a large trade balance in our favour, a lot of Canadians might prefer the *status quo*, but I say it is not realistic. The United States Congress is moving aggressively toward a more protectionist stance. We must take action.

Everyone agrees that certain areas would have to be excluded from any trade agreement but that secure access to the United States market would be a good thing. However, agreement breaks down over the costs of adjustments, whether they are acceptable, and what government should do to make them less difficult.

If we are unsuccessful and United States protectionism grows, I believe the costs of adjustment will be much greater than would be the case if we were to negotiate a trade agreement. Job losses may not only be larger, they may indeed be more concentrated regionally leaving little scope for job creation in other sectors. Those who argue that a free trade agreement will cost jobs must also look at the other side of the coin. What will United States protectionism cost?

There remains the concern about political and economic absorption. That issue concerns all of us. I see it more in the context of foreign ownership than trade. After all, Canada participated actively in reducing tariff barriers during the Tokyo Round. Has anyone suggested that because 80 per cent of our trade with the United States will be tariff-free by 1987 that our sovereignty will then be in danger? If so, surely we should have debated the issue a decade ago.

The answer lies in controlling foreign investment and competition in the cultural area and maintaining our independence in all major social and economic policy areas.

If the opportunities for trade enhancement are well managed, the benefits for Canada could be substantial. If the opportunities are bungled, the losses could be even greater.

Fifth, government must play a central role in allaying the fears of those who see themselves threatened by new technologies, the steamshovels.

Government working with the labour movement and with industry must provide mechanisms to ensure that those people who might be hurt are protected.[10] Unless workers know that such measures are in place, they will fight the introduction of new technologies. Who could blame them for trying to protect their jobs, the only reliable source of income they know? At the same time, resistance to new technology would destroy any chance of our becoming more competitive and increasing our share of world trade.

To that end, the Trudeau government sponsored the establishment of the Canadian Labour Market and Productivity Centre. The Centre is an independent forum within which labour and management are to bring forward suggestions for resolving the problems, conflicts and challenges that will exist by virtue of these new technologies being introduced into the work place. It is too early to reach conclusions about its effectiveness but it certainly makes a lot of sense.

There is more government can do to facilitate the adjustment of workers. We know of the Japanese experience whereby textile workers became skilled in a sector foreign to them, namely cosmetics, in a matter of months. Why can't we do the same? Because our workers are less educated. How do we upgrade the skills of workers in shoe factories in Richmond, Quebec, asbestos workers in Thetford Mines or shoe factory employees in Hamilton, Ontario? They are of all ages. Some have many years of productive work ahead. Add to them our unemployed youth who have not even found a first job. The answer must be a massive investment in education akin to that provided our young veterans after World War II. Educational SWAT teams could invade communities like Richmond, Quebec. Temporary facilities, teachers, equipment would all be brought in. Relevant skills would be taught to provide a flexible workforce that might attract other industries. In any event, the individuals would be able to adapt and move to better employment opportunities, elsewhere, if necessary.

Graduates of this exercise right across Canada would emerge with pride and self-confidence. They would be able to operate the steamshovel, service it, build it and perhaps even design the machine that will soon replace it. What an exciting and creative investment of taxpayers' dollars such a program would be. Would most Canadians not prefer this use of their money to buying and operating more gas stations?

Sixth, the government should finally bring coherence and purpose to regional development. In Canada this subject has been a confusion of competing interests with political considerations usually winning the day. Hundreds of millions of dollars injected into public works, thought to pay political dividends, dot the Gaspé and the Atlantic Provinces. The economic disparity with the rest of Canada persists. In most cases it has widened.

I have heard some politicians declare that Canadians should be able to find the work of their choice in the regions where they live. That is a ridiculous notion but it spawned efforts to make it happen.

Money was thought to be able to solve the problem. Roads, wharfs, airports, parks, marinas—the list seemed endless. Many temporary jobs were created and some good infrastructure put in place. The economic disparities and unemployment remained. Many government programs neutralized economic forces but brought no long-term benefit. Adjustments were not made.

As Minister of State for Economic and Regional Development, I grew to appreciate the extraordinary strengths of our provinces. The trick is to build on those strengths and not to search vainly about to attract industries which are unable to profit from a region's comparative advantages.

Public money spent on direct job creation is usually of limited value. The time has come for a new approach, one that takes advantage of new technologies; one that recognizes that the post industrial economy with its accent on information and knowledge can at last bring an end to the heartland-hinterland psychology. Smoke-stack industries do not migrate; brains do. More important, ideas and knowledge will.

The information network of tomorrow will replace the roads and railroads of yesterday.[11] In the past, our governments connected isolated communities to each other by railways, roads, airlines, post offices, telephone and tele-

238

communication systems and a national broadcast network; all Canadians were seen as having the right to be served in these ways regardless of how remote their community. Those initiatives, combined with equalization payments, were the very cornerstone of sensible regional development. This publicly financed communications system should now be extended to information: the best available, as soon as possible after its creation, and the know-how to use the information.

An information network would make the geographically isolated fishing villages of British Columbia and Newfoundland as close to the centre of activity as Toronto and Montreal. Thousands of miles would shrink to milliseconds. Canada is a leader in communication technology including satellite communications and ground station expertise. Once established here, this technology could be exported around the world.

Whatever the subject—agriculture, fishing, forestry, business management, international market conditions, investments, health or social services—citizens could tap in to a mammoth national repository of information. It would also be a vehicle for education, including ongoing adult education.

A government procurement program could develop new technologies and refine old ones. The know-how, technology and hardware could find enormous export opportunities as we move closer and closer to McLuhan's global village.

With these information networks in place we could begin to exploit the know-how that the technological revolution has brought to us.

The key to economic growth is human capital. Given the right intellectual environment, skilled people can easily be attracted to regions where the quality of life for many holds much more promise than in Canada's industrial centre. The kind of information network I have described liberates the professional from the necessity of living in central Canada. Journalists, writers and others like Bruce Hutchison and Peter Newman in Victoria, Dalton Camp in New Brunswick, George Bain and Eric Kierans in Nova Scotia already exploit these opportunities. Each has maintained a national presence while distancing himself from the heartland.

I am also enthusiastic about the prospect of developing regionally-based centres of excellence. Each would have a university or a research centre (or both, if possible) as its nucleus and would attract industries based on advanced technology to locate nearby.

A good example in Canada of such a complex is in Halifax where universities, advanced technology companies and all necessary infrastructure are already in place including a medical centre of international standing. Another is being developed in St. John's, Newfoundland around Memorial University where a national and international centre of Cold Water Engineering has already begun to attract industry. There are similar examples in each province. One of the most striking is in Saskatoon where the University of Saskatchewan serves as the catalyst for several areas of advanced technology, notably biotechnology and high energy physics.

The critical role for government in this is to establish research centres, located all across the country. This is how I believe government should be spending our money to promote industry and commerce. Instead of giving taxpayers' money directly to corporations, it should be invested to create the kind of environment that produces innovation and encourages Canadian industries to be among the most advanced and competitive in the world.

We cannot afford to spread our resources too thinly, however. They are too scarce and too precious. With good "networking" among researchers, all Canadians will benefit from the work done in regional centres. Meanwhile, the regions themselves will be strengthened by the added research and development activity.

If there is to be a global village why should we not have the model right here in Canada?

XVII

Attacking the Mountain

*"It is tragic to see how far the authority of the
people has been eroded, how Parliament has
been emasculated and how open accountable
government in theory, has become closeted secretive government in fact."*

If you think we have caught sight of the promised land in
earlier pages, then I suspect a big question has formed in your
mind. How do we get there from here?

For example, in the aftermath of the failure of two Canadian chartered banks, I was on a hotline show in Montreal. A
seemingly intelligent and well-informed caller asked why a
committee of laymen could not be appointed to oversee government activity in order to prevent a recurrence of the kind
of bad decision-making that brought us the bank debacle. I
reminded her that such a body already exists—the voters' representatives in the House of Commons. In reflection, however, and knowing how uninformed Parliamentarians are on
such government actions, I can sympathize with that caller
who wanted to find a better way to protect her interests.

Sitting in Parliament since 1978 has made me increasingly
cynical about the capacity of our institutions to respond to
society's needs and demands. In many ways, Parliament has
become irrelevant in that process.

The electorate is disenchanted with Parliament.[1] Television exposure of the posturing of MPs during Question Period
has not helped; nor have the annual reports of the Auditor
General. Government management has improved but the media naturally highlight those juicy parts of the Auditor Gener-

241

al's report which sell newspapers and stop viewers from switching channels. It will be ever thus. Yet, in the case of the House of Commons, the public's perception is quite close to the mark: elected representatives are not playing their roles.

I know my views are not shared by all. Many seem to think the Parliamentary process is in great shape. For example, in his recent book, Jean Chrétien attributes an exalted role to the Member based on his own experience which is far different than my own.[2] During my time in Parliament I managed a stint on the government backbenches (1978-1979), a period in Opposition when I chaired the Public Accounts Committee (1979-1980), over four years in Cabinet (1980-1984) and now find myself once more on the benches of the Official Opposition. From these vantage points I have reflected upon the undeniable truth that the House of Commons has become more an object of scorn and sardonic humour than an institution respected as an instrument of public policy.

As a rookie backbencher I was deeply disturbed by what I saw. Today I am drawn to the conclusion that for our country to surge ahead with a coherent set of programs like those described in preceding chapters, major barriers at the institutional levels of government must be overcome.

The recommendations set forth in this chapter proceed on one fundamental principle we seem to have forgotten: the government belongs to the people; it is *our* instrument to serve *our* needs. Our only access to that instrument is through our elected MPs. Remember, the people do not even elect the Prime Minister in our system. It follows that our MPs must be invested with the power and authority to carry out their mandate on behalf of the people of Canada. The Cabinet must be truly responsible to the House of Commons. All other institutions should exist first and foremost to serve that body and, through it, the people.

It is tragic to see how far the authority of the people has been eroded, how Parliament has been emasculated and how open accountable government in theory, has become closeted secretive government in fact.

To make Parliament an informed body of public debate capable of bringing radical changes to public policy of the kind Canadians demand, our MPs must be given the tools to do the job. For that purpose the Auditor General and the public service are critical. In these pages I have also elected to raise issues that touch the Constitution, Cabinet and the Senate, never forgetting that the people speaking through their MPs must *always* have the last word.

The Constitution

In a confederation such as ours, federal-provincial relations can make the country work well or they can drag us all down. During the last mandate of Pierre Trudeau, relations were generally poor. There was too much baggage around the conference table; too many old scores to settle. It worked both ways. Our ministers viewed many premiers and provincial ministers with scorn and contempt. Too often they found themselves denied credit for initiatives taken to support their provincial colleagues. For many there was little goodwill left.

Some federal politicians and probably some bureaucrats were prepared to resort to competitive federalism, having concluded that co-operative federalism would not work. It must be made to work, however, because all politicians, whether federal, provincial or municipal, serve only one client, only one public interest, and we must never forget it.

But there will always be conflict of some kind and there should be. Each level of government represents different interests. As the Macdonald Commission stated, the challenge is to establish instruments for co-operative action.[4]

Quebec did not sign the agreement leading to the Constitution Act, 1982. While not signed, its provisions bind the Province. We would all like to see that signature but action on the economic and social priorities facing the country and the Province are in no way compromised by its absence. To reopen a national debate on that question at this stage seems to me to be a waste of time, more likely to reopen old wounds than to solve problems.

Robert Bourassa returned to power in Quebec on a platform of strong economic renewal. The Constitution was not an issue in his election campaign. He received a massive mandate, 99 of 122 seats, with no concern being expressed by the electorate on constitutional issues. To meander from his economic mandate into the treacherous swamp of the Constitution which will provide no more than emotional comfort for some and anguish for others would be sheer folly. He should not allow himself to be dragged into that quicksand.

Pierre Trudeau fought to bring Quebec into the main-stream of Canada's economic and social evolution. To do so he pushed his official language policy at great political cost to ensure that Quebec did not become ghettoized, a distinct fran-cophone society unto itself. He wanted the Jean Chrétiens, Marc Lalondes, Monique Bégins, their colleagues and succes-sors to apply their ideas and talents at the national level. To be rooted in a constitutionally distinct society, a province not like the others, would make that kind of participation difficult for the rest of Canada to accept. Why should Quebec politicians create policies for Ontario which could not apply to Quebec? Their roles as national policy makers would be seriously un-dermined. That is not the way to build a strong federation.

To declare in the preamble to the Constitution that Quebec is a distinct society, the centre for Canadian francophones, is a harmless statement of the obvious. To enshrine it in the Con-stitution as the Macdonald Commission recommends in order to placate Quebec nationalists, not knowing where that legal distinctiveness is likely to take us in years hence, is another matter. To accommodate Quebec's perceived interests and pre-serve equality, the Macdonald Commission proposed that each province be allowed to opt out of any constitutional amend-ments transferring legislative powers from the provinces to Ottawa, *with full compensation in all cases*. In any event, such an amendment would require the support of two-thirds of the provinces representing fifty per cent of the total population.

Since the seven provinces needed to adopt the amendment would have to include either Ontario or Quebec, one of the latter plus another province could opt out with full compensa-tion. The theoretical potential for a national checkerboard is alarming.

On the issue of veto, it *is* important to protect Quebec's interests in national institutions, such as the Supreme Court of Canada where current Quebec membership is now guaranteed because of the civil law system of that province. A veto on such issues would be appropriate.

In summary, living in the Province of Quebec and work-ing with French-speaking colleagues of all ages, I sense a yearning for economic success. The City of Montreal and the province itself seem poised for a robust economic renewal.

244

Business is the preoccupation, not the Constitution. We are told that in 1985 nearly forty per cent of students at Canadian universities seeking their Masters of Business Administration degrees were from Quebec.

Young Quebecers are joining the mainstream of the Canadian economy, the North American economy and the international economy. Their linguistic capabilities are helpful in doing so. This generation of Quebecers has accepted Trudeau's challenge. Retreating behind the constitutional "special status" of a "distinct society" seems singularly inappropriate for the exciting, dynamic, self-confident Quebec that has liberated itself from the Péquiste yoke.

The Senate

The Senate is regarded by many Canadians as an expensive joke. That view has been reinforced by some of the appointments which lend credence to the Senate's role as a pasture of political patronage more than a chamber of sober second thought. As a result, much of the good work done by the Senate passes unnoticed as does much diligent work by individual Senators.

Most Senate reformers seem to favour the process of regional elections to the Senate.[5] I believe that good regional representation can be accomplished by reforming the House of Commons. What would be the point of an *elected* Senate? An elected body must have power. Would the Commons give it up to enhance the role of a second Chamber? At the moment, with the Commons itself powerless in fact, to add one more elected body would simply compound impotence, add cost and probably reinforce negative public perceptions.

My own first-hand experience as a witness before Senate Committees leads me to believe in the value of our appointed body. Some of their work and especially some reports have been first class. The challenge is to develop a method of appointments which would furnish the experience and representation for that needed sober second thought.

Many people in our society enjoy careers that make them excellent candidates for such a body. Often they are people who shrink from the prospect of elected office, although others have held elected office within their own organizations.

A majority of members of the Senate I envisage would be the graduates of other offices. For example:

- heads of major education institutions, post secondary and secondary;
- intellectual leaders from a variety of fields;
- heads of scientific research institutes and hospitals;
- community leaders and heads of major volunteer organizations;
- leaders from industry and commerce as well as former presidents of trade or professional associations in the arts and culture, medicine, law and accountancy;
- former labour leaders; for example, the outgoing President of the Canadian Labour Congress would be expected to be named to the Senate;
- representatives of constituencies such as the fishery, agriculture and forestry sectors;
- religious leaders;
- former members of the fifth estate;
- retiring Provincial Premiers.

This list is intended to be illustrative only. Some would also be named by the government of the day. However, they should be more than grateful recipients of political patronage. The government's nominees beyond defined categories should not exceed one-third of the Senators and all nominees should be subject to approval by an all-party joint Parliamentary Committee.

Many of the current Senators would meet these criteria. Some transitional measures should be introduced to move to a body of which we could all be proud. A few "golden handshakes," while expensive, would be worth the price.

As far as powers are concerned, I would support a suspensive veto and language protection as recommended by the Macdonald Commission. But the Senate's true value would lie, not in its powers, but in the experience and wisdom its members would bring to the complex issues facing our country. Its composition would somewhat resemble the Roman Senate in the latter period of the Empire, some appointed and some the previous holders of important office.

The Cabinet

The Cabinet as a whole had lost much of its clout as a decision-making body by the time I arrived early in 1980. Full Cabinet with between twenty and forty Ministers was an impossible forum within which to have meaningful debates. Opinions were simply expressed and might or might not be commented upon by the Prime Minister in reaching a conclusion. One seldom knew. Anyone with committee experience recognizes that a decision-making body should not exceed twelve in number. When it does, absolute authority rests with the Chairman.

The executive committee of Cabinet, Priorities and Planning (P&P), was where any power rested that was not assumed by the Prime Minister himself. The decisions of that "inner Cabinet" prevailed and could circumvent the full Cabinet process. As a general rule, especially significant items came forward to Cabinet as well. That agenda was determined by the Prime Minister and his advisers. Therefore, a major question like the Petrofina acquisition might not make it to full Cabinet.

The Cabinet committee system was, in theory, designed to streamline the process with decisions of each committee subject to automatic approval at either P&P or full Cabinet unless an objection had been registered by a dissenting minister in advance.

Funding allocations were also delegated to these policy committees of Cabinet. Theoretically they were responsible for the allocation of funds to new program initiatives. Under the envelope system, Treasury Board was confined to managing the budgets of departments for ongoing programs. New initiatives had to be funded from reserves administered by the policy committees and this brought about the undignified haggling amongst ministers.

From the viewpoint of ministers, the structure was unwieldy, inefficient and time consuming. The notion of confining new policy initiatives to a common reserve within a

247

specific envelope, namely, the amount allocated to a particular committee, created serious conflicts. The committee only had power to replenish the reserve from existing resources within departments represented on the committee. Ministers were disinclined to make internal cuts simply to free up funds for other departments to spend.

In my view, the whole approach needs to be revised:

The Cabinet should be reduced to not more than twelve ministers, some presiding over a number of Ministries of State. For example, the Minister of Transport would assume responsibility for overall transportation policy. That minister could be assisted by a Minister of State for air transport, a Minister of State for marine transport and a Minister of State for surface transport. They would all report under the umbrella of the Ministry of Transport itself.

Each Ministry at the level of Cabinet would have its own spending envelope. Priorities and funding would be established at Cabinet level and each minister would then assume responsibility for his or her department and all Ministries of State associated with it.

Any number of models might be considered. The machinery of government should never be cast in stone. Each Prime Minister will remodel the system to his or her taste. Nonetheless, most Prime Ministers are likely to tread cautiously on systems that appear to be working. The model I have suggested here, while a substantial move from the existing machinery, could be easily accommodated. It would combine more ministerial independence and authority with a lean Cabinet and a reduced number of central agencies. It would also make Cabinet itself an effective working committee. Each minister, in consultation with the Prime Minister could delegate authority to one or a number of junior ministers of state. Some important functions should be reserved for the Prime Minister, notably Science and the Environment. These need not be headed by ministers. There could and should however be professional advisers appointed to provide input directly to the Prime Minister and all other ministers.

For me, this scaled down Cabinet is the essence of what must be accomplished.

Well-wishers at the beginning of 1978 campaign. Left to right are: *Robert Cowling, Claire Dayan, Diana Weatherall, Sam Berger, author, Heather, Marcel Prud'homme and Brenda Norris.*

Author with campaign manager James Grant at the filing of nomination papers, 1978.

Kicking off 1978 by-election campaign with MPs Fernand Leblanc, Gérard Loiselle, Warren Allmand, provincial Member George Springate, Marcel Prud'homme and Jacques Guilbault.

top: *With George Springate, then provincial deputy for Westmount and Mike Duffy of CBC, 1981.*

above: *Fête au Village, St. Henri, 1981. Tony Volikakis, author, René Paris.*

251

left: *Author consoling John McEnroe at Player's Pro-Am Tournament, 1983*

below: *With Heather, June 1984, at a press reception during the Liberal leadership race. (Canapress Photo)*

left: *Playing tennis the day I received my black eye, Montreal, April, 1984. (Canapress Photo)*

right: *McPherson cartoon. Toronto Star, April 1984.*

bottom: *Three young supporters who would rather fight than switch sport the "Johnston" black eye. Vancouver, April, 1984. (Canapress Photo)*

At the leadership convention.

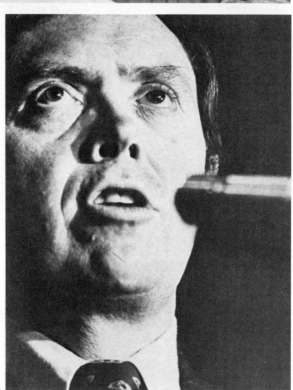

Addressing the issues.

Serving up "nerf" balls at the leadership convention, June 1984.

With party leader John Turner at the benefit held to help pay my leadership deficit. Montreal, 1984. (Canapress Photo)

The Public Service

All initiatives of the peoples' elected representatives can be thwarted without a devoted public service through which policy must be implemented.

The permament Public Service of Canada has grown dramatically in the post-war period. If we use its widest definition, that is, the public service actually controlled by the Treasury Board, plus the employees of wholly-owned Crown corporations, the non-controlled sector which is financed from the public purse, and the armed services, the number exceeds 500,000. Knowing the bureaucratic organization required in even a mid-sized commercial corporation, one can appreciate the challenge of effectively managing a bureaucratic army of this magnitude. Nonetheless the same management tasks apply—maintaining efficiency, maximizing productivity and minimizing waste. The shareholders are the taxpayers of Canada and like any corporate owners they have an absolute right to receive value for their investment. Through Parliament, they have hired The Auditor General to report waste and inefficiency to them. Here is my own report:

From the perch of a minister I found it really difficult to penetrate the inner workings of the vast public service, never mind the Crown corporations. I base my judgements on those I have known and worked with. For the most part these are deputy ministers, assistant deputy ministers, other senior managers and heads of Crown agencies and Crown corporations. The same in turn is true for deputy ministers themselves, who penetrate the bureaucratic pyramid to a greater depth than ministers but seldom to the point where they are cognizant of day-to-day happenings at the field level. That is where the bureaucracy comes in direct contact with its shareholders, the people of Canada. That is where public perceptions of the public service are found. It is the teller, not the bank president, who forms your view of the bank.

At senior levels I was impressed. Canadians should know that the senior bureaucrats are generally dedicated, reliable, able and hard working. If those people are representative of future generations of public servants rising through the system, Canada will be well served.

Yes, there is some waste; yes, there is inefficiency; yes, improvements can be made. Inevitably there will be interdepartmental conflicts and jealousies that tend to throw monkey wrenches into the machinery of government. Yet the merit system and the role of the Public Service Commission, which for generations has removed public service employment from political influence, have provided Canada with an outstanding public service. It is worthy of our pride.

There has recently been some talk of politicising the public service. In the United States a change of administration brings several new layers of senior officials. Not so in Canada, where professional bureaucrats serve the government of the day. I believe ours is a better system. Our bureacracy is perceived by many Tories as having a strong Liberal bias. I do not believe that to be the case. My colleague Jean Chrétien is of the same view. Judging by the limited number of changes made by Brian Mulroney, it appears that he is also satisfied with the political neutrality of public servants.

No government can be permitted to stack the bureaucracy with its own political bias. Governments must inevitably change and the new political regime must be provided with an even-handed and effective instrument through which its power must be exercised and its policies implemented. Public service obstructionism cannot be tolerated no matter how distasteful the new government's policies may be to particular civil servants. Their choice is to serve or to resign. While the thought of purging the public service with each change of government has appeal to many, I believe it would be a disaster.

A permanent civil service, its senior members living in the isolation of Ottawa, does tend to lose touch with the Canadian constituency. Contact with the private sector must be maintained. To do that, we should intensify exchange programs and encourage more young Canadians to devote at least a few years to public service.

A moment ago I raised the problem of managing hundreds of thousands of public servants. I was satisfied that the way to do it is through a strong management team. Such a team can impart a consistent management philosophy from the top of the bureaucratic pyramid to the bottom. Whether it be the customs officer, the tax inspector or the clerk in a manpower and immigration office, there must be some uniformity of attitude, philosophy and service. There must be a sense of service to the customer, attitudes critical to the success of all retail traders and service businesses. An expanded management group supported by a strong philosophy of "public service" is the way that can be accomplished. We created such a management group when I was at Treasury Board. A philosophy of management was issued under my successor, Herb Gray. Those initiatives should be built upon.

The introduction of collective bargaining with the concomitant right to strike dealt a serious blow to perceptions of Canada's public service. Resulting strikes all but destroyed the traditional image of the public servant in the eyes of Canadians. Had I been in government in 1967 I would have supported collective bargaining but fought the right to strike. Unfortunately, the right was given. I had to confront several serious strike situations as President of the Treasury Board.

In any circumstance a strike is a cruel weapon of last resort. It becomes more so when the principal bargaining chip is the public interest. By no means does it serve the majority of members of the public service unions well. For example, at one point I was faced with strikes by the postal workers on the one hand and the translators on the other. The contrast in how the right to strike served them is worth noting.

Whenever postal workers go on strike the public outcry is overwhelming and has often forced an unreasonable settlement at great public expense or, alternatively, the strikers are legislated back to work. The former solution is unfair to the public. The latter is a denial of the very right which has been given. Neither is reasonable.

On the other hand when the translators were out on strike the general public would have been prepared to see them strike forever. "Translators! Who cares?" some asked. That placed the translators at the mercy of government negotiators.

In either case, the right to strike is inappropriate. The market forces at play in a private sector strike where the economic interests of the employer are competing with those of the employees does not find its place in the public sector. The right to strike by public employees should be withdrawn.

We must introduce a better system to resolve disputes as quickly as possible; a system that will protect collective bargaining; that will provide for quick, fair and equitable settlements and which protects the public interest. Many formulae have been proposed. I would caution those who believe that binding arbitration in its simplest form is the only alternative. It too has serious drawbacks because a major cost of government, namely the payroll of the public service, is simply handed to third parties for decision. The taxpayers need better protection. Therefore, I suggest we consider binding arbitration with established parameters beyond those which now exist to ensure that settlements always follow and not lead the comparable areas of the private sector. In doing so, due weight should be given to the measure of job security that exists in the public sector.

Auditor General

Unlike many former Cabinet colleagues, I am strongly in favour of expanding the role of the Auditor General.

My first contact with the Auditor General came shortly after my election in 1978 when MPs Lloyd Francis and Tom Lefebvre encouraged me to join the Public Accounts Committee. It was chaired by Ron Huntingdon, the Tory MP from Capilano at that time.

The Auditor General of the day, Jim Macdonell, gave strong support to the role of the Public Accounts Committee and frequently attended its sessions. Other members of his department, in particular Michael Rayner, now the Comptroller General of Canada, and Deputy Auditors General Larry Meyers and Ray Dubois, were very helpful to members on the committee.

James J. Macdonell was an auditor by training but a management consultant by profession. It was his long association with business management that brought a fresh approach to the role of the Auditor General. Compliance and substantive auditing of the accounts of the Government of Canada, standards applicable in the commercial world, would not satisfy Jim Macdonell. He had to be satisfied that the Canadian taxpayer he represented was getting value for money.

In his 1976 report Jim Macdonell declared: "I am deeply concerned that Parliament, and indeed the government, has

lost, or is close to losing, effective control of the public purse."
Was he right? It certainly appeared that way if one were to
study the increases in spending and the growing list of white
elephants which seemed to dot the federal public sector land-
scape. Macdonell had done the job he was hired to do. He was
not much appreciated by many public servants and certainly
not by members of the government. He was flamboyant and
colourful. His language caught the media's attention. He succeeded in making a giant leap forward in providing the people
of Canada with value-for-money auditing. Unlike his predecessors, he was more interested in how well the management systems were working. While horses on the payroll might be fun
for the media, Macdonell was more interested in installing systems that would prevent them from being rehired.[6]

I developed a close working relationship with Macdonell.
When I assumed my responsibilities as President of the Trea-
sury Board our relationship was already well established.
Upon his retirement in 1980, I hosted a black tie dinner in the
Confederation Room of the West Block. Former associates and
professional colleagues came from across Canada. I am sure
that Macdonell was especially pleased to see our Speaker,
Jeanne Sauvé, former Prime Minister Joe Clark, Flora
Macdonald and former Presidents of the Treasury Board, Bob
Andras and Bud Drury, in attendance. It was a grand evening.

Canadian taxpayers lost a great friend when Jim
Macdonell passed away in 1983. Never had their interests been
in better hands.

Prime Minister Trudeau asked me to find a successor. I
put forward the name of Ken Dye[7] and Trudeau accepted my
recommendation.

Dye has moved forward with Macdonell's reforms, not
hesitating to cross swords with both the bureaucracy and the
government. I sense that his relationship with his client departments is more co-operative and perhaps even more constructive than was Macdonell's.

My view is that the Auditor General's role should be
strengthened, particularly with respect to Crown corporations.
The post-war period has witnessed the expansion of a second
public service through our Crown corporations not subject to
the stringent controls of Treasury Board nor subject to the

261

detailed reviews of the Auditor General. Extravagant abuses have gone unchecked. The shares and funds of those corporations are held in trust for the people of Canada and are as much a part of the public balance sheet as are those of the Department of National Defence.

As far as taxpayers' dollars are concerned, the political passion for secrecy has no place except where there are matters of national security at stake. The office of the Auditor General should be the ultimate, unfettered, independent watch dog of MPs on the expenditure of tax dollars. By the same token, the Auditor General must limit his public comments to a factual appraisal. He should not venture into the evaluation of political decisions. It is the role of the Opposition to do that, with the electorate acting as the ultimate judge. The Auditor General should also be the designated auditor of all Crown corporations. This would not preclude private sector auditors where the Auditor General deems it appropriate.

The House of Commons

Our first task is to ensure that Parliament does its job. It is Parliament that must express the public will and implement the legislative measures necessary to give policy the flesh of legal reality. Before it is too late we must establish it as a theatre of informed debate; an instrument for efficient and rapid policy implementation, a forum respected if not revered by all Canadians. What kind of reform is necessary?

Discussions of parliamentary reform have focussed around the rules of debate, prearranged schedules for sittings, electronic voting, expanding the role of members and of committees in the House, better research assistants and policy experts to support committees, more joint committees of the House and the Senate and so on. Independent observers have done good work in this area.[8] Most important, a Special Committee of the House itself advised:

"rigid discipline is hardly compatible with the philosophy of a democratic political party, and reasonable latitude consistent with loyalty to the party should be permitted to individual members of any party."

The thrust of the committee's recommendations is that confidence votes be limited by the government to measures central to its administration. The report supports the value of dissent and the positive effects it can have on Parliament. It makes the fundamental point that changes of attitude are necessary and concludes that:

> "if the necessary changes of attitude come about, not only would the role of the private member become more meaningful, but parliamentary government itself would become more effective".[9]

I have previously spoken about the importance of making one adjustment which will carry with it a wave of other corrections. I put it forward in the context of a tennis coach. Nowhere is it more applicable than in the House of Commons. This one recommendation is the most important of all. It is the self-correcting concept which could make the House of Commons an effective legislative instrument. It would be an understatement to say I was thrilled by the Committee's recommendation. It was in line with my own submission to the Committee where I emphasized the importance of strengthening the role of individual members.

The imposition of party discipline in the House of Commons has eroded the value of the institution. It has turned intelligent, vigorous, creative members into eunuchs. It has depreciated the value of the standing committees. It has permitted Cabinet to arrogate all meaningful policy development. Worse, it has permitted the Prime Minister's Office (PMO) to emasculate even the Cabinet. With such concentration of power in the PMO it was inevitable that the bureaucratic support system, especially the Privy Council Office (PCO) would assume responsibility and authority over the affairs of the nation far beyond anything vested in the elected representatives of the people. This evolution is unacceptable and dangerous.

The consequences of party discipline in the House of Commons reach far beyond Parliament itself. The pyramidical nature of the party apparatus breaks down as the power and influence becomes invested in a smaller and smaller coterie of politicians, bureaucrats and advisers who form the entourage of the Prime Minister. In the interests of good government, we should heed the lessons history has taught us and make a change.

The role of a Member of Parliament will never be self-fulfilling, will never properly take advantage of the potential of members, until the heavy hand of the party whip is relaxed.

Individual members of the Liberal caucus expressed their disgust to me during the final years of the Trudeau government. They felt irrelevant. They were irrelevant. They felt exploited. They were exploited. They knew that the few goodies to be dished out, such as parliamentary secretaryships or international trips, would be reserved for those who toed the line. They realized any dissenter was considered a maverick and mavericks seldom made it to the Cabinet table. Can you imagine the initiative that was destroyed when they saw that having the courage of their convictions made them superfluous to the mechanism of the very government they sought to serve?

During my political lifetime I hope to see MPs reinvested with the responsibility and the confidence that tens of thousands of Canadian electors have entrusted to each of them.

Included in the reform I recommend would be maintenance of non-confidence votes on budgetary bills, the Speech from the Throne and rare issues the government considers pivotal to its mandate; modifications of the rules of budgetary secrecy so as to permit the government of the day to strike a consensus in the government caucus; and, subject to the exceptions referred to, *freedom to vote as a member wishes.*

What would this accomplish in terms of correcting the unacceptable situation which now exists?

First, the party's consensus underlying policy directions would be genuine and not simply a product of discipline.

Second, it would greatly enhance the role and self-respect of the backbencher who would become more fully committed to discharging the responsibilities that are in theory encumbent upon him or her.

Third, it would radically reduce the power of the Prime Minister, his advisers, the PCO and the Cabinet. Policy which originates in the bureaucracy and around the Cabinet table would have to be sold, not only to caucus members on the government benches, but often to caucus members of other parties. I am convinced that, had these conditions prevailed when the National Energy Program and the Western Transportation Initiative were introduced, coalitions would have been struck. Necessary amendments to forge compromise would have greatly improved the final product. In the end, the legislation, instead of dividing the country, could have brought it together.

Making those trade-offs and compromises in order to secure the support of a cross-section of parliamentarians from all parties is what good government should be all about. Canadians are tired and resentful of government policy being railroaded through the House of Commons on the strength of a government majority and party discipline.

Fourth, the elimination of party discipline would give every region a voice in the House of Commons regardless of the election results. During the last Parliament, the Tories had been virtually wiped out in Quebec with only Roch LaSalle holding onto the riding of Joliette. In western Canada, Liberals were not represented west of St. Boniface, Manitoba. Whenever such lack of representation exists the federation seems threatened. Western Canada argued that it was not represented in the House of Commons. Of course it was, but not on government benches. Were there not party discipline, cross-party alliances could have permitted western Conservative and NDP members to influence legislation in the House and in Committee. Western Canadians would have seen their views being heard and acted upon, especially in the energy and transportation sectors. Party discipline ruled out that possibility. As a result the appeal of major changes such as proportional representation gained momentum. I reject the notion of proportional representation. I see it as the last resort of a political party which has failed to establish a national base and be representative of all regions. When that failure takes place as it did with the Liberals from 1980 to 1984, the answer is the elimination of party discipline, not proportional representation.

Fifth, I recommend a much enhanced role for committee chairmen who would be elected on a free vote by their peers. The chairmen of standing committees should enjoy the same prestige, level of remuneration and perquisites as junior ministers. Even today the responsibility of some chairmen exceeds that of several junior ministers.

On October 9, 1985 the government responded to the Special Committee's recommendation in these terms:

265

"The Government endorses the recommendations in principle. The Government will seek to have a definition of confidence written into the Standing Orders to make it clear which votes are critical tests of a Government's ability to maintain the confidence of the House (e.g. Speech from the Throne and Budget). The Government will determine what legislation it will consider a matter of confidence.

"The Government will also seek to have confirmed in the Standing Orders the practice of votes independent of party position."

Where this "endorsement in principle" will take the matter is difficult to assess. One cannot change the whole culture of the institution simply by rewriting the Standing Orders. A commitment to make free votes the rule, not the exception, is necessary. That implies a major change in attitude. For example, dissenters from party policy should not be penalized. In principle, it could mean a dilution of the power of the Cabinet and the Prime Minister. But with 211 seats there could be a lot of dissent before that would happen. Therefore, this is in many ways the ideal time to move on this vital issue.

Finally, I turn to one last controversial issue in parliamentary reform. Nobody should be an MP for more than twelve consecutive years.

In Canada we see career politicians; individual men and women who look to the political arena as others look to career opportunities in journalism, law, business, medicine and so on.

When I ran for office in 1978, I declared my intention to participate for a limited period of time as an elected representative of the people. I did so because I believed then, and believe even more firmly now, that the professional career politician is more of a liability than an asset. True, there are many exceptions, some sitting in the House at the present time. But the loss to Canada by truncating their political careers would be more than offset by the benefits derived from seeing more people participating as elected representatives. They would bring their fresh, innovative ideas not burdened with the baggage and the prejudices of years of parliamentary debate. Nor, after many years of office, would they settle into the comfortable parliamentary existence, seeking every opportunity to tour the world at public expense and not tending to the nation's business. Knowing their terms were limited they would tend to look to the long-term good of the nation rather than the short-term run to the next election. This would be particularly true during their last four-year mandate.

The concern of most career politicians is understandably to further their political careers. That means scoring political points, not good government. In opposition, the challenge is to assume or reassume power at the first opportunity. Whether there is a policy agenda to lay before the Canadian public before that takes place seems to many to be completely irrelevant.

The career politician wants to ensure that his or her livelihood is protected. That means an inordinate concentration of effort on stroking constituents. While it is important to attend to the problems of constituents and represent their interests, the large expenditure of time and money on much political activity is wasteful of taxpayers' dollars and damaging to the system. For example, the printing and mailing of four separate pamphlets to each household in the constituency each year at taxpayer expense is an extravagant luxury. Worse still, there have been MPs who have made virtually no contribution at the national level, preferring to devote their time to their number one priority, getting re-elected. Barbecues and baptisms might be well attended; the nation's business forgotten.

There is another good reason for shorter terms. Unless we create a greater flow of elected representatives into and out of Parliament, those sectors of our society which are badly underrepresented, especially women, will continue to be underrepresented. When women occupy their share of seats in the House of Commons and at the Cabinet table, the feminist movement, the women's commissions of political parties, affirmative action programs, equal pay for equal work and all the other mechanisms designed to bring about equality and employment equity will fade into history. But if access to the House of Commons is barred through the longevity of incumbent members who have become comfortable with the environment and the lifestyle of Parliament, unequal representation will be perpetuated for many years to come.

I recognize that many support the *status quo*, arguing that the people will decide whether a member has ceased to be useful at the next election. In an ideal system that might hold. Today it is seldom, if ever, a candidate's election. It is a national contest between leaders and the most unworthy candidates win on the leader's coattails.

As far as the rest of the reform recommendations are concerned, I would leave them very much to be decided by MPs using their judgement, freed from the dictatorship of the PMO and Cabinet. How they strengthen the role of committees, how they improve research, how they remunerate committee members, should be in their own hands.

There is one further issue that concerns me: the shortcomings of MPs. It is not a criticism of their abilities but rather of their lack of knowledge about Canada. I thought I knew my country reasonably well when I was first elected. How skimpy my knowledge turned out to be! Mere travel and sightseeing is not enough. It requires direct contact with people in all sectors in each region as well as much study.

The issues in agriculture, energy, mining, communications and so on differ dramatically from region to region. Even the agricultural sectors in the adjacent provinces of Saskatchewan and Alberta are substantially different, the one with a dominant role in red meat exports, the other in grains.

Add the grievances and claims of aboriginal peoples, the plight of our fisheries, the environmental challenges of northern development, trade, taxation, federal-provincial relations, labour-management issues, research and development, immigration, financial institutions, the list is endless. How many MPs are able to assess intelligently the policy options in these areas, many as foreign to them as the problems of sheep herdsmen in Outer Mongolia?

Many MPs go abroad either on Parliamentary delegations or with ministers on official business. I will wager that most of them have never visited all our provinces or Canada's north. Knowing the world is important but knowing the country in which you are an MP should come first. I recall lunching with the Unites States Ambassador Paul Robinson just after his return from an extended trip to Canada's north with other foreign diplomats. The trip is an annual event sponsored by the Canadian government, the taxpayers of Canada. Imagine how I felt admitting that I had never visited the North!

One of the best investments Canadian taxpayers could make would be in the education of our MPs. Each should, immediately following election, have the benefit of a comprehensive course such as a condensed version of the fine course offered by the National Defence College in Kingston, Ontario. They should also visit all regions, meeting with representatives of significant sectors, learning of their problems and their opportunities.

The richest legacy of all that I will carry from public life is a better knowledge and understanding of my country: its majesty, its wilderness, its oceans, mountains, rivers and plains, its institutions, its cities, towns and villages, its untapped natural riches and, above all, its people. They are our greatest resource. They give me confidence that my children and theirs could see a future of prosperity and happiness my generation only dared to dream of. We have the opportunity and the obligation to make that future a reality.

Epilogue

We have travelled a long journey together through the pages of this book. For me it has been a bit like a trip through an exciting foreign country, the dilemma always deciding what to leave off the itinerary, not what to put on. But if the scope becomes too ambitious we run the risk of missing the essential. It is the latter that I have tried to capture in the preceding pages.

Now as I sit writing these last words watching a heavy snowfall cast its mantle of silence and beauty on my city as it has each winter for hundreds of years I wonder, will it ever be different? And generations ago were there not men and women in this same place watching the snow gently fall who thought they saw a better way? Why were they unable to make it happen? With so many needed reforms, why the inertia? Did they waste their time and am I wasting mine?

Sometimes I have thought so. The way Parliament functions has not helped. But I detect encouraging signs that make me want to keep trying. This book is part of that effort. The parable of the foolish old man who removed mountains is apt. We must have patience; we must persevere.

By reading this book I hope more Canadians will be moved to active political involvement. There is one unshakable truth: every democracy gets the government it deserves.

Think about this statement as your mood darkens over the morning headlines, as you fill out your income tax return, as you fight with the bureaucracy and as you complain over the state of the nation as if the country's problems belonged to someone else. If you think enough about it, you may just drop that next bridge game, postpone watching that home video movie and instead go down to a political meeting and make your views known. If you do you may well catch the political disease. It is highly contagious—produces feverish activity, can be physically exhausting but is mentally very healthy. If you have read this far, you already have revealing symptoms.

Donald J. Johnston
Montreal, Quebec,
January, 1986

271

Notes

I. Tough Choices

1. John Maynard Keynes, *The End of Laissez-Faire* (London: Leonard and Virginia Woolf, Hogarth Press, 1926), 46-47.
2. In *Maximes politiques*, written by Duc Gaston de Lévis in the early 1800s.

II. Into the Fray

1. Donald J. Johnston, *Fiscalamity: How to Survive Canada's Tax Chaos*, (PaperJacks, a Division of General Publishing Company, Limited, 1974). A revised and updated edition was published in 1975 under the title *How to Survive Canada's Tax Chaos* and a revised third edition appeared in 1977.

IV. Countdown to Defeat

1. Jean Chrétien, *Straight from the Heart* (Key Porter Books Limited, 1985), p. 117.
2. Tom Axworthy, "After 1984: A Liberal Revival," *Canadian Forum*, (November 1984) **64**, 5-7.
3. The Constitutional Resolution was adopted by the House of Commons on December 2, 1981 and by the Senate on December 8, 1981. The Constitution Act 1982 was proclaimed on April 17, 1982.
4. Economic and Regional Development Agreements were signed with seven provinces for the first time in 1983-1984: Manitoba, Nov. 25, 1983; Saskatchewan, Jan. 30, 1984; New Brunswick, Apr. 13, 1984; Newfoundland, May 4, 1984; Alberta, June 8, 1984; Nova Scotia, June 11, 1984; and Prince Edward Island, June 13, 1984.
5. Pierre de Bané succeeded Romeo LeBlanc as Minister of Fisheries. As a result of his legendary tenacity, de Bané eventually recovered authority for the Atlantic Fishery.
6. *House of Commons Debates* (Nov. 5, 1982), 20444-20445.
7. The Royal Commission on the Economic Union and Development Prospects for Canada (more commonly called "The Macdonald Commission"), chaired by the Honourable Donald S. Macdonald, delivered its report on September 5, 1985. In its three volumes it dealt with a vast range of subjects touching the long-term economic potential, prospects and challenges facing Canada. *Macdonald Commission Report*

(Canadian Government Publishing Centre, Supply and Services, Ottawa, Canada K1A 0S9).

V. On the Record

1. At the time of the NEP, oil and gas rights had been issued for the bulk of productive areas in Canadian territory beyond provincial jurisdiction (Canada Lands). Numerous provisions had existed to provide revenues to the federal government from those areas. Most recently there was the "checkerboard" where an exploration permit was granted, then a production licence covering 50 per cent of the area in defined squares (the "checkerboard"). The balance would revert to the government. Subsequently, a royalty arrangement replaced the checkerboard. The Progressive Incremental Royalty (PIR) required the payment of a royalty to the government of 10 per cent plus 40 per cent of the net profit beyond a 25 per cent floor. The NEP preserved the PIR and added the 25 per cent back-in which was convertible to a working interest at any time prior to production.
2. Mr. Justice Allan Gold is now Chief Justice of the Quebec Superior Court.
3. The air traffic controllers were legislated back to work on August 10, 1977, after a three-day strike.
4. Jean Chrétien, *op. cit.*, 126-127.

VI. Who was Pierre Elliott Trudeau?

1. "Business leaders lean to Tories," *Financial Post* (May 5, 1979), pp. 1 and 12.
2. Marc Lalonde, "Challenges and Achievements: Canada's Economic Record Since 1968," a speech to the Outaouais Chamber of Commerce (Hull, Quebec; March 28, 1984).
3. Laurier, 1917, cited by O. D. Skelton, *Life and Letters of Sir Wilfrid Laurier* (Toronto: Gundy, Oxford University Press, 1921) **II**, 542.
4. *Ibid.*, **II**, 381.
5. *Ibid.*, **II**, 380.
6. Richard Gwyn, *The Northern Magus: Pierre Trudeau and Canadians* (Toronto: McLelland and Stewart, 1980).
7. Editor's note: In the tapes, U.S. President Richard Nixon referred to Trudeau as "that asshole".
8. *House of Commons Debates* (December 15, 1978), 2167.
9. "Pierre Elliott Trudeau, by the nobility of his thoughts, his sense of history and his understanding of today's realities, has conferred upon Canada an importance which truly matches its size." (*translation*)

VII. Lessons for Losers

1. "Paving a Long Road Back: Q & A, John Turner," an interview by Peter C. Newman, *Maclean's* (Nov. 19, 1984), 10.

VIII. Laurier's Legacy

1. Laurier, June 26, 1877, speech on political Liberalism to the Club Canadien of Quebec, *op. cit.*, **I**, 148.
2. Laurier, 1919, *Ibid.*, **II**, 554-555.
3. Throne Speech, April 14, 1980: "Therefore, in employing the limited resources available, my ministers will help first those who need help most."

IX. Rapids of Change

1. (a)   In 1980 Canada had the fifth highest standard of living among OECD nations based on GDP per capita ($10,760 US) and the second highest standard based on purchasing power ($11,430 US). Peter Hill, *Real Gross Domestic Product in OECD Countries and Associated Purchasing Power Parities*, Working Paper Number 17 (Paris: OECD, 1984), Table 1; as cited in *Macdonald Commission Report*, **II**, 560.

1. (b)   In 1981 Canada ranked third among OECD countries in life expectancy (75 years) and fourth in infant mortality (10 deaths per thousand prior to the first birthday). *World Development Report 1983* (New York: Oxford University Press for the World Bank, 1983), Table 23; as cited in *Macdonald Commission Report* **II**, 561.

1. (c)   In the period 1981-84, there was a net loss of 154,000 jobs from Canada's manufacturing sector. Net losses were also recorded in agriculture, forestry, fishing, mining, construction and transportation. Job increases occurred in non-resource sectors: community services (216,000), trade (45,000), finance (37,000) and public administration (23,000). Judith Maxwell, "The battle of the ages," *Report on Business Magazine* (June 1985), 19-20. (See also *Macdonald Commission Report*, **II**, 404 and 408.)

1. (d)   "The engine of resource development has been slowing relative to other sectors for several decades... Exports of food (mainly wheat) and crude and fabricated materials accounted for 84 per cent of Canada's exports in 1964 and only 56 per cent in 1984." Judith Maxwell, "The inevitable move away from resources," *The Report on Business* (May 1985), 11-14. See also *Macdonald Commission Report*, **II**, 407.

1. (e)   "Science is pushing toward products that are knowledge-intensive rather than raw material-intensive." Stuart Smith of the Science Council of Canada in a speech to the Canadian Association of Physicists, April 25, 1984.

1. (f)　　Between 1982 and 1984 China increased its corn production by 15 per cent, rice by 20 per cent and wheat by 40 per cent. In 1984-85 China produced 13.9 per cent of the world's wheat and coarse grains, just one per cent less than the 14.9 per cent of the total world supply consumed by China. Barbara Insel, "A World Awash in Grain," *Foreign Affairs* (Spring 1985) **63**, 892-911.

1. (g)　　Canada's population was 3.7 million in 1871 and roughly doubled during each of the three succeeding 40-year intervals. If fertility remains constant at 1.7 births per woman and net immigration stays in the vicinity of 50,000 per year, our population will peak at 30 million in 2021 and decline gradually thereafter. *Population Projections for Canada, Provinces and Territories, 1984-2006* (Statistics Canada, Catalogue 91-520).

1. (h)　　The portion of Canada's population which is 65 years old or older has grown from 4.8 per cent in 1921 to 7.8 per cent in 1951 to 9.7 per cent in 1981. By the year 2030 it will have increased to somewhere in the range 18.8 to 26.2 per cent depending on fertility and net immigration levels in Canada between now and then. *Macdonald Commission Report*, **II**, 11 and 54-58.

1. (i)　　In November of 1985 more than 430,000 young Canadians aged 15 to 24 could not find jobs. This represented 16.9 per cent of the labour force in that age group. The unemployment rate for the entire work force was 9.8 per cent. Statistics Canada, *The Labour Force* (November 1985, Catalogue 71-001).

1. (j)　　A majority of Canada's working poor are single-parent families headed by women. In 1981 there were 714,000 single-parent families (82 per cent headed by women), representing 11.3 per cent of all families. The fact that divorce rates almost doubled between 1970 and 1981 may, in part, explain the trend to greater numbers of single-parent families. It is interesting to note, however, that in 1931, 13.6 per cent of families had only one parent. In the next three decades it fell (1941, 12.2 per cent; 1951, 9.9 per cent; and 1961, 8.4 per cent) and then began to climb again (1971, 9.4 per cent; 1981 11.3 per cent). Statistics Canada, *Canada's Lone-Parent Families* (Catalogue 99-933; 1984) and *Women in Canada: A Statistical Report* (Catalogue 89-503E, March 1985), pp. 7 and 64.

1. (k)　　Progress in closing the wage gap between men and women has been slow. Women in full time jobs in 1971 earned, on average, only 59.7 per cent as much as men in full time jobs. This had only improved to 64.0 per cent by 1982. Statistics Canada, *Women in Canada: A Statistical Report* (Catalogue 89-503E; March 1985).

1. (l)　　For every one hundred 18-year-olds in Canada, there were 55 high school graduates in 1972 and 63 in 1982. Statistics Canada, *Education in Canada: A Statistical Review for 1982-83* (Catalogue 81-229; June 1984), 33.

1. (m)　　Women received 38.0 per cent of Bachelor's and first professional degrees awarded in Canada in 1971. This had risen to 50.9 per cent

by 1982. Fields of study in which women still accounted for less than one-third of the degrees in 1982 were mathematics and physical sciences (28.5), economics (28.4), computer sciences (26.4), dentistry (19.8) and engineering and applied sciences (9.3). Statistics Canada, *Women in Canada: A Statistical Report* (Catalogue 89-503E, March 1985), 31.

1. (n)   The long-term trend in Canada is toward higher levels of education. University degrees were held by only one per cent of our adult population (age 15 and over) in 1941 and by 8 per cent in 1981. The proportion with some post-secondary education rose from 17.1 per cent in 1971 to 27.6 per cent in 1981. *Macdonald Commission Report*, **II**, 562-563.

1. (o)   In the past few years, however, there has been a slight decline in the number of degrees granted per capita. The number of Bachelor's degrees earned per 100,000 Canadians fell from 380 in 1978 to 350 in 1982. Master's degree recipients decreased from 54 to 53 per 100,000 and Doctorates fell from 7.7. to 6.9 per 100,000. Statistics Canada, *Education in Canada: A Statistical Review for 1982-83* (Catalogue 81-229, June 1984), 148.

1. (p)   Union membership has decreased slightly in recent years for men and increased slightly for women. In 1982, 37.3 per cent of employed men (2,069,000) belonged to union organizations and 24.5 per cent of women (985,000). Statistics Canada, *Women in Canada: A Statistical Report* (Catalogue 89-503E, March 1985), 53.

1. (q)   Ownership of Canadian businesses is highly concentrated. A March 1985 report stated that nine families control stock worth 46 per cent of the value of the 300 "TSE 300" companies. Diane Francis, "Nine families said to control stock worth 46 per cent of value of the TSE300," *Toronto Star* (March 19, 1985), A1 and A15. The Toronto Stock Exchange estimates that 11 per cent of Canadians owned shares in publicly-traded corporations in 1983 (half the level in the U.S. according to the New York Stock Exchange). Over 40 per cent purchased their first stocks since 1976 and over 60 per cent had incomes below $35,000. Toronto Stock Exchange, *Canadian Shareholders: Their Profile and Attitudes* (1984).

1. (r)   The debt-to-equity ratio of large Canadian industrial corporations rose from 1.24 to 1.53 between 1978 and 1982, substantially increasing their vulnerability to rising interest rates. Since 1982 the ratio has begun a gradual decline. *Economic Review* (Canada: Department of Finance, 1984), 27.

1. (s)   Real interest rates in Canada since the onset of the recession in the early 1980s have been high, ranging from 4 to 7 per cent. During the previous two decades it was much lower, usually less than 4 per cent and in the 1970s even going down to minus one and two per cent (when the rate of inflation was actually higher than the interest rate charged on bank loans).

1. (t) In 1982 Canada's resource sectors contributed 14.2 per cent to the Gross Domestic Product ($46.8 billion). *Macdonald Commission Report*, **II**, 404.

2. In 1984 the Baikal-Amur Mainline (BAM) railway across Siberia began operation. This permits the Soviet Union to tap vast resources in Eastern Siberia including coal, iron ore, gas, gold, diamonds, copper, titanium, tin, zinc, lead, tungsten, molybdenum and one-fifth of Russia's timber. Fred Pearce, "A Permanent Way Across the Permafrost," *New Scientist* (November 1, 1984), 10-11.

3. Our forests are being used up much more quickly than they are being replenished; our soil on agricultural lands, especially in the west, is being depleted and blown away; and the increasing burden of pollutants in the air, particularly acids created by sulphur and nitrogen oxide emissions of industry and automobiles ("acid rain"), is damaging our lakes, forests, crops, farm land, and even our health. Ted Schrecker, *The Conserver Society Revisited* (Ottawa: Science Council of Canada, Discussion Paper D83/3, May 1983). T. G. Honer, *Assessing Change in Canada's Forest Resource 1977-1981* (a paper presented at the annual meeting, Canadian Institute of Forestry, September 23-26, Winnipeg, Manitoba). *Soil at Risk: Canada's Eroding Future*, a report on soil conservation by the Standing Committee on Agriculture, Fisheries, and Forestry, to the Senate of Canada (Hon. H. O. Sparrow, Chairman; June 1984). "Erosion causes soil's vanishing act," *New Scientist* (No. 1482, November 14, 1985), 46. *Still Waters*, a report of the House of Commons Subcommittee on Acid Rain (1983).

X. Global Imperative

1. Trudeau presented his suffocation proposal in a speech delivered May 26, 1978 to the General Assembly of the United Nations during the *Tenth Special Session* which was devoted to disarmament (May 23 to June 30, 1978).

2. A line from the song entitled "Russians" released by Sting in 1985.

3. Gerard Piel, "Re-entering Paradise: the Mechanization of Work," *Challenge* (September-October 1983), 4-11.

4. Robert B. Reich, "Toward a New Public Philosophy," *The Atlantic Monthly* (May 1985) **255**, 68-79.

5. India's GNP per capita of $260 (US) in 1982 grew at an average of 1.3 per cent per year between 1960 and 1982 while Canada's GNP per capita of $11,320 (US) in 1982, a full 44 times higher than India's, grew at 3.1 per cent per year, two-and-a-half times the rate of India's. *World Development Report 1984* (published for The World Bank by Oxford University Press), 218-219.

6. The per capita GNP (in constant US dollars) for all developing countries grew from $340 in 1955 to $730 in 1980. During this same period, that for all industrial market economies grew from $4,940 to $10,610. The gap had widened from $4,600 to $9,880. At the same time, the portion of

the world's population in developing countries grew from 68.1 to 73.6 per cent and that of the industrial market economies decreased from 19.3 to 15.4 per cent. *World Development Report* (World Bank, 1982).

7. *Trout*, a quarterly magazine circulated to members of Trout Unlimited (Canadian Headquarters: P. O. Box 1014, Station Q, Toronto, Ontario M4T 2P2).

8. Phosphorous from laundry detergents in sewage effluent, fertilizers in land run-off and industrial sources was promoting excessive growth of plant life in Lake Erie. This in turn used up the oxygen needed to support fish. In 1972 the International Joint Commission (a joint U.S.-Canada body overseeing Great Lakes water quality) began a clean-up effort aimed at reducing industrial and municipal discharge into the lake. While good progress has been made in reducing the phosphorous, other pollutants, some of them thought to cause cancer, have been discovered. Much work remains to be done. *Great Lakes Water Quality Agreement 1978* (International Joint Commission, United States and Canada); *Report to the International Joint Commission* (Great Lakes Water Quality Board, 1985); and *Environment Canada 1985-86 Estimates, Part III, Expenditure Plan* (Government of Canada), 18-19.

9. From a speech by the Hon. Charles Caccia, former Minister of the Environment (1983-1984), to the World Industrial Conference on Environmental Management, November 14-16, 1984, in Versailles, France.

XI. Fiscal Imperative

1. In the ten years between 1976 and 1986, Canada's gross public debt will have quadrupled from $59.4 billion to $265 billion. *The Fiscal Plan*, (Ottawa: Department of Finance, May 23, 1985). In just six years, from 1976 to 1982, the portion of total federal government revenue spent to pay the interest on the public debt more than doubled, growing from 11 per cent in 1976 and reaching 22.2 per cent in 1982. If this trend continues, we would spend 44 per cent of federal government revenues to service the debt in 1988, 88 per cent in 1994, and well over 100 per cent by the year 2000. *The National Finances 1984-85* (Toronto: Canadian Tax Foundation, 1985), pp. 32 and 294-297.

2. For example, estimates for 1984 show that, although Canada's economy grew 4.8 per cent, British Columbia's grew only 1.2 per cent; Alberta's economy actually decreased by 0.2 per cent; Saskatchewan's grew 1.1 per cent; Manitoba's grew 4.8 per cent; Ontario, 7.5 per cent; Quebec, 6.6 per cent; New Brunswick, 5.5 per cent; Nova Scotia, 5.6 per cent; Prince Edward Island, 2.7 per cent; and Newfoundland, 2.2 per cent. Informetrica, *Monthly Economic Review*, **Vol. 4** (September 1985), No. 4.

3. Although only 2.7 per cent of our public debt was owed to non-residents in 1975, the figure had grown to 8.9 per cent in 1983 representing a debt of $12.3 billion. If the public debt reaches $265 billion in 1986, this figure would grow to over $23 billion and interest payments of more than $2 billion would leave the country annually. *The National Finances 1984-85*, (Toronto: Canadian Tax Foundation, 1985), 7.

4. George Guess and Kenneth Koford, "Inflation, Recession and the Federal Budget Deficit (or, Blaming Economic Problems on a Statistical Mirage)," *Policy Sciences* **17** (December 1984), 385-402.

XII. An End to Welfare

1. Mary Janigan, "The Growing Ranks of the Homeless," *Maclean's* (January 13, 1986), 28-29. "Study finds 1 in 5 Montrealers is poor," *Globe and Mail* (July 11, 1985).

2. a)   "In the long run, responding to the incipient threat of technological unemployment, public policy should aim at securing equitable distribution of work and income, taking care not to obstruct technological progress even indirectly." Wassily W. Leontief, "The Distribution of Work and Income," *Scientific American* **247** (September 1982), 188-204.

2. (b)   "The intensive use of automation over the next twenty years will make it possible to conserve about 10 per cent of the labor that would have been required to produce the same bill of goods in the absence of increased automation." Wassily Leontief and Faye Duchin, "The Impacts of Automation on Employment, 1963-2000".

2. (c)   "As the steam engine displaced human muscle from production of goods, the communications technologies displace the human nervous system from the services as well as from goods production." Gerard Piel, "Re-entering Paradise: the Mechanization of Work," *Challenge* (September-October 1983), 4-11.

2. (d)   Martin Feldstein, Former Chairman of the Council of Economic Advisers to the President of the United States, and Professor of Economics at Harvard University believes that advancing technology will create more jobs than it eliminates.

2. (e)   "(Improving productivity) is the only way to improve incomes and sustain healthy employment growth . . . The choice must be taken to forge ahead and quickly adapt to technological change if we are to meet Canadians' long-term expectation that tomorrow will be better than today." M. C. McCracken and C. A. Sonnen, "Technology, Labour Markets and the Economy," *Canada Tomorrow Conference: Commissioned Papers* (Canada: Ministry of State for Science and Technology, November 6-9, 1983).

3. Marc Lalonde, Minister of National Health and Welfare, *Working Paper on Social Security in Canada*, "The Orange Paper" (Government of Canada; April 18, 1973).

4. I have suggested the name CISS for a comprehensive income support system in Canada. In the Orange Paper of 1973, Lalonde (*Ibid.*, p. 30) used the term "general income supplementation plan," while it was called a "universal income security program" (UISP) in the *Macdonald Commission Report*, **II**, 794.

5. A total of $58.9 billion was spent on social security programs in Canada in 1984-85. The federal government contributed 78 per cent ($45.9 billion) in the form of 19 separate programs (Canada Assistance Plan, Veterans' Allowance, Social Assistance to on-reserve Indians, Guaranteed Income Supplement and Spouses Allowance, Child Tax Credit, Social Housing, Child Care Expense Deduction, Family Allowance, Child Tax Exemption, Married and Equivalent to Married, Unemployment Insurance, Training Allowance, Employment Expense Deduction, Canada Pension Plan, Old Age Security, Tax Assistance (RRSP, RPP, CPP), Age Exemption, Pension deduction, Veterans' Pensions. The provincial governments carried 22 per cent of the burden ($13 billion), covering a portion of some federal programs in addition to Provincial Tax Credits and Workers' Compensation. *Macdonald Commission Report*, **II**, 772.

6. For a thorough discussion of Canada's current income security system and selected options for reform, see *Macdonald Commission Report*, **II**, 769-803.

XIII. Who Pays the Piper?

1. Canada Royal Commission on Taxation, *Report of the Royal Commission on Taxation* (Ottawa: Queen's Printer, 1966, 7 volumes) **I**, 3.

2. In November, 1984, the United States introduced tax reform measures intended to shift the tax burden away from individuals onto corporations by, among other things, repealing accelerated depreciation write-offs and terminating special low tax rates for capital gains. However, the impact of these and other measures is to tax those earning less than $40,000 at 29 per cent, those between $40,000 and $80,000 at 25 per cent, and those above at 17.5 per cent. Robert S. McIntyre, "Inside the Sellout: Tax reform for the rich," *The New Republic* (June 24, 1985), 9-11.

3. Canadian Tax Foundation, *The National Finances, 1984-85*, (Toronto, 1985), Tables 4.1 and 4.3, pp. 41-42 and 44.

4. Ernie Lightman, "A Flat-Rate Tax," *Policy Options*, **5** (November 1984), 35-37. John Evans, M. P., *Canadian Tax News* (Coopers and Lybrand, Donald Huggett, ed., December 1983) **Vol. XI**, No. 7.

5. "... an expenditure tax ... would tax the sources of people's spending ... would be a practical way of bringing spending from wealth into the tax net ... raise the same amount of revenue with lower rates ... (and) would be far simpler for taxpayers to understand and comply with ..." "Better Taxes," *The Economist* (September 17, 1983), 11-12. See also a series of three articles in the same publication entitled "Britain: The Case for Tax Reform," (September 17, 1983), 41-46; "Britain: Revamping Company Tax," (September 24, 1983), 41-46; and "Britain: The Welfare Muddle," (October 1, 1983), 35-39.

6. For example, the dairy products marketing board, which operates through supply management, benefits producers through the use of quotas and subsidies by $670 million annually. Consumers lose this amount in the purchase price of the product and taxpayers lose an additional

$300 million per year. (This problem does not arise with marketing boards, such as those for hogs and vegetables, which do not operate on a quota system.) *Reforming Regulation* (Ottawa: Economic Council of Canada, 1981), 61-64.

XIV. Why Replace Robots?

1. "Census data for 1981 show that for those without high school diplomas or equivalent trade certificates, unemployment rates were 72 per cent higher than for other groups with those qualifications or better." Claude E. Forget (former Minister of Education in the Province of Quebec), "Education Policy in Canada: the Urgent Issues," *Commentary* (C. D. Howe Institute, January 1985). Furthermore, in 1983 when national levels of unemployment of men and women were 12.1 and 11.6 per cent, respectively, the unemployment rates for those with less than grade 9 education were 13.6 and 13.1; for those with post-secondary certificates of diplomas, 9.2 and 8.6; and for those with a university degree, 4.7 and 5.9 per cent. Statistics Canada, *Women in Canada; A Statistical Report* (March 1985, Catalogue 89-503E), 39.

2. The National Commission on Excellence in Education, *A Nation at Risk: the Imperative for Educational Reform* (U. S. Department of Education, April 1983).

3. Dr. Eric Bates, senior spokesman in Britain's Department of Trade and Industry, as cited by David Dickson in "Britain Debates Science Education Reforms," *Science*, **222** (October 28, 1983), 397-399.

4. Claude E. Forget, *op. cit.*.

5. Thomas P. Rohlen, *Japan's High Schools* (Berkeley: University of California Press, 1983) as cited by James R. Bartholomew in "Secondary Education in Japan," *Science*, **224** (May 18, 1984), 714-715. Will and Ariel Durant, *The Story of Civilization VII: The Age of Reason Begins* (New York: Simon and Schuster, Inc., 1961), 51.

6. *Macdonald Commission Report*, **II**, 738-740.

7. The "Bovey Commission" the Commission on the Future Development of the Universities of Ontario, was established January 20, 1984 by the Ontario government with Edmund C. Bovey as Chairman "to present the Government a plan of action to better enable the universities of Ontario to adjust to changing social and economic conditions." The Commission's report, *Ontario Universities: Options and futures*, was presented in December 1984.

8. (a)   "The years since 1977 have seen a decline in constant dollar-per-student expenditures on post-secondary education in almost all provinces . . ." *Macdonald Commission Report*, **II**, 742.

8. (b)   The Commissioners found that representatives of the education sector lacked innovative ideas about post-secondary education and "tended to deal less with how they could help Canadians adjust to a changing world than with how badly they needed more money." *Ibid.*, **II**, 747.

8. (c) The Commissioners suggest that making money directly available to students for post-secondary education would "greatly fortify the consumer power of these students and thus strengthen the competition among universities to attract them and consequently encourage the development of centres of excellence." *Macdonald Commission Report*, **II**, 750.

8. (d) A 1985 federal study on financing of post-secondary education, however, argues against the voucher system. A. W. Johnson, *Giving Greater Point and Purpose to the Federal Financing of Post-Secondary Education and Research in Canada*, a report prepared for the Secretary of State of Canada (February 15, 1985), 39-44.

9. In 1983, 51.2 per cent of all jobs held by women were clerical (32.6) or service (18.6). Only 17.7 per cent of men were employed in these two sectors. Statistics Canada, *Women in the Labour Force* (March 1985, Catalogue 89-503E), 51.

10. In the twenty years between 1961 and 1981, however, the number of women in a number of traditionally male occupations has increased significantly. For example, the number of female university teachers, psychologists, physicians and surgeons has more than doubled, the number of female biologists and socialists has more than tripled, the number of female economists, agriculturalists and related scientists has quadrupled, the number of female engineers, systems analysts and computer programmers has gone up more than five-fold, and the number of female lawyers and notaries has increased by a factor of 6.5. Statistics Canada, *1981 Census of Canada* as cited in "Closeup on Canada," *The Gazette* (Montreal: July 3, 1985), 1.

11. Claude E. Forget, *op. cit.*, 6. *Macdonald Commission Report*, **II**, 739-740.

12. Financing of foreign students should be considered in the context of our foreign aid programs. See Chapter 10.

XV. Teaspoons or Steamshovels?

1. The 1985 Annual Review of the Economic Council deals extensively with the question of Total Factor Productivity (TFP) recognizing that much more than labour input is to be taken into account in measuring the overall productivity of our economy. The Review points out that "increases in output can be attributed (conceptually, if not always statistically) to some net increase in a composite of all the individual elements engaged in the process of production. They range beyond labour to include capital, materials, energy, and many other 'factors' (or 'inputs')." Economic Council of Canada, *Strengthening Growth: Options and Constraints* (Twenty-Second Annual Review, 1985), 21-23.

2. (a) *Ibid.*, 23-30.

2. (b) Canada's absolute productivity (real gross domestic product per employed person) rose from 88.1 to 94.0 between 1960 and 1973 relative to the United States (on a scale where the absolute produc-

tivity of the U.S. is set at 100.0). There has been a slight decline to 92.8 in 1981 and 92.3 in 1982. During the same period, Japan increased steadily from 26.2 in 1960 to 56.3 in 1973, 70.3 in 1981 and 72.4 in 1982. In 1982 only the United States (100.0), France (94.7) and Belgium (92.7) had higher levels of absolute productivity than Canada. Michael J. Daly and P. Someshwar Rao, "Some myths and realities concerning Canada's recent productivity slowdown, and their policy implications," *Canadian Public Policy*, **XI** (1985), 206-217 (see Table 2, p. 208).

2. (c) Canada's productivity in manufacturing (output per hour), on the other hand, is only about 70 per cent that of the United States. Japan increased from 28 per cent of the U.S. level in 1960 to 80 per cent in 1983, passing Canada in absolute productivity in the manufacturing sector in about 1980. *Competitiveness and Security: Directions for Canada's International Relations* (Canada: Secretary of State for External Affairs, 1985), 21-22.

3. Daly and Rao, *op. cit.*.

4. Peter F. Drucker, "Our entrepreneurial economy," *Harvard Business Review* (January-February, 1984), 59-64.

5. In 1921 one-third of the Canadian labour force was employed in agriculture. This had fallen to 11.2 per cent in 1961 and 4.4 per cent by 1981. Productivity rose steadily, however, growing from $1.7 billion in 1961 to $11.2 billion in 1981 (expressed in constant 1983 dollars). In terms of output per worker, this represents an increase from $2,430 per year in 1961 to $23,110 per year in 1983 (expressed in constant 1983 dollars). The manufacturing sector, which employed 26.5 per cent of the labour force in 1951 and only 17.6 per cent in 1983, is following the same trend. *Macdonald Commission Report* **III**, 404 and 408. Conference Board of Canada, *Handbook of Canadian Consumer Markets* (1984).

6. Thomas J. Peters and Robert H. Waterman, Jr., *In Search of Excellence: Lessons from America's Best Run Companies* (New York: Harper & Row, 1982). As the sequel has shown, however, these companies will remain a minority.

7. From 1978 to 1982, 65.7 per cent (483,085 jobs) of all jobs created in Canada in the private sector were created by businesses with fewer than 20 employees. Businesses with 20 to 100 employees suffered a net loss of 2.7 per cent (-20,125 jobs) and those with more than 100 employees created 37 per cent of the jobs (271,806 jobs). While there was a net loss of jobs in manufacturing (-72,113 jobs), this was a result of losses from the medium and large business sectors. Small businesses actually created 52,434 manufacturing jobs. As expected, the service sector gave rise to most of the new jobs, accounting for 73.1 per cent if business and personal services (24.6 per cent), community services (23.1), retail trade (20.8) and finance (4.6) are combined. *Macdonald Commission Report*, **II**, 121.

8. "Professionals would make up almost 20 per cent of the labor force in the year 2000 if the new technology is adopted, whereas they would make up only 14.5 per cent under the old technology." See page 39 of Wassily Leontief, "The Choice of Technology," *Scientific American* **252** (June 1985), 37-45.

9. "A fraction of small firms creates all new jobs created by small firms . . . between 12 and 15 per cent depending on the study examined." David E. Gumpert, "Scrap scattershot backing of small business," *The Wall Street Journal* (February 6, 1985), 26.

10. McKinsey and Company, *The Winning Performance of the Midsized Growth Companies* (American Business Corporation, May 1983).

11. Guy P. F. Steed, *Threshold Firms: Backing Canada's Winners* (Ottawa: Science Council of Canada, Background Study 48, July 1982).

12. By the year 2000 many new occupations will come into existence. For example, there will be careers for hazardous waste management technicians (30,000 jobs), industrial robot production technicians (80,000 jobs), energy auditors (18,000 jobs) and computerized vocational training technicians (30,000 jobs) to name just a few. Marvin J. Cetron, "Getting Ready for the Jobs of the Future," *The Futurist* (June 1983), 15-22. S. Norman Feingold, "Emerging Careers: Occupations for Post-Industrial Society," *The Futurist* (February 1984), 9-16.

13. (a) "Canada's forest products industries yielded a positive trade balance of more than $11 billion in 1980. They support more than 300,000 jobs directly, and account directly or indirectly for one Canadian job in every ten. The industries are key employers in most provinces and support 28 per cent of Canada's 400-plus single-industry communities." Ted Schrecker, *The Conserver Society Revisited* (Ottawa: Science Council of Canada, Discussion Paper D83/3, 1983), 19.

13. (b) "In proportion to its area of forested land, Canada has less than half as many professional foresters as Sweden and one-fifth as many as Norway." *Ibid.*, 20.

13. (c) A major long-term commitment to forest management could allow Canada to increase its national allowable cut by 40 per cent over the next two decades. This would create additional exports of $12 billion per year and 75,000 to 100,000 new jobs. *Ibid.*, 20. See also *A Forest Sector Strategy for Canada* (Ottawa: Environment Canada, Discussion Paper, September 1981).

13. (d) The study identifies trends toward energy conservation, alternative energy use and pollution control as a potential source of new industrial activity for Canada. It also points out that we can only capitalize on these developments if we design, build and market Canadian equipment for these applications. Ted Schrecker, *op. cit.*, 26-33.

XVI. Getting in Gear

1. "The available evidence does suggest, however, that these plans are associated with improved productivity and/or profitability, more satisfactory communication between employers and employees, improved labour/management relations, and better employee morale. *Macdonald Commission Report* **II**, 713-716.

2. Robert Reich, "How Wheeling and Dealing Limit Our Prosperity," *The Washington Monthly* (1980).

3. *Strengthening Growth: Options and Constraints* (Ottawa, Economic Council of Canada, Twenty-Second Annual Review, 1985), pp. 30, 46 and 85-86.

4. (a) The National Research Council has three programs which aid the diffusion of technology: IRAP, Industrial Research Assistance Program; CISTI, Canada Institute for Scientific and Technical Information; and PILP, Program for Industry/Laboratory Projects.

4. (b) Canada has only six science counsellors abroad. They are stationed in Bonn, Brussels, London, Paris, Tokyo, and Washington.

5. "One of the most basic choices facing Canadians is whether to remain an outward looking trading nation, fully participating in the international economy, or to go in the direction of self-sufficiency and protectionism. I have no difficulty with this choice, nor do I think that Canadians have much doubt where their longer-run interests lie. The benefits of international trade are simply too apparent, and outweigh the costs of adjustment to changes in world markets." Donald J. Johnston, Minister of State for Economic and Regional Development, *Submission to the Royal Commission on the Economic Union and Development Prospects for Canada.*

6. *Competitiveness and Security: Directions for Canada's International Relations* (Ottawa: Secretary of State for External Affairs, 1985), 16.

7. Zhao Deyan, "China emerging as a trading nation," *Canadian Business Review* **12** (Spring 1985), 56-62.

8. *World Development Report 1984* (published for The World Bank by Oxford University Press), 218-219.

9. (a) Canada East-West Centre Ltd., *The Trade Issue*, (a Discussion Paper prepared for the National Liberal Caucus Research Bureau, September 1985). *Macdonald Commission Report* **I**, 233-238.

9. (b) Canada East-West Centre Ltd., *op. cit..* Catherine Harris, "Trade barriers all over the map," *Financial Post* (November 10, 1984). *Macdonald Commission Report* **I**, 279-295.

9. (c) Canada West Foundation, *The Canadian Common Market: Interprovincial Trade and International Competitiveness* (Calgary, 1985), 6.

10. The Macdonald Commissioners proposed the creation of a Transitional Adjustment Assistance Program (TAAP) to provide (i) more funding of on-the-job training programs, (ii) portable wage-subsidy programs, (iii)

early retirement plans, (iv) mobility grants and (v) special projects funding. *Macdonald Commission Report*, **II**, 616-619.

11. Says Dr. Ian Stewart, noted economist, author, former Deputy Minister of Finance with the Government of Canada, and former Deputy Minister of Energy, Mines and Resources.

XVII. Attacking the Mountain

1. Douglas Fisher, "No Reformers Here," *Executive*, **26** (December 1984), 47-48; and "The Six O'clock Scandal," *Executive* (April 1985), 71-72. Furthermore, a Gallup poll taken in July of 1983 showed that 45 per cent of Canadians saw big government as "the biggest threat to Canada in years to come," with 34 per cent identifying big labour as the biggest threat and 14 per cent choosing big business (7 per cent did not know).

2. Jean Chrétien, *Straight From The Heart* (Key Porter Books Limited, 1985).

3. *Macdonald Commission Report* **III**, 325-408.

4. *Ibid.*, **III**, 330.

5. Among those speaking in favour of an elected Senate have been Senators Duff Roblin, Michael Pitfield and Royce Frith; Gordon Robertson and Edward McWhinney; the Canada West Foundation; the Macdonald Commission; and the Joint Committee on Senate Reform chaired by Senator Gil Molgat and Paul Cosgrove, MP.

6. George Selkirk Currie, *Report on the Canadian Army Works Services with special reference to the irregularities uncovered at Camp Petawawa*, House of Commons Debates, December 15, 1952.

7. I selected Ken Dye after consultation with Comptroller General Harry Rogers, Fred Drummie of the Privy Council Office and Marcel Caron, President of the Canadian Institute of Chartered Accountants.

8. For example, the Business Council on National Issues has explored the subject in some detail and in 1983 published a study on the subject entitled *Parliamentary Democracy in Canada, Issues for Reform*. The Council calls for more latitude for Members of Parliament to follow their own best judgement by recommending that "the leaders of both the government and opposition parties recognize and adopt in practice a less stringent approach to the question of party discipline and the rules covering confidence."

9. This was one of the most significant recommendations of the McGrath Committee. It is found in Chapter 2 of *The Report of the Special Committee on Reform of the House of Commons* (June 1985).

Bibliography

Abernathy, William J., Kim B. Clark, and Alan M. Kantrow. *Industrial Renaissance: Producing a Competitive Future for America.* Basic Books, New York, 1983.

Anderson, Ronald. "Consumers Take Back Seat to Special Interest Groups." *Globe and Mail*, May 7, 1985.

Axworthy, Tom. "After 1984: A Liberal Revival." *Canadian Forum*, **64** November 1984.

Bartholomew, James R. "Secondary Education in Japan." *Science*, **224** May 18, 1984.

Bruce, Neil, and Douglas D. Purvis. *Evaluating the Deficit: The Case for Budget Cuts.* C. D. Howe Institute, Toronto, 1984.

Business Council on National Issues. *Parliamentary Democracy in Canada, Issues for Reform.*

Canada. Department of Finance. *Economic Review*. Ottawa, 1984.

Canada. Department of Finance. *The Fiscal Plan*. Budget papers, May 23, 1985.

Canada. (The Carter Commission). *Report of the Royal Commission on Taxation,* 7 vols. Ottawa, 1966.

Canada. Environment Canada. *A Forest Sector Strategy for Canada.* Environment Canada Discussion Paper, Ottawa, September 1981.

Canada. House of Commons. *Still Waters.* A report by the Subcommittee on Acid Rain. Ottawa, 1981.

Canada. (McGrath Committee), *Report of the Special Committee on Reform of the House of Commons*, June 1985.

Canada. Ministry of State for Science and Technology. *Research, Development and Economic Growth.* Background paper for the National Economic Conference, Ottawa, 1985.

Canada. *Report of the Royal Commission on the Economic Union and Development Prospects for Canada.* 3 Vols, Ottawa, September 1985.

Canada. Secretary of State. *Giving Greater Point and Purpose to the Federal Financing of Post-Secondary Education and Research in Canada.* Ottawa, 1985.

Canada. Statistics Canada. *Canada's Lone-Parent Families.* Catalogue 99-933, Ottawa, 1984.

Canada. Statistics Canada. *Education in Canada: A Statistical Review for 1982-83.* Catalogue 81-229. Ottawa, June 1984. .

Canada. Statistics Canada. *The Labour Force.* Catalogue 71-001. Ottawa, November 1985.

289

Canada. Statistics Canada. *Population Projections for Canada, Provinces and Territories, 1984-2006,* Catalogue 91-520. Ottawa, 1984.

Canada. Statistics Canada. *Women in Canada: A Statistical Report,* Catalogue 89-503E. Ottawa, 1985.

Canada East-West Centre, Ltd. *The Trade Issue.* A discussion paper prepared for the National Liberal Caucus Research Bureau, September 1985.

Canada West Foundation. *The Canadian Common Market: Interprovincial Trade and International Competitiveness.* Calgary, 1985.

Canadian Institute of Chartered Accountants. "A Framework for Tax Simplification." Paper submitted to Minister of Finance, Michael Wilson, March 29, 1985.

Canadian Institute of Public Opinion. "Over Four in Ten See Threat From 'Big' Government." *The Gallup Report.* Toronto, December 2, 1981.

Canadian Manufacturers' Association. *Competing in the Global Village: Self-Help is the Best Help.* Canadian Manufacturers' Association, Ottawa, 1982.

Canadian Tax Foundation. *The National Finances 1984-85.* Canadian Tax Foundation, Toronto, 1985.

Carmichael, Edward A. *Tackling the Federal Deficit.* C.D. Howe Institute, Toronto, 1984.

Cetron, Marvin J. "Getting Ready for the Jobs of the Future." *The Futurist,* **17** June 1983

Choate, Pat, and Susan Walter. *America in Ruins: Beyond the Public Works Pork Barrel.* Council of State Planning Agencies, Washington, DC, 1981.

Chrétien, Jean. *Straight from the Heart.* Key Porter Books Limited, Toronto, 1985.

Clark, The Hon. Joe. *Competitiveness and Security: Directions for Canada's International Relations.* ("The Grey Paper") Department of External Affairs, 1985, Ottawa.

Cohen, Dian, and Kristin Shannon. *The Next Canadian Economy.* Eden Press, Montreal, 1984.

Conference Board of Canada. *Canada's Output Growth: Performance and Potential, 1966-92.* A Technical Paper, April 1983.

Conference Board of Canada. *Handbook of Canadian Consumer Markets,* 1984.

Currie, George Selkirk. *Report on the Canadian Army Works Services with special reference to the irregularities uncovered at Camp Petawawa.* House of Commons Debates, December 15, 1952.

D'Aquino, Thomas, G. Bruce Doern, and Cassandra Blair. *Parliamentary Democracy in Canada: Issues for Reform.* Methuen, Toronto, 1983.

Daly, Michael J., and P. Someshwar Rao. "Some myths and realities concerning Canada's recent productivity slowdown, and their policy implications." *Canadian Public Policy,* **XI** (1985).

Denton, Frank T., and Byron G. Spencer. "Population Aging and Future Health Costs in Canada." *Canadian Public Policy.* **9,** June 1983.

Deyan, Zhao. "China Emerging as a Trading Nation." *Canadian Business Review*, **12**, Spring 1985.

Dickson, David. "Britain Debates Science Education Reforms." *Science*, **222** October 28, 1983.

Dorfman, Nancy S. "Route 128: The Development of a Regional High Technology Economy." *Research Policy*, **12** (1983).

Drucker, Peter F. "Our Entrepreneurial Economy." *Harvard Business Review*, **62**, January-February 1984.

Drucker, Peter F. "Schumpeter and Keynes." *Forbes*, **131**, May 23, 1983.

Durant, Will and Ariel. *The Story of Civilization VII: The Age of Reason Begins*. Simon and Schuster Inc., New York, 1951.

Economic Council of Canada. *Intervention and Efficiency: A Study of Government Credit Guarantees to the Private Sector*. The Council, Ottawa, 1982.

Economic Council of Canada. *Reforming Regulation*. Ottawa: The Council, 1981.

Economic Council of Canada. *Strengthening Growth: Options and Constraints*, Twenty-Second Annual Review. The Council, Ottawa, 1985.

The Economist "America Cannot Afford its Cost of Capital." (April 30, 1983)

The Economist. "Better Taxes," September 17, 1983.

The Economist. "Britain: The Case for Tax Reform," September 17, 1983.

The Economist. "Britain: Revamping Company Tax," September 24, 1983.

The Economist. "Britain: The Welfare Muddle," October 1, 1983.

Evans, John, M.P. *Canadian Tax News*, ed. Donald Huggett, Coopers and Lybrand, **Vol. XI**, No. 7. December 1983.

Feather, Frank. "Are We Missing Out on China Trade?" *Toronto Star*, March 31, 1985.

Feingold, S. Norman. "Emerging Careers: Occupations for Post-Industrial Society." *The Futurist*, February 1984.

Financial Post. "Business leaders lean to Tories," May 5, 1979.

Fisher, Douglas. "No Reformers Here." *Executive*, December 26, 1984.

Fisher, Douglas. "The Six O'clock Scandal." *Executive*, April 1985.

Foot, David K. *Canada's Population Outlook: Demographic Futures and Economic Changes*. Canadian Institute of Economic Policy, Ottawa, 1982.

Forget, Claude E. "Education Policy in Canada: The Urgent Issues." *Commentary*. C. D. Howe Institute, January 1985.

Fortin, Pierre, and John McCallum. "Ottawa devrait adopter une politique monétatire expansioniste." *Le Devoir*, April 22, 1985.

Francis, Diane. "Nine Families Said to Control Stock Worth 46% of Value of the TSE 300." *Toronto Star*, March 19, 1985.

Fullerton, Douglas. " 'Poverty Line' Formula is Artificial and Questionable." *The Ottawa Citizen*, May 8, 1982.

Globe and Mail. "Study finds 1 in 5 Montrealers is poor." July 11, 1985.

Great Lakes Water Quality Board. *Report to the International Joint Commission*, 1985.

Guess, George, and Kenneth Koford. "Inflation, Recession and the Federal Budget Deficit (or, Blaming Economic Problems on a Statistical Mirage)." *Policy Sciences*, **17**, December 1984.

Gumpert, David E. "Scrap scattershot backing of small business." *The Wall Street Journal*, February 6, 1985.

Gwyn, Richard. *The Northern Magus: Pierre Trudeau and Canadians*. McClelland and Stewart, Toronto, 1980.

Handy, Charles. *The Future of Work: A Guide to a Changing Society*. Basil Blackwell, Oxford, 1984.

Harris, Catherine. "Trade Barriers All Over the Map." *Financial Post*, November 10, 1984.

Hill, Peter. *Real Gross Domestic Product in OECD Countries and Associated Purchasing Power Parities*. Working Paper Number 17, OECD. Paris, 1984.

Honer, T. G. *Assessing Change in Canada's Forest Resource 1977-1981*. A paper presented at the annual meeting, Canadian Institute of Forestry. Winnipeg, Manitoba, September 23-26, 1982

House of Commons. *Still Waters*. A report by the House of Commons Subcommittee on Acid Rain, 1983.

Informetrica. *Monthly Economic Review*, **4**, September 1985.

International Joint Commission, United States and Canada. *Great Lakes Water Quality Agreement 1978*.

Insel, Barbara. "A World Awash in Grain." *Foreign Affairs*, **63**, Spring 1985.

Janigan, Mary. "The Growing Ranks of the Homeless." *Maclean's*, January 13, 1986.

Johnson, A. W. *Giving Greater Point and Purpose to the Federal Financing of Post-Secondary Education and Research in Canada*. A report prepared for the Secretary of State of Canada, February 15, 1985.

Johnston, Donald J. "Banquet Speech." In *Report of the Proceedings of the 35th Tax Conference*. Canadian Tax Foundation, Toronto, 1983.

Johnston, Donald J. *Fiscalamity: How to Survive Canada's Tax Chaos*. PaperJacks, Toronto, 1974, revised editions 1975, 1977.

Johnston, Donald J. "Government and Business: a Personal Perspective." *Viewpoint*. Liberal Party of Canada, Ottawa, March 1982.

Johnston, Donald J. Submission to the Royal Commission on the Economic Union and Development Prospects for Canada. Macdonald Commission, Ottawa, 1985.

Keynes, John Maynard. *The End of Laissez-Faire*. Hogarth Press, London, 1926.

Kierans, Tom. "Commercial Crowns: the Canadian Situation Calls for Privatization if Necessary But Not Necessarily Privatization." *Policy Options*, **5**, November 1984.

Kuttner, Bob. "The Declining Middle." *The Atlantic Monthly*, July 1984.

Lalonde, Marc. *Challenges and Achievements: Canada's Economic Record Since 1968*. Speech to the Outaouais Chamber of Commerce, Hull, Quebec, March 29, 1984.

Lalonde, Marc. *Working Paper on Social Security in Canada*. ("The Orange Paper") National Health and Welfare, Ottawa, 1973.

Lang, Otto. "The Fundamental Principal for the Liberal Party is the Worth and Dignity of the Individual." Paper delivered at the annual General Meeting of the Liberal Party of Manitoba, Winnipeg, March 9, 1985.

Leontief, Wassily W. "The Choice of Technology." *Scientific American*, **252**, June 1985.

Leontief, Wassily W. "The Distribution of Work and Income." *Scientific American*, **247**, September 1982.

Leontief, Wassily W., and Faye Duchin. *The Impacts of Automation on Employment, 1963-2000*.

Liberal Party. *The Liberal Way: A Record of Opinion on Canadian Problems as Expressed and Discussed at the First Liberal Summer Conference*. J.M. Dent and Sons, Toronto, 1933.

Lightman, Ernie. "A Flat-Rate Tax." *Policy Options*, **5**, November 1984.

Lipovenko, Dorothy. "Four Million Seniors by 2000, Report Says." *Globe and Mail*, June 5, 1985.

Malthus, Thomas Robert. *On Population*. Modern Library, New York, 1860.

Macdonald Commission. See The Royal Commission on the Economic Union and Development Prospects for Canada.

Marchetti, Cesare. "Swings, Cycles and the Global Economy." *New Scientist*, May 2, 1985.

Maxwell, Judith. "The battle of the ages." *Report on Business Magazine*, June 1985.

Maxwell, Judith. "The Inevitable Move Away From Resources." *Report on Business Magazine*, May 1985.

McCall-Newman, Christina. "Michael Pitfield and the politics of mismanagement." *Saturday Night*, October 1982.

McCracken, M. C., and C. A. Sonnen. "Technology, Labour Markets and the Economy." *Canada Tomorow Conference: Commissioned Papers*. Canada: Ministry of State for Science and Technology, November 6-9, 1983.

McIntyre, Robert S. "Inside the Sellout: Tax Reform For the Rich." *The New Republic*, June 24, 1985.

McKinsey & Company. *The Winning Performance of the Midsized Growth Companies*. American Business Corporation, May 1983.

Natural Sciences and Engineering Research Council of Canada. *Completing the Bridge to the 90s: NSERC's Second Five-Year Plan*. Ottawa, 1985.

New Scientist. "Erosion causes soil's vanishing act." November 14, 1985:.

Newman, Peter C. "Paving a Long Road Back: Q & A, John Turner." *Maclean's*, November 19, 1984.

North-South Institute. "Aid Evaluation." *North South News*, May 1983.

North-South Institute. *Third World Markets and Exports Financing: Onto a Sounder Footing*. Submitted to the Minister of Finance and the Minister for International Trade, 1985.

293

O'Hara, Jane. "The Billion Dollar Problem." *Maclean's*, **98**, May 20, 1985.

Olson, Mancur. *The Rise and Decline of Nations: Economic Growth, Stagflation and Social Rigidities*. Yale University Press, New Haven, Connecticut, 1982.

Ontario. *Ontario Universities: Options and Futures*. A report of the Commission on the Future Development of the Universities of Ontario (The Bovey Commission). Ministry of Colleges and Universities, Toronto, December 1984.

Owens, Jeffrey. "Direct Tax Burdens: An International Comparison." *OECD Observer*, **133**, March 1985.

Pearce, Fred. "A Permanent Way Across the Permafrost." *New Scientist*, **104**, November 1984.

Peters, Thomas J., and Nancy Austin. *A Passion for Excellence: The Leadership Difference*. Random House, New York, 1985.

Peters, Thomas J., and Robert H. Waterman, Jr. *In Search of Excellence: Lessons from America's Best Run Companies*. Harper & Row, New York, 1982.

Piel, Gerard. "Re-entering Paradise: the Mechanization of Work." *Challenge*, **26**, September-October 1983.

Province of Quebec. *White Paper on the Personal Tax and Transfer Systems*. Ministere des Finances, Gouvernement de Québec, 1984.

Reich, Robert B. "How Wheeling and Dealing Limit Our Prosperity." *The Washington Monthly*, 1980.

Reich, Robert B. "Toward a New Public Policy." *The Atlantic Monthly*. **255**, May 1985.

Ricardo, David. *Principles of Political Economics and Taxation*. G. Bell and Sons, London, 1891.

Royal Commission on the Economic Union and Development Prospects for Canada. *Macdonald Commission Report*. Canadian Government Publishing Centre, Supply and Services, Ottawa, 1985.

Schrecker, Ted. *The Conserver Society Revisited*. Science Council of Canada, Discussion Paper D83/3, Ottawa, May 1983.

Senate of Canada. Standing Committee on Agriculture, Fisheries and Forestry (Chairman: Hon. H. O. Sparrow). *Soil at Risk: Canada's Eroding Future*. A report to the Senate of Canada, June 1984.

Servan-Schreiber, Jean-Jacques. *The World Challenge*. Simon and Schuster, New York, 1980.

Sharwood, Gordon R. *The New Entrepreneurial Society*. Speech given at Northern Institute for Resource Studies conference, "Investment and Growth in British Columbia: The Challenge to 1990," British Columbia, May 7, 1985.

Sharwood, Gordon R. *The Rise of Entrepreneurship*. Speech given to Canadian Manufacturers Association, January 29, 1985.

Sinclair, Sonja. *Cordial But Not Cozy: A History of the Office of the Auditor General*. McClelland and Stewart, 1979.

Skelton, Oscar Douglas. *Life and Letters of Sir Wilfrid Laurier*. 2 Vols., Oxford University Press, Toronto, 1921.

Smith, Adam. *An Inquiry into the Nature and Causes of the Wealth of Nations*. Clarendon Press, Oxford, 1869.

Smith, Stuart. "High Technology Can Mean Wealth and Jobs." *Toronto Star*, March 17, 1985.

"Social Expenditure: Erosion or Evolution?" *OECD Observer*, **128**, January 1984.

Steed, Guy P. F. *Threshold Firms: Backing Canada's Winners*. Science Council of Canada, Background Study 48, Ottawa, 1982.

Strassman, Paul A. *Information Payoff: The Transformation of Work in the Electronic Age*. The Free Press, New York, 1985.

Task Force on Federal Policies and Programs for Technology Development. *A Report to the Minister of State, Science and Technology*, ("The Wright Report") July 1984.

Thurow, Lester C. "The Disappearance of the Middle Class: It's Not Just Demographics." *New York Times*, February 5, 1984.

Toronto Stock Exhange. *Canadian Shareholders: Their Profile and Attitudes*. Toronto Stock Exchange, Toronto, 1984.

Trout Unlimited. *Trout*. A quarterly magazine circulated to members of Trout Unlimited (Canadian Headquarters: P. O. Box 1014, Station Q, Toronto, Ontario M4T 2P2).

Trudeau, Pierre Elliott. News conference, Economic Summit, Williamsburg, Virginia, May 30, 1983.

United States, National Commission on Excellence in Education. *A Nation at Risk: The Imperative for Educational Reform*, United States Department of Education, April 1983.

Weidenbaum, Murray, and Michael Munger. "Protectionism: Who Gets Protected?" *Consumers' Research Magazine*, October 1983.

Wilson, Michael H. *The Fiscal Plan*. Department of Finance, Ottawa, 1985.

World Bank. *World Development Report*. Oxford University Press, New York, 1983.

Index